WORLD'S ULTIMATE CYCLING RACES

WORLD'S ULTIMATE CYCLING RACES

Collins
An imprint of HarperCollins Publishers
Westerhill Road
Bishopbriggs
Glasgow G64 2QT

First Edition 2012

Printed in China

British Library Cataloguing in Publication Data
A catalogue record for this book is available from the British Library

ISBN 978-0-00-748281-8
Imp 001

All mapping in this publication is generated from CollinsBartholomew digital databases.
Collins Bartholomew, the UK's leading independent geographical information supplier,
can provide a digital, custom, and premium mapping service to a variety of markets.
For further information:
Tel: +44 (0) 208 307 4515
e-mail: collinsbartholomew@harpercollins.co.uk
or visit our website at: www.collinsbartholomew.com

If you would like to comment on any aspect of this book, please write to
Collins Maps, HarperCollins Publishers, Westerhill Road, Bishopbriggs, Glasgow G64 2QT
e-mail: collinsmaps@harpercollins.co.uk
or visit our website at: www.collinsmaps.com
Follow us on Twitter @CollinsMaps
Search Facebook for "World's Ultimate Cycling Races"

WORLD'S
ULTIMATE
CYCLING
RACES

Collins

Contents

Foreword

I have been a participant, a commentator, and supporter of cycling races throughout the world for over thirty years. These days, more than ever, I'm amazed by the variety of races both in terms of type and location. This book showcases that variety, bringing the greatest races from around the world together in one unique volume.

The highlight of the cycling calendar is without doubt the Tour de France. The first Tour de France was organised and sponsored by struggling newspaper L'Auto as a publicity event. Today the race has no problems generating publicity and is broadcast to millions throughout the world. It continues to be the showcase race for cycling, but this should not distract from the many other superb races held throughout the year.

Races such as Paris–Nice, Milan–San Remo, Paris–Roubaix and Liège–Bastogne–Liège are significant races in their own right. They are all included in this book as some of the World's Ultimate Cycling Races.

Road racing is not just a European obsession, however. At the time of writing, I have recently returned from covering another successful Tour of California in the US. Australia and South Africa also have successful and thriving bike racing scenes, including two of my favourite races the Santos Tour Down Under and Cape Argus Pick n Pay Cycle Tour, which

has 35,000 riders! It is also wonderful to see that the Middle East is hosting some great pro races, such as the Tour of Qatar and Tour of Oman. The desert scenery provides an amazing backdrop for these stage races and some great conditions for fast racing.

Following the pro cyclist races around the world is one thing, but the real excitement begins when you get out there and do it yourself. One of the best ways to do this is to try a sportive. These massed-start events recreate what it feels like to be in the middle of a speeding pro peloton – just with the speed and suffering turned down a notch or two. Most sportive events offer two or three distance options, so there's something for everyone, whatever your level. Whilst not officially races – although in mainland Europe road rules do allow the front runners to battle it out – these are still great events, and you will find plenty that suit your ability and experience in these pages.

When I started covering cycling, mountain biking was barely recognised as a sport. It was the underground, seldom talked about cousin of road racing. Since mountain bikes have become cheaper and more widely available however, it has started to find its place in the mainstream. An established circuit of mountain bike races now exists, with some amazing races to look out for. The Leadville

Trail 100 climbs and descends through the Colorado Rockies; the Crocodile Trophy takes on the Australian Outback in North Queensland; and the Craft Bike TransAlp leads riders through the mountains of Germany, Austria and Italy. The most exhausting of them all is the Cape Epic that runs through the beauty of South Africa's Garden Route.

If you still like the idea of cycling on thin wheels and with drop handlebars, then you can always turn to cyclo-cross. For anyone unfamiliar with the discipline, it falls somewhere between mountain biking and road cycling. The races are usually held on closed circuits in parks, although there are exceptions, such as the infamous Three Peaks in the Yorkshire Dales in northern England, where the hills can be so steep competitors are at times forced to carry their bikes.

Whether you are a 24-hour racer, a sprinter or a stage racer, this book is full of top-quality races and rides for you to watch and try. The events are helpfully flagged up as 'professional', 'take part' or 'race against the pros' to help you gauge the level of the races.

Let's face it, now there really are no excuses to stop you getting on your bike, and finding your perfect race.

Phil Liggett

Introduction

Cycling, as a sport, pastime and means of transport, is enjoying a renaissance all around the world. People are increasingly recognising its health benefits, its relative cheapness and the sheer amount of fun there is to be had riding a bike, competitively or otherwise.

This book brings together 300 organised rides and races taking place across the globe, which you can either ride, race or watch. For those who have never been to watch a professional race, the experience is every bit as exciting as you might imagine. It also stirs up feelings of wishing you were riding your own bike too. Therefore more and more race organisers are organising 'cyclosportives' that follow the same route as the pro events, but which cater for enthusiastic amateur riders who want to experience what their heroes go through.

This list is by no means exhaustive; it can't be, as new sportives – or 'gran fondos' as they are usually called in Italy and the USA – are being organised around the globe nearly every weekend. On the other hand, the number of pro races out there isn't growing at quite the same rate, and indeed some of the smaller ones are in fact disappearing.

All the more reason to go along and support these races as a spectator. While the Tour de France or the Giro d'Italia will always attract a large crowd, it's at the smaller races that the stars of tomorrow are moulded. To be able to say you saw a young Bradley Wiggins win a stage of the Tour de l'Avenir while you were on holiday in France in 2003, for example, gains you instant kudos among your club-mates at the pub.

The intention, too, has been to select events from all over the world – from mountain-bike epics in South America, to pro stage races in Australia, to the most mountainous sportives in Europe. We've tried to include a number of smaller, more intimate, unusual and fun events, too – all 'ultimate' in their own way, be it their originality, location, uniqueness or terrain, or because they are great star-spotting occasions where you're guaranteed to bag an autograph from your favourite rider at the start.

Of course, a decent map, some willing legs and a bit of time on your hands are all you need to plan your own rides, but at organised events you get closed – or at least semi-closed – roads, feed stations, marshals, route markers and, most importantly of all, an excited, colourful, noisy peloton of like-minded riders to experience it all with.

However, cycling doesn't always have to be about going full bore, so we've also included a number of events that offer shorter-distance options more suitable for beginners or younger riders.

There's something for everyone, then. We've indicated whether each event is open to everyone to 'take part' in, or if it's a 'professional race', or thirdly if it's an event where you can 'race against the pros', with the last being a mix of the previous two – events where you actually get to line up with professional athletes to show them what you've got.

For so long, working weeks around the world have ended with a sociable Friday-night drink with colleagues politely asking each other, "So, what are you up to this weekend?" Too often, the cyclist has told their work-mates that they're off to ride a sportive the next day, or that they have a race on Sunday, and that has been the end of it. So if you are that cyclist, why not next time tag a question on to the end of your answer? "Do you want to come, too?"

The more people there are cycling, the safer it makes our roads, as drivers who also ride empathise with what it's like to be on two wheels. The more people there are cycling, the more people will discover cycling as a competitive sport and will go to watch professional cycling events, helping to attract sponsorship and keep those races alive. The more people there are cycling, the healthier and happier people will be, too.

This book will help you choose your own cycling adventure: something close to home, something a little further afield, that pro race you've always wanted to watch in person, or that event that will take you completely outside of your comfort zone, which will require training, planning, drive and commitment, but which will be something you'll return home from enriched and emboldened, and enthusiastic for more.

Ellis Bacon

How to use this book

The page on which the information on a race can be found is accessed in a number of ways – by consulting the continent maps on which all the races are located, or by reference to either the alphabetical, country or race category index. All race entries are presented in a similar manner and are arranged by the month in which they take place.

The diagram below indicates the individual components of each entry.

Race category icon
gives, at a glance, the category of the race. For full category list, see pages 10–11

Race type
shows the race level.

Locator map
shows the location of the race in a wider region.

Race title
gives the race name for each entry.

Race location
indicates the principal country where the race takes place.

Race category
indicates the type of race.

Summary
gives a short synopsis of each race.

Main text
gives concise descriptions and information about each race.

Month indicator
highlights the month in which the race takes place.

Extra information
about each race supplements the details in the main text. The most recent information has been used, however, is subject to change depending on the race route for that year.

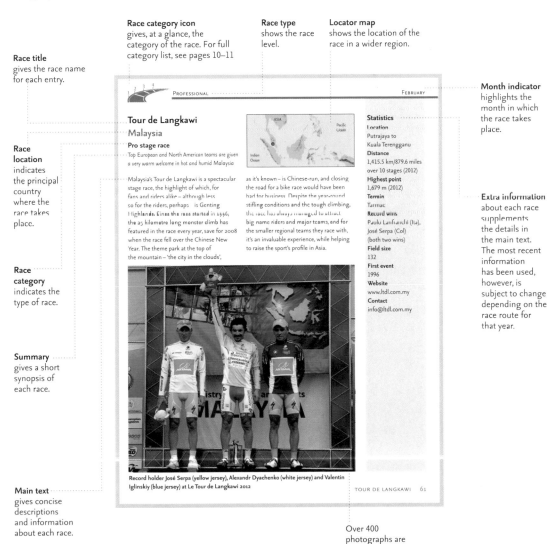

1 2 3 4 PROFESSIONAL FEBRUARY

Tour de Langkawi
Malaysia
Pro stage race
Top European and North American teams are given a very warm welcome in hot and humid Malaysia

Malaysia's Tour de Langkawi is a spectacular stage race, the highlight of which, for fans and riders alike – although less so for the riders, perhaps – is Genting Highlands. Since the race started in 1996, the 45 kilometre long monster climb has featured in the race every year, save for 2008 when the race fell over the Chinese New Year. The theme park at the top of the mountain – 'the city in the clouds',

as it's known – is Chinese-run, and closing the road for a bike race would have been bad for business. Despite the year-round stifling conditions and the tough climbing, the race has always managed to attract big name riders and major teams, and for the smaller regional teams they race with, it's an invaluable experience, while helping to raise the sport's profile in Asia.

Statistics
Location
Putrajaya to Kuala Terengganu
Distance
1,415.5 km/879.6 miles over 10 stages (2012)
Highest point
1,679 m (2012)
Terrain
Tarmac
Record wins
Paolo Lanfranchi (Ita), José Serpa (Col) (both two wins)
Field size
132
First event
1996
Website
www.ltdl.com.my
Contact
info@ltdl.com.my

Record holder José Serpa (yellow jersey), Alexandr Dyachenko (white jersey) and Valentin Iglinskiy (blue jersey) at Le Tour de Langkawi 2012

TOUR DE LANGKAWI   61

Over 400 photographs are included in the book.

Race Categories

Pro stage race

These are multi-day races for professional riders, which challenge participants over varied terrain, and often also against the clock in a time-trial stage, with a leader's jersey awarded at the end of each day to the rider with the shortest accumulated time for the race to that point. The Tour de France, the Giro d'Italia and the Vuelta a España – collectively known as the 'grand tours' – are the biggest and best examples, but there are hundreds more to discover...

Road

This term covers by far the majority of sportives and gran fondos, and the majority of events covered in this book. These are rides for road bikes, where the road surfaces are normally tarmac – although are sometimes cobbles or dirt roads – and which often cover the same roads as the professional races.

Mountain bike

This category covers off-road events or urban downhill events in which competitors use mountain bikes, although some mountain-bike events included in this book do fall into 'long distance' or, in the case of the popular 24-hour MTB races, 'night'.

Night

This covers events – both road and off-road – that require a set of lights to help you on your way, whether it's a 24-hour event in which you try to complete as many laps of a course as you can or a fun, under-cover-of-darkness ride designed to take advantage of quiet roads and challenge your senses.

Pro one-day race

Professional road races held over the course of one day, which, unless you're good enough to turn pro, you'll only ever be watching on the television or, even better, at the roadside. These include the so-called 'Classics' – cycling's oldest and most prestigious events, often held on routes as tough as when the races were held for the first time.

Cyclo-cross

A cycling discipline that combines both off-road riding and running – the latter with your bike on your shoulder. The bikes used are more akin to road bikes than mountain bikes, making them light enough to carry over obstacles and up hills too steep to ride. As a competitive sport it's huge in Belgium, where it's as popular as road racing and second only to football.

Long distance

We've defined 'long distance' as cycling events that total over 300 km – whether single-day rides or events held over a number of days. This rules out any professional one-day races, which all fall below 300 km, while pro stage races also have a separate category.

Track

Events held in velodromes – both indoors and out – which are oval tracks for cycling, generally banked to allow for a constant high speed, on which riders complete multiple laps in a variety of different events. It's cycling's equivalent of athletics.

Key to map pages

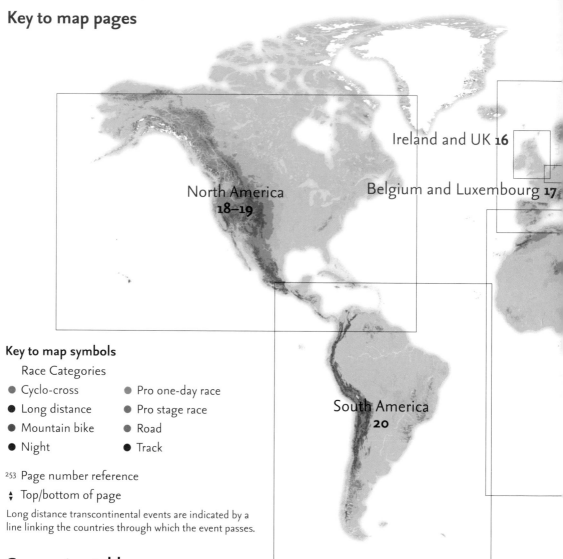

Ireland and UK **16**

North America
18–19

Belgium and Luxembourg **17**

South America
20

Key to map symbols

Race Categories

- ● Cyclo-cross
- ● Long distance
- ● Mountain bike
- ● Night

- ● Pro one-day race
- ● Pro stage race
- ● Road
- ● Track

²⁵³ Page number reference

↕ Top/bottom of page

Long distance transcontinental events are indicated by a
line linking the countries through which the event passes.

Conversion tables

Metres	1	5	10	25	50	75	100	250	500	1,000	5,000	10,000	20,000
Feet	3.3	16.4	32.8	82.0	164.0	246.1	328.1	820.2	1,640.4	3,280.8	16,404.2	32,808.4	65,616.8
Miles	0.0006	0.003	0.006	0.016	0.031	0.047	0.062	0.156	0.311	0.621	3.107	6.214	12.427

Metres

0	1,000		5,000		10,000			20,000
0	1		3		6			12

Miles

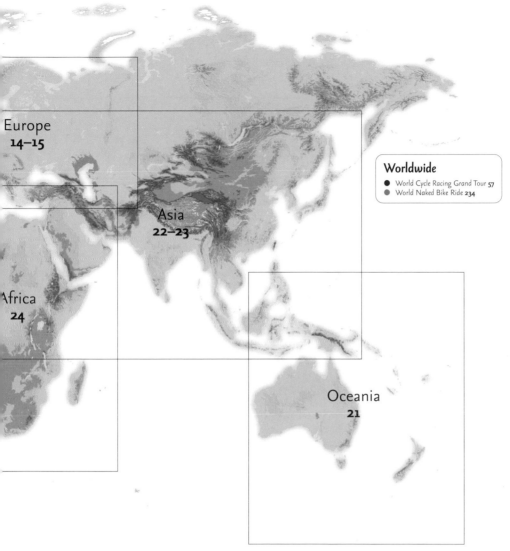

Europe
14–15

Asia
22–23

Africa
24

Oceania
21

Worldwide
- World Cycle Racing Grand Tour **57**
- World Naked Bike Ride **234**

Kilometres	1	5	10	20	50	100	250	500	1,000
Miles	0.621	3.107	6.214	12.427	31.069	62.137	155.343	310.686	621.371

Kilometres

| 0 | 50 | 100 | | 500 | | | 1,000 |

| 0 | 50 | 100 | | 300 | | | 600 |

Miles

Miles	1	5	10	20	50	100	250	500	1,000
Kilometres	1.609	8.047	16.093	32.187	80.467	160.934	402.336	804.672	1,609.34

Miles

| 0 | 50 | 100 | | 500 | | | 1,000 |

| 0 | 100 | 250 | 500 | 750 | 1,000 | | 1,500 |

Kilometres

Height

Metres		Feet
6,000	20,000	
5,000	15,000	
4,000	10,000	
3,000		
2,000	5,000	
1,000		
0	0	

ICELAND

NORWAY

SWEDEN

FINLAN

Faroe Islands
(Denmark)

ESTONI

LATVIA

see page 16

222

255

343 348

LITHUANIA

RUSSIA

380

363
349

284

DENMARK

352 354

239 244

POLAND

NETHERLANDS

382

324

252

118

GERMANY

310 312

296

154

250

98▼ 128

105, 125▲

119

250

389

164

408

150 151

116

76 398

121

262

360 196

CZECH REPUBLIC

SLOVAKIA

388

424

132

124▼

107

227

419

298 202

276

250

368

362

98▲

364

334

298

376

AUSTRIA

HUNGARY

84▼

442

188

370

143

366

298

377

298

253

456

464

436

330

356

366

239

133

SLOVENIA

238

FRANCE

272

328

392

242

174 260

228

301

250

CROATIA

342

224

286

459

237

250

250

184

372

82, 418, 422

438

256

216

426

290

250

85▼

198

ROMAN

47

52 58

452

74

440

156

254

269

41 401

127

78

ITALY

BOSNIA

HERZEGOVINA

SERBIA

340

123

106

344

266

92

426

MONTENEGRO

318

99

86

KOSOVO

THE FORMER

YUGOSLAV

REPUBLIC

OF MACEDONIA

BULGA

SPAIN

50

126, 136

PORTUGAL

73

GREECE

MALTA

60

56▼

250

14

see page 17

Europe

IRELAND

UNITED KINGDOM

35
268▲
365

166

207
218

314

412
115
280

161
160

170
470

430
192

64

189
168
165

404
94▲

246
40▼
146
257

374
315

176
402
307

264
172

120
104

236
206, 232, 268▼
185, 258, 262, 302, 482

56▲
226
112

472
379
466
446

220
378
306
409
448
69

437
46▼
177
336
320, 400

294
194
261

396

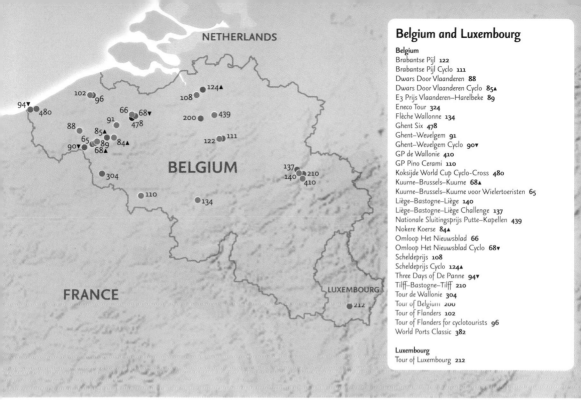

Ireland and United Kingdom (page 16)

USA

180 428 300
390
29
142

CANADA

285
313

UNITED STATES
OF AMERICA

251
338   394
406   346
130
462   125▼
322
208   415 162 190
414   90   248
223 90▲
326
331
332 308
204 358
292
416
142▼ 144
178   152

477

MEXICO

CUBA   DOMINICAN
REPUBLIC

BELIZE   JAMAICA   Puerto
HONDURAS   Rico
                        (USA)

GUATEMALA
  EL SALVADOR   NICARAGUA

                PANAMA
COSTA RICA 476

VENEZUELA

GUYANA

COLOMBIA

SURINAME

ECUADOR

PERU

B R A Z I L

BOLIVIA

PARAGUAY

●28

62 ● ● ●444

CHILE ●37

URUGUAY

ARGENTINA

●36

Falkland
Islands
(UK)

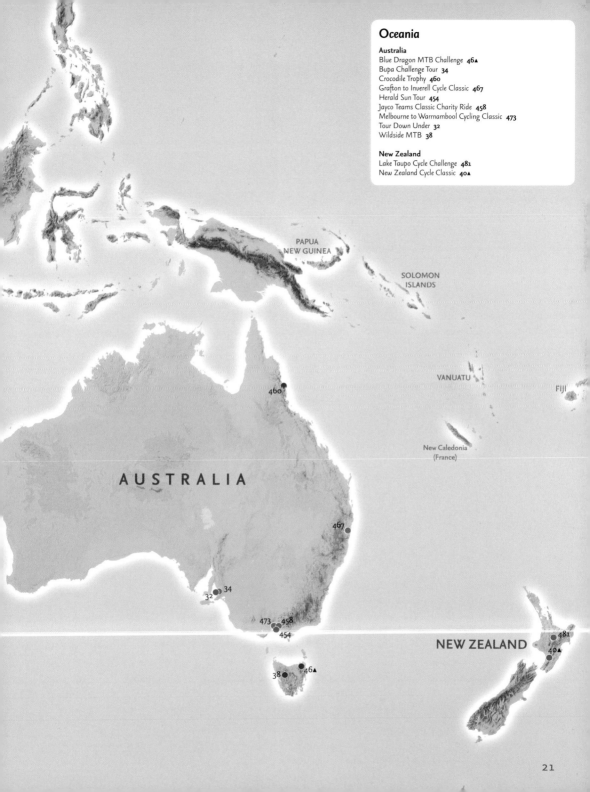

PAPUA
NEW GUINEA

SOLOMON
ISLANDS

VANUATU

FIJI

460

New Caledonia
(France)

AUSTRALIA

467

32 34

473 458
454

NEW ZEALAND 481
49▲

38 46▲

R U S S I

KAZAKHSTAN

GEORGIA

186

TURKEY

UZBEKISTAN

KYRGYZSTAN
186

186

ARMENIA

AZERBAIJAN

TURKMENISTAN
186

TAJIKISTAN
186

138

CYPRUS

SYRIA

LEBANON

ISRAEL

IRAQ

IRAN
186

AFGHANISTAN

JORDAN

KUWAIT

PAKISTAN

NEP

BAHRAIN

SAUDI
ARABIA

QATAR
48 44

UNITED
ARAB
EMIRATES

INDIA

54

OMAN

SRI LANKA

YEMEN

Asia

A

MONGOLIA

CHINA

●450

○295

BANGLADESH

MYANMAR

LAOS

THAILAND

VIETNAM

CAMBODIA

MALAYSIA

SINGAPORE

●61

BRUNEI

PHILIPPINES

PALAU

INDONESIA

EAST TIMOR

NORTH
KOREA

SOUTH
KOREA

JAPAN

●468

175
186

23

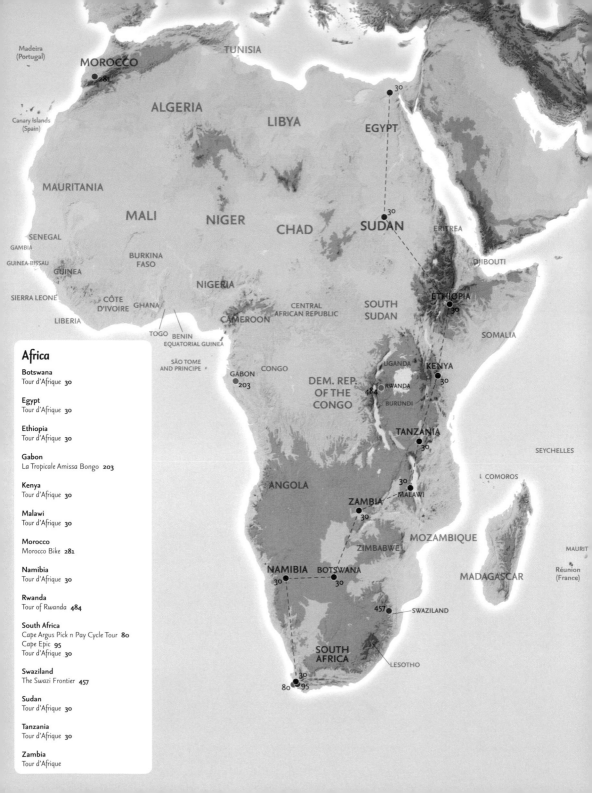

Madeira
(Portugal)

TUNISIA

MOROCCO
● 281

ALGERIA

LIBYA

EGYPT
● 30

Canary Islands
(Spain)

MAURITANIA

MALI

NIGER

CHAD

SUDAN
● 30

ERITREA

DJIBOUTI

SENEGAL
GAMBIA
GUINEA-BISSAU
GUINEA
SIERRA LEONE
LIBERIA
CÔTE
D'IVOIRE
GHANA
TOGO
BENIN
EQUATORIAL GUINEA
SÃO TOME
AND PRINCIPE

BURKINA
FASO

NIGERIA

CAMEROON

CENTRAL
AFRICAN REPUBLIC

SOUTH
SUDAN

ETHIOPIA
● 30

SOMALIA

GABON
● 203

CONGO

DEM. REP.
OF THE
CONGO

UGANDA

RWANDA
484 ●
BURUNDI

KENYA
● 30

SEYCHELLES

ANGOLA

TANZANIA
● 30

● 30

MALAWI

ZAMBIA
● 30

COMOROS

MOZAMBIQUE

MAURIT
Réunion
(France)

ZIMBABWE

MADAGASCAR

NAMIBIA
● 30

BOTSWANA
● 30

457 ● — SWAZILAND

SOUTH
AFRICA

LESOTHO

● 30
80 ● ● 95

The world's 300 ultimate cycling races,
ordered by month.

Vuelta Chile
Chile
Pro stage race

A truly international pro stage race showcasing Chile's spectacular scenery

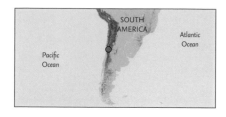

Cycling is a popular pastime in Chile, and a combination of that passion, the terrain and the weather makes the Vuelta Chile a popular race for local enthusiasts to watch and foreign teams to participate in alike. Since 1976, the race has openly welcomed teams from all over the world, with the infamous Festina team dominating the race in the late 1990s. However, despite strong competition from abroad, South Americans have met with plenty of success, with Chile and Colombia tied on eight wins per nation until 2012 when local boy Patricio Almonacid swung it in Chile's favour.

After a four-year hiatus, the race had returned bigger and better than ever in 2011, and made special efforts to take the race to the people across the whole country, ensuring varied but always spectacular terrain, with the stand-out feature of the 2012 edition being the 1,822 m summit finish at the ski resort of Farellones on the penultimate day.

The use of regional artists to design the race leaders' jerseys makes for arguably the most spectacular leaders' jerseys out there, and there's even a competition to vote for the race's handsomest rider, which appeared to be going the way of Chile's own Freddy Mena for 2012 at last count, not-really-that-closely followed by race winner Almonacid's Clos de Pirque-Trek team-mate Cristopher Mansilla.

Statistics

Location
La Serena to Santiago (2012)

Distance
1,348 km/837.6 miles over 10 stages (2012)

Highest point
1,822 m (2012)

Terrain
Tarmac

Record wins
Luis Fernando Sepulveda (Chi), Marco Arriagada (Chi) (both two wins)

Field size
120

First event
1976

Website
www.vueltachile.cl/en

Contact
Via website

Jersey designed by local artists

5 CIUDADES | 10 ETAPAS | 1400 KMS

INVITA

VUELTA
CHILE

vtr.com

Tour d'Afrique
Africa

Long distance

An epic event through ten African countries – and yes, it is a race if you want it to be

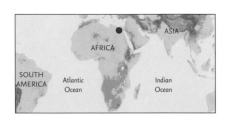

From Cairo to Cape Town, the Tour d'Afrique takes you through the most eclectic mix of terrain, weather and cultures, and although it sounds a lot like the trip of a lifetime – which it is – it's also a bona fide bike race. Far from the organisers trying to play down the competitive element, it's most definitely there for those who want it, but equally you can take your time – within reason! – and just enjoy the challenge of traversing the world's second-largest continent by bike.

Starting out from the Great Pyramid of Giza in Egypt and crossing though eight other countries before arriving in South Africa, the Tour d'Afrique is open to cyclists of all abilities. Of course, riding your bike almost every day for a third of a year requires at least some prior knowledge of how life is going to be; a commute to work this isn't. In fact, you couldn't be further away from the hustle and bustle of city life, and participants are encouraged to embrace the local culture of each country and, as you pass through relatively leisurely on two wheels, it's hard not to. Support vehicles carry your luggage, and food is provided along the way on all riding days, while accommodation is a tent most nights.

Riders experience the vast and varying wonders of Africa as they traverse the continent

Statistics

Location
Cairo, Egypt to Cape Town, South Africa via Sudan, Ethiopia, Kenya, Tanzania, Malawi, Zambia, Botswana and Namibia

Distance
11,693 km/7,261 miles over four months (2012)

Terrain
Tarmac and dirt roads

Field size
16 full-tour riders/ 36 racers in 2012

First event
2003

Website
www.tourdafrique.com

Contact
info@tourdafrique.com

Tour Down Under
Australia
Pro stage race

The first major stage race on the international calendar provides the pros with a good dose of sunshine

This six-day stage race, which takes place in and around Adelaide, South Australia, has gone from strength to strength since it began in 1999, and enjoyed a real surge in popularity when it joined the Tour de France as part of international cycling's WorldTour circuit in 2008, welcoming Lance Armstrong to the following year's edition of the race.

Riders, team staff and the media appreciate the convenience of an event based at the Hilton hotel right at the heart of Adelaide, and the race convoy heads off from there each morning to various start and finish venues in and around the city, with regulars on the route including picturesque Victor Harbor, the Germanic village of Hahndorf and the wine paradise that is the Barossa Valley.

Simon Gerrans – a member of Australia's first top-division pro team, GreenEDGE, and the 2012 Australian road race champion – won the TDU, as it's known, in both 2006 and 2012, and shares the record of titles won with German André Greipel and local hero Stuart O'Grady.

"It's a big opportunity to race in front of family and friends at such a big event when you normally race in Europe," Gerrans says. "It's also really rider-friendly and well run, plus you're staying at the same hotel each night and then there's the great weather..."

That great weather is almost as famous as the race itself, and the riders have enjoyed – or, rather, endured – temperatures in recent years way above the historic

monthly average for January.

"Back in 2006, I remember it being well over 30 °C all the time, and it almost touched 50 °C at times," says Gerrans. "When it's extreme like that, it's really not pleasant, but I seem to be able to handle it fairly well." Sprinters have tended to dominate the race, despite some short, sharp climbs, such as 'Adelaide's Alpe d'Huez', Old Willunga Hill, which is a regular feature of the race. For 2012, the route organisers decided to mix things up, with the race featuring its first uphill finish on the climb, where Spain's Alejandro Valverde pipped Gerrans for the win on stage five, although it was Gerrans who took control of the overall classification and never let go.

Lance Armstrong

Statistics
Location
Adelaide,
South Australia
Distance
803.3 km/499.1 miles
over 6 stages (2012)
Terrain
Tarmac
Record wins
Stuart O'Grady (Aus),
André Greipel (Ger),
Simon Gerrans (Aus)
(all two wins)
Field size
133
First run
1999
Website
www.tourdown
under.com.au
Contact
tourdownunder@
tourism.sa.com

The Tour Down Under attracts a host of international cyclists ▶

Bupa Challenge Tour
Australia
Road

The Tour Down Under's answer to the Etape du Tour

The Bupa Challenge Tour has seen various sponsor changes since its first edition in 2003, but the concept remains the same: the chance to ride the same route as the pros over one of the stages of the Tour Down Under, with the added pressure of it being run on the same day that the pros ride it.

With the world's best riders hot on your heels, there's no time for hanging about, although the organisers insist that this is a 'challenge' rather than a race but try telling that to 7,500 revved-up riders.

Along for the ride in 2012, and helping, no doubt, to further bring out that competitive streak in people, was none other than Eddy Merckx – arguably the world's greatest-ever cyclist thanks to 525 career wins, including five Tour de France victories. The Belgian joined participants on the route of stage four of the Tour Down Under, between Norwood in Adelaide and Tanunda out in the Barossa Valley, tackling a number of climbs on the full 138 km route, including TDU regular Menglers Hill, which also featured on the three shorter ride options.

A coach transfer with your bike back to the start is the kind of service that all sportive-style point-to-point events would provide in an ideal world, and here there's even a choice of two return times: one post-ride and another leaving after the pro race has finished, catering for those riders who wish to rest their legs in the almost-guaranteed sunshine and watch the pros come home.

Statistics

Location
Between Norwood and Tanunda (2012)
Distance
138 km/85.7 miles (2012)
Terrain
Tarmac
Field size
7,500
First event
2003
Website
www.tourdown under.com.au
Contact
tourdownunder@ tourism.sa.com

Riders take in a stage of the Tour Down Under

Strathpuffer 24
United Kingdom

Mountain bike

Twenty-four hour mountain-bike madness in the Highlands of Scotland

Torrachilty Forest, near Strathpeffer in the Scottish Highlands, is the stunning venue for the Strathpuffer 24 mountain bike race. Fantastic event-name puns aside, and despite only having run since 2005, the Strathpuffer has quickly become one of those must-ride races among off-road fanatics as solos, pairs and teams of four compete to complete as many laps of a challenging 11 km circuit within 24 hours as they can. One of the real draws, perversely, is the weather, and January in the Highlands often means freezing, snowy conditions, made all-the-more fun in the dark at 4am.

The Puffer Lite takes place in July on the same course over 'just' 12 hours and, taking place in summer as it does, is the ideal introduction to, and training for, January's main event.

Statistics

Location
Torrachilty Forest, near Strathpeffer, Scotland

Distance
Laps of an 11 km/ 6.8 mile course

Terrain
Off-road, fire-tracks

Field size
362

First event
2005

Website
www.strathpuffer.co.uk

Contact
Via website form

Racing through Torrachilty Forest

Trans Andes Challenge
Chile
Long distance

A tough, multi-stage mountain-bike challenge through the Andes mountains in Chile

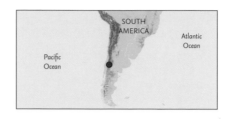

"The best six mountain-bike days of your life" is quite a claim by the organisers, but then taking on the Andes mountains in Chilean Patagonia by bike is going to be up there in anyone's book. Racing in pairs or individually, this is not an event for the faint of heart, made up as it is of challenging off-road terrain, long, lung-bursting climbs and technical descents, while your accommodation each night is a tent – although cabins and hotels are also available should it all get too much. However, the pain is only temporary, while the stunning views of imposing volcanoes and picture-perfect lakes will stay with you forever. Distances vary between 60 and 100 km across six stages, although the Half Trans Andes Challenge covers only the final three stages, and is a good place to start out if you're not quite ready to go the whole hog.

Statistics

Location
Andes Mountains, Chilean Patagonia
Distance
419 km/260 miles over 6 stages (2012)
Terrain
Off-road, single-track, jeep roads and technical terrain
Field size
250
First event
2009
Website
www.transandes challenge.com
Contact
info@transandes challenge.com

Villarrica Volcano, Pucon, Chile

Tour de San Luis
Argentina
Pro stage race

Argentina's premier stage race, which attracts the world's top pro teams

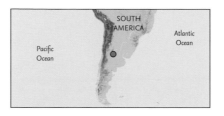

Many of the top European pro teams heading to the ever-increasing number of top-end South American stage races for the first time are surprised by the warmth and enthusiasm of fans for what has always been a traditionally European sport. They're quickly sold, and are then first in line to return year after year. Argentina's Tour de San Luis is a prime example: in 2012 it hosted squads from Saxo Bank, Movistar, Liquigas and Ag2r, whose riders enjoyed not only a warm welcome but pleasant, warm weather – the heavy downpour on stage one notwithstanding – while the tough route in the foothills of the Andes mountains helped set them up for the tough season ahead.

However, it was Omega Pharma-Quick Step's American star, Levi Leipheimer, who triumphed overall in San Luis, in central Argentina, having matched Spain's Alberto Contador on the race's steep climbs and then overpowered him in the 20 km time trial on stage four.

It was quite a race for Omega Pharma as, apart from Leipheimer's stage win and overall victory, the Belgian team also notched up victories in the opening two stages for their Italian sprinter Francesco Chicchi, and a fourth through Tom Boonen on the final stage, warming up nicely ahead of his spring Classics campaign back in Europe.

Statistics
Location
San Luis
Distance
1,051 km/653.1 miles over 7 stages (2012)
Terrain
Tarmac
Field size
168
First event
2007
Website
www.tour-san luis.com.ar
Contact
Via website

Levi Leipheimer

Wildside MTB
Australia
Mountain bike

Experience the best of Tasmania in this mountain bike stage race

The perfect chance to ride with, and even take on, some of the world's best mountain bikers, the Wildside shows off the best Tasmania has to offer through a combination of untimed 'cruise' stages and relatively short competitive stages over four days. There really is something for everyone, from suspension-bridge crossings through rainforests, to racing along unspoilt sandy beaches, to a dual time trial stage where, as its name suggests, riders set off two at a time to blast over a 6 km stage that takes them underground through the old railway tunnel at the former silver-mining town of Zeehan.

There are a number of age categories, as well as a single-speed category and a three-person team event, so even if you're not in the hunt for the top prize, there's always someone to compete against. Or indeed take it a little bit more leisurely and enjoy the stunning scenery, although you do still have to make the time cut each day.

If you thought the finish of the 1989 Tour de France was exciting, when Greg LeMond beat Laurent Fignon to win by just 8 seconds, try 2012 Wildside winner Sid Taberlay puncturing and having to ride the last 3 km of the final stage on his wheel rim, and winning the event overall – for the fifth time, we hasten to add – by just 2 seconds after more than 200 km of riding.

Statistics

Location
Tasmania

Distance
210 km/130.5 miles over four days, timed and untimed (2012)

Terrain
Off-road

Record wins
Sid Taberlay (Aus) (five wins)

Field size
450

First event
2002

Website
www.wildside mtb.com

Contact
race@wildside mtb.com

Riders contend with varying off-road terrain

New Zealand Cycle Classic
New Zealand

Pro stage race

New Zealand's sole UCI men's event that
attracts the cream of Andtipodean cycling

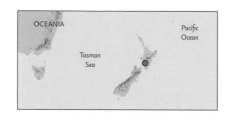

Since 1988, the New Zealand Cycle Classic –
formerly known as the Tour of Wellington –
has welcomed Australia and New Zealand's
top cycling teams to the North Island, and
celebrated its 25th anniversary in 2012,
with top honours falling to up-and-coming
Australian talent Jay McCarthy of the
Jayco-AIS squad.

The race, which in 2012 stuck exclusively
to the windy region of Manawatu-
Wanganui, with stages based around the
regional capital of Palmerston North, is the
only men's event in New Zealand that is part
of the International Cycling Federation's
(UCI) calendar.

A women's version of the race takes place
in February – the NZCT Women's Tour of
New Zealand – which also allows cycling
enthusiasts to ride a stage of the race at the
Mitre 10 Mega gran fondo.

Statistics
Location
Manawatu
Distance
535.2 km/332.6 miles
over 5 stages (2012)
Terrain
Tarmac
Record wins
Brian Fowler (Nzl)
(four wins)
Field size
105
First event
1988
Website
www.cycletournz.com
Contact
jorge@ihug.co.nz

TAKE PART

CX Sportives
United Kingdom

Cyclo-cross

A perfect antidote for restless summer-sportive
riders looking to stay fit through the colder months

Although the organisers encourage all
types of bikes, and go as far as suggesting
your mum's shopper if you really feel like
a challenge, a proper cyclo-cross – or CX –
bike is going to serve you best at either of
these two events. The popularity of the first
running of January's Woodcote CX event, in
Oxfordshire in 2011, prompted organisers
to add the South Downs CX, with its HQ in
Duncton, West Sussex, for 2012, which takes
in sections of the South Downs Way.

With mechanical assistance and feed
stations at both events, these truly are
off-road sportives, while for those worried
about the cold, on-site catering boasting
hot food and drink is also available. A nice,
restorative cup of tea will soon have your
cockles warmed up again afterwards.

Statistics
Location
Woodcote and Duncton
Distance
80/60/40 km
49.7/37.3/24.9 miles
(2012)
Highest point
211 m (Woodcote),
228 m (South Downs)
Terrain
Tarmac, bridleways and
off-road tracks
Field size
400 (2012)
First event
2011
Website
www.cxsportive.com
Contact
info@cxsportive.com

GP La Marseillaise
France
Pro one-day race

The traditional curtain-raiser to the European race season

The Grand Prix d'Ouverture La Marseillaise, to give this one-day race its full name in all its grandeur, heralds the start of the European road-racing season. Despite being a one-day event in its own right, it usually falls two days before the start of the Etoile de Bessèges, and features the same field, effectively acting as a warm-up for the stage race.

'Warm-up' perhaps isn't quite the best way to describe it as even in southern France the weather isn't exactly balmy at this time of year, and cycling fans' first glimpse of the pros in their spanking-brand-new team kits is usually with the addition of arm and leg warmers at the very least, if not jackets. It's a far cry from those sun-soaked pro events taking place in Australia and South America at the same time.

Although there are worse places to be on a crisp, sunny morning than Marseille, from where the race heads inland to take on the climbs around Aubagne and Trets, including the Col de l'Espigoulier – a 14 km climb with an average gradient of 5 per cent, which also regularly features on the route of the Tour of the Mediterranean and is a good leg-loosener at this early point in the season. However, there's still usually a relatively large front group that stays intact to barrel back into the city for a sprint royale in front of the Stade Vélodrome – Olympique de Marseille football club's home ground.

Statistics

Location
Marseille
Distance
148 km/92 miles (2012)
Highest point
723 m
Terrain
Tarmac
Record wins
Baden Cooke (Aus),
Edwig Van
Hooydonck (Bel),
Eddy Planckaert (Bel)
(all two wins)
Field size
144
First event
1980
Website
www.lamarseillaise.fr
Contact
journal.lamarseillaise@
gmail.com

Marseille

Ladies' Tour of Qatar
Qatar
Pro stage race

The world's fastest women battle both the wind and each other in this three-day stage race

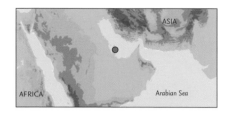

The Ladies' Tour of Qatar takes place on the same roads as the men's event that directly follows it later in the week, and shares the same race organisation, amazing hotel and the windy conditions out on the road – in fact, the only difference is that the women's event is slightly shorter at three days instead of six. A collaboration between the Qatar cycling federation, Eddy Merckx and Tour de France organisers ASO, it's a race that attracts the very best international women's teams, and the strong support for the event since its first edition in 2009 is indicative of the Qataris' love of sport.

In 2012, two-time Qatar champion Kirsten Wild of the Netherlands looked on course to make it a hat-trick after taking the opening stage. That is, until Germany's Judith Arndt and Trixi Worrack put more than two minutes into chasers Wild and compatriot Adrie Visser, with the peloton almost three minutes down on a blustery stage two. While Worrack took the stage win, Arndt took over the race lead. With the German's strong GreenEDGE-AIS squad controlling the race on the final stage, the golden jersey was in the bag, while Wild had to console herself with a second stage win on the day, which also gave her the points title.

Statistics
Location
Doha
Distance
304 km/188.9 miles over 3 stages (2012)
Terrain
Tarmac
Record wins
Kirsten Wild (Ned) (two wins)
Field size
90
First event
2009
Website
www.letour.fr
Contact
cyclisme@aso.fr

Top international teams annually compete in Doha

2012 Tour of Qatar winner Judith Arndt ▶

Blue Dragon MTB Challenge Australia

Mountain bike

Riders are encouraged to slow down just a little to enjoy the stunning Blue Tier Forest Reserve

The Blue Dragon MTB Challenge is Tasmania's second major mountain-bike event, along with January's Wildside MTB, and it's nice to see both events actively helping to publicise each other – either as an alternative if one is sold out, or to even suggest you make a proper holiday of it in Tasmania by riding the Wildside and then sticking around for the Blue Dragon, too!

The Blue Dragon takes you to the northeast of the island, and although you compete over two days, there's still a strong emphasis on encouraging you to remember where you are and to enjoy what you're doing – and, as you are riding in pairs, to try to share the experience with your riding partner, too.

Statistics

Location
Derby, Tasmania
Distance
100 km/62 miles over 2 stages (2012)
Highest point
910 m (2012)
Terrain
4WD tracks, single-track, gravel roads
Field size
400 (200 pairs)
First event
2009
Website
www.wildwheel promotions.com.au
Contact
wildwheel promotions@gmail.com

 RACE AGAINST THE PROS

Perfs Pedal Race
United Kingdom

Road

And they're off! British road-race season opener in Hampshire

While the mainland European season is kicked off with the GP La Marseillaise in the chilly but sunny south of France, the Perfs Pedal Race near Portsmouth in the southeast of England is traditionally the first event of the British road-racing season.

Almost anyone who's anyone among British cycling's road-race elite has raced here – past winners include Sean Yates, Julian Winn and Alex Dowsett – with Mick Waite of VC St. Raphael having organised every edition since 1964. An early-season event in the UK brings its own problems, and Mick has had his fair share of battles with ice, snow, flooding and roadworks, but getting on for half a century later, this remains one of the UK's best known and best loved road races.

Statistics

Location
Southwick, Portsmouth
Distance
75 km/46.6 miles (shortened to 60 km due to ice, 2012)
Terrain
Tarmac
Record wins
Graham Moore (Gbr), Tim Harris (Gbr) (both three wins)
Field size
85
First event
1964
Website
www.british cycling.org.uk
Contact
vcstraphael@hotmail.com

Etoile de Bessèges
France
Pro stage race

France's first major stage race of the year that traditionally brings the sprinters out in force

Traditionally the preserve of the sprinters, the addition of a short, sharp time trial to the 2012 edition changed the dynamic of this French stage race so that it became a battle between two of France's brightest young hopes: Pierre Rolland – the winner of the young rider's jersey at the 2011 Tour de France – and Saur-Sojasun's

Jérôme Coppel. Rolland had scored his Europcar squad's first victory of the season on stage three, and taken the overall lead, but it was Coppel who had the best legs on the final 3 km, 16 per cent climb of the closing 10 km time trial, and it was enough for him to win both the stage and steal the leader's jersey from Rolland.

Statistics

Location
Beaucaire to Alès

Distance
690 km/428 miles over 6 stages (2012)

Highest point
631 m (2012)

Terrain
Tarmac

Record wins
Jean-Luc Molineris (Fra), Jo Planckaert (Bel) (both two wins)

Field size
136

First event
1971

Website
www.etoilede besseges.com

Contact
etoiledebesseges@ wanadoo.fr

Race finished in the town of Alès in 2012

Tour of Qatar
Qatar
Pro stage race

The race that put the Middle East on the pro cycling map

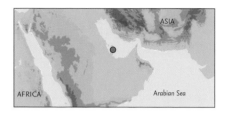

Now that everyone seems to have fallen back in love with sprinting thanks to riders like Mark Cavendish, the Tour of Qatar appears to have enjoyed a new lease of life. In its early years it was accused of being "flat and boring, and it always ends in a sprint". Now that everyone wants bunch sprints again, the peloton is literally up against it, as what has always been a windy race appears to be getting even windier. That means echelons. Echelons are formed when there is a side wind, and riders line up side-by-side to shelter from it, rather than one behind the other. It means that someone ends up running out of road, which means that they have to start a new echelon, which takes both time and strength, and which in turn means gaps open up between echelon groups on the road. It makes for fantastic television, and some very hard racing for the riders. Nevertheless, with the spring Classics on their minds, they need all the hardship they can get, as they certainly have it easy when it comes to accommodation for the week: the whole race – including a very grateful press corps, with easy access to more interviews than they can shake a Dictaphone at – stays in the luxurious surroundings of the Ritz-Carlton, Doha. As a result, it's a popular race with teams and press alike.

Statistics

Location
Doha

Distance
727 km/451.7 miles over 6 stages (2012)

Terrain
Tarmac

Record wins
Tom Boonen (Bel) (four wins)

Field size
128

First event
2002

Website
www.letour.fr

Contact
cyclisme@aso.fr

Four-times winner Tom Boonen and Qatar cycling federatio president Sheikh Khali bin Ali al-Thani

Arnaud Demare celebrates after winning the final stage in 2012

Tour of Mallorca
Spain
Pro one-day race (x4)
Fast racing, tough climbing and almost guaranteed sunshine – except when it snows

The Tour of Mallorca was always unique among stage races in that riders could drop in and out of 'stages' as they chose, with each pro team normally using a football-inspired squad rotation system to try out different combinations of riders this early in the season, and ensure that everyone gets a chance to race. Only those who rode all the events counted for the unofficial general classification. However, as of 2010, the organisers of what is these days also called the Mallorca Challenge did away with the general classification, and it's now essentially just four back-to-back one-day races, or trofeos.

The Balearic island is a favourite with northern European club cyclists, and February is a popular time to get a cheap flight with your bike, stay at an off-peak-price hotel, get some sunny kilometres under your belt and watch some pro racing. Appropriately enough, popular holiday destination as it is, Mallorca had a very British slant to it in 2012 thanks to Brit Andy Fenn winning the Trofeo Palma – his very first pro race – and then the Trofeo Migjorn the next day, while Lars-Petter Nordhaug, one of British team Sky's Norwegian imports, won the Trofeo Deia.

However, the fourth and last day of competition – the Trofeo Serra de Tramuntana, which featured the well-known climbs of the Col de Soller and Puig Major – had to be cancelled due to heavy snow. What's nearly always a cyclist's paradise can still have its moments in February after all.

Statistics
Location
Mallorca – various towns
Distance
439 km/272.8 miles over three days (fourth day cancelled) (2012)
Terrain
Tarmac
First event
1992
Website
www.vuelta mallorca.com
Contact
info@unisport consulting.com

Approach to the Col de Soller

Spectacular Puig Major ▶

Tour of the Mediterranean
France
Pro stage race

2012 champ Tiernan-Locke used YouTube to familiarise himself with the stage race's climbs

In winning the 2012 edition of the Tour of the Med, Britain's Jonathan Tiernan-Locke joined an illustrious list of past winners, among them Tony Rominger, Gianni Bugno and Eddy Merckx.

However, it's highly unlikely that any of them used the wonders of YouTube to train for the race's traditional summit finish on Mont Faron.

The stunning climb watches over the old naval port of Toulon, and had obviously made quite an impression on the Devon man, too.

"The Tour of the Med is a race I've wanted to do well in since watching the CSC team dominate on Mont Faron in the early 2000s," says Tiernan-Locke. "So I started watching videos of it on YouTube to prepare myself for what was to come, picking out and memorising landmarks to familiarise myself with it.

"I actually based my whole winter's training on being ready for Mont Faron," continues Tiernan-Locke, and having proven his good form by unexpectedly winning the race's opening stage, the Endura rider went into the fourth and final stage full of confidence, albeit by then 10 seconds behind new race leader Michel Kreder.

Then disaster struck. Due to snow – a very real possibility on higher ground in February, even in the south of France – the climb was dropped from the route.

"My heart just sank when I heard the news," says Tiernan-Locke, "as I assumed they'd just make it a flat, sprinters' finish instead." However, affable organiser Lucien Aimar – a home winner of the Tour de France in 1966 – and his team had an ace up their sleeve: the lesser known Col de Garde, which already featured on the stage's original route, but was upgraded to become the race's alternative summit finish.

"I knew I'd just have to go hard right from the bottom, as I knew that Kreder was pretty good," says Tiernan-Locke, which is exactly what he did, winning the stage alone, 17 seconds ahead of Spanish climber Daniel Navarro and 2000 Giro d'Italia winner Stefano Garzelli, and putting enough time into Dutch Garmin rider Kreder to win the race overall by a commanding 27 seconds – and becoming the first British winner of the race in the process.

Toulon from Mont Faron

Statistics

Location
Pertuis to Mont Faron, Toulon

Distance
482 km/299.5 miles over 4 stages (shortened due to snow, 2012)

Highest point
452 m (2012)

Terrain
Tarmac

Record wins
Gerrie Knetemann (Ned) (three wins)

Field size
144

First event
1974

Website
http://letourmed.fr

Contact
occostebelle@wanadoo.fr

Jonathan Tiernan-Locke celebrates winning the 2012 race ▶

Tour of Oman
Oman

Pro stage race

A new, top-level international stage race full of eastern promise

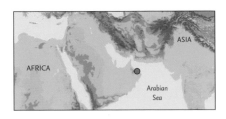

With the Sultanate of Oman only having welcomed the world's top pro riders to its stage race since 2010, with many riders coming directly from the Tour of Qatar that takes place just a couple of days before, just a short plane ride away, this is one of the newer events on the international calendar. Part of the International Cycling Federation's (UCI) push to further 'internationalise' cycling, the Tour of Oman is organised by none other than Eddy Merckx, ably backed up by Tour de France organisers ASO, ensuring that riders feel quite at home when it comes to the running of the event.

Teams often change very few of the riders on their rosters between Qatar – also organised by Merckx – and Oman, and both races provide those riders targeting the spring Classics, in particular, with a good level of fitness before they return to the cold and wet of northern Europe. Indeed, it does no harm at all that the racing out in Oman is in what are normally very pleasantly warm temperatures, and that teams, the press and the organisation all stay in the lap of luxury at the Shangri-La Barr Al Jissah resort on the coast near the capital city of Muscat.

For the 2011 edition of the race, the Oman organisers introduced the cycling world to Jabal al Akhdar – Green Mountain – and the addition of the climb really helped make the race come alive after what had

already been a very promising start in its inaugural year.

For many riders, it was their first proper climb of the season in competition, and eventual overall race winner Robert Gesink of Rabobank was the emotional winner of the stage, the Dutch climber dedicating his victory to his father who had passed away following a mountain-bike accident the year before.

With the climb on the route again for the 2012 edition, it looks as though it's a feature of the race that's there to stay, and this time it was Italian Vincenzo Nibali showing Omega Pharma-Quick Step's Peter Velits a clean pair of heels to win by 10 seconds from the Slovakian, although it was Velits who went on to take the overall crown in Muscat the next day.

Marcel Kittel won stage six in 2012

Statistics
Location
Muscat
Distance
875 km/543.7 miles
over 6 stages (2012)
Highest point
1,235 m (2012)
Terrain
Tarmac
Field size
128
First event
2010
Website
www.tourofoman.om
Contact
Via website

Competitors make their way from the Royal Opera House to Al Jabal Al Akhdar during stage 5 ▶

Red Bull Hill Chasers
United Kingdom
Night

Head-to-head hill-climbing excitement in Bristol city centre

The Red Bull Hill Chasers is a hill-climb with a difference – and not only in that it comes at the start of the season rather than the traditional end-of-season slot. Park Street is the venue for the event that pitches pairs of riders head-to-head up the steep hill in the centre of Bristol in front of thousands of screaming spectators on a February evening: sixteen elite-level riders from different cycling disciplines versus the best sixteen amateur riders from a qualifying session that same morning. The elimination battles whittle things down until the best, but exhausted, final two go up against each other for the top honours, won in 2012 by Wiggle's Ben Simmons, while Liquigas pro Ted King went out in the first round. If the crowd's enthusiasm is anything to go by, could this be the future for hill-climbs?

Statistics

Location
Bristol
Distance
200 m/0.12 miles (2012)
Terrain
Tarmac
Field size
32 (16 elite cyclists and 16 amateur cyclists)
First event
2011
Website
www.redbull.co.uk
Contact
Via website

 PROFESSIONAL

Ruta del Sol
Spain
Pro stage race

This Spanish stage race gives riders a chance to blow out the cobwebs and size up the competition

With a first edition in 1925, the Vuelta a Andalucia – or the Ruta del Sol as it is best known – is one of Europe's older stage races, although after that inaugural event it was another 30 years until the second edition in 1955. Since then, though, the stage race around Spain's southernmost region has consistently attracted the top pro teams, eager to find their stage-racing legs on the race's challenging terrain in some early-season warm weather. Like the neighbouring Tour of the Algarve, the race draws the big names out of hibernation and gives them a chance to size up their rivals for the first time on what are some very tough climbs, with anyone carrying any excess winter weight cruelly exposed.

Statistics

Location
Andalucia
Distance
642 km/398.9 miles over 5 stages (2012)
Highest point
924 m (2012)
Terrain
Tarmac
Record wins
Rolf Gölz (Ger), Freddy Maertens (Bel), Dietrich Thurau (Ger), Stefano Della Santa (Ita) (all two wins)
Field size
112
Website
www.vueltaandalucia.es
Contact
Via website

World Cycle Racing Grand Tour Worldwide

Long distance

An unsupported bike race around the world

The ultimate bike ride and the ultimate bike race rolled into one. Cycling around the world requires slightly more than a banana and a puncture repair kit in your pocket, but to actually race against other riders on top of the logistics and problems of lugging yourself and your steed around the globe truly is mind-boggling. There are a few house rules to abide by under the World Cycle Racing Grand Tour manifesto, though, and they include that entrants will ride completely unassisted, that they'll ride a minimum of 29,000 km in one direction – although they can choose whether to head east or west – and that the start and finish points are the same location. All this while trying to beat each other – and ideally set a new world record in the process. Nine riders set out from London's Greenwich Park in February 2012, with another setting off from the Isle of Man and one from New Zealand.

An event of this magnitude has been threatening to get off the ground for a while. Plans for a Global Bicycle Race, organised by former record holder Vin Cox, have been shelved, while Mark Beaumont – whose record Cox beat in 2010 – has been involved with organising a fully-supported round-the-world trip for 30 riders called the World Cycle Challenge, set to depart in September 2012.

Statistics

Location
Greenwich Park, London

Distance
29,000 km/18,020 miles (minimum) (2012)

Terrain
Tarmac and dirt roads

Field size
11 (nine from London, two 'independents')

First event
2012

Website
www.worldcycle racing.com

Contact
Via website

Setting off on the gruelling journey

Tour du Haut Var
France
Pro stage race
A tough two-day pro race in springtime Provence

EUROPE

Atlantic
Ocean

The Tour du Haut Var may only be over two stages, but distances are long for such an early-season race over such tough terrain. However, Endura Racing's Jonathan Tiernan-Locke, winner of the 2012 edition, was always ready.

"I was confident as I'm used to training for long hours, and I also know the area a bit from having raced there as an amateur," the Devon-born climber explains.

It also didn't do him any harm that he headed to the Provençal race having won two stages and the overall at the Tour of the Mediterranean less than a week before, either.

"They're the kinds of races that suit me down to the ground, with really punchy climbs," he says.

With a lot of the same riders there who also took part in the Tour of the Med, Tiernan-Locke knew what he was capable of. "I'd targeted these races in particular, as I knew that if we could do well early on in the season, it would lead to more invites for the team to other, bigger races later on."

While more experienced pros shiver in the cold of early-season races like the Tour of the Med and Haut Var, 'JTL' simply knuckles down to business; for him the solution is a simple one: "Just wear more clothing!"

Having finished third on the opening stage between Draguignan and La Croix Valmer, Tiernan-Locke took control on the second and final day's summit finish at Fayence. He held off Team Type 1's Julien El Fares on the leg-sapping climb, which featured sections of 20 per cent, and took the overall win from the Frenchman by 6 seconds, showing many of Europe's top riders another clean pair of heels.

Haut Var started life as a one-day race, but it grew to become a two-dayer in 2009, and there are rumours now that the race could grow yet further, adding a third day – likely to be a time trial on the opening day – and even become part of the International Cycling Federation's (UCI) top-tier WorldTour circuit.

Thomas Voeckler on his way to victory in 2011

Statistics
Location
Draguignan to Fayence
Distance
395 km/245.4 miles over 2 stages (2012)
Terrain
Tarmac
Record wins
Joop Zoetemelk (Ned) (three wins)
Field size
176
First event
1969
Website
www.tourdu hautvar.com
Contact
tourduhautvar@free.fr

Joop Zoetemelk has won the event a record three times ▶

Tour of the Algarve
Portugal

Pro stage race

Many of the sport's biggest names start their season at this stage race that has something for everyone

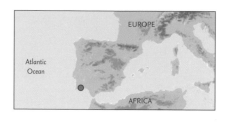

British holidaymakers able to tear themselves away from their sun loungers just long enough to enjoy the spectacle that is the professional peloton coming by were in for a treat in the 2012 edition of the race. Team Sky's Aussie import, Richie Porte, brought home the bacon in the form of overall victory in the south of Portugal, while roadside British fans would have been even more keen to see Tour de France hopeful Bradley Wiggins in action for the first time.

Portugal's flagship cycling event is often a season opener for many of the world's top riders targeting the spring and summer stage races, and a good place for them to get a good look at each other, too, making it a great star-spotting event for fans.

Statistics

Location
Algarve
Distance
745 km/462.9 miles
over 5 stages (2012)
Terrain
Tarmac
Record wins
Belmiro Silva (Por)
(three wins)
Field size
160
First event
1960
Website
www.volta
algarve.com
Contact
nunos.scsports@
gmail.com

Riders and spectators enjoy the picturesque Algarve

Tour de Langkawi
Malaysia
Pro stage race

Top European and North American teams are given a very warm welcome in hot and humid Malaysia

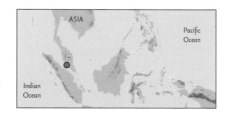

Malaysia's Tour de Langkawi is a spectacular stage race, the highlight of which, for fans and riders alike – although less so for the riders, perhaps – is Genting Highlands. Since the race started in 1996, the 25-kilometre-long monster climb has featured in the race every year, save for 2008 when the race fell over the Chinese New Year. The theme park at the top of the mountain – 'the city in the clouds',

as it's known – is Chinese-run, and closing the road for a bike race would have been bad for business. Despite the year-round stifling conditions and the tough climbing, the race has always managed to attract big-name riders and major teams, and for the smaller regional teams they race with, it's an invaluable experience, while helping to raise the sport's profile in Asia.

Statistics

Location
Putrajaya to
Kuala Terengganu

Distance
1,415.5 km/879.6 miles
over 10 stages (2012)

Highest point
1,679 m (2012)

Terrain
Tarmac

Record wins
Paolo Lanfranchi (Ita),
José Serpa (Col)
(both two wins)

Field size
132

First event
1996

Website
www.ltdl.com.my

Contact
info@ltdl.com.my

Record holder José Serpa (yellow jersey), Alexandr Dyachenko (white jersey) and Valentin Iglinskiy (blue jersey) at Le Tour de Langkawi 2012

Valparaiso Cerro Abajo
Chile

Mountain bike
Going downhill fast in central Valparaiso, Chile

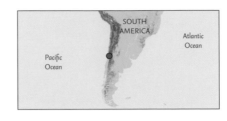

Ever wanted to know what careering down a long flight of steps on two wheels is like? If so, why not join the large crowds who turn out in their thousands to watch some of the most technically skilled downhill mountain bikers in the business do their thing at this urban downhill in the city of Valparaiso?

Cerro Abajo is downhill mountain biking with a difference, taking place on a mile-long course made up of a mixture of natural and man-made obstacles, with massive jumps, stone steps and even wall rides. Riders who stray too close to the walls of the buildings at other times, though, are certainly going to know about it, as there's no space for run-offs and certainly no soft landings if you don't get your timing spot-on.

That danger element is magnified even further by the fact that competitors don't get the opportunity to pre-ride the course; this is a living, breathing, working city, and a UNESCO World Heritage Site at that, so when the riders do get on the course, it's to race, and enjoying the colourful building façades or the stunning sea views is the preserve of the spectators. Trust us, it's the better side of the fence to be on.

Statistics
Location
Valparaiso
Distance
1.6 km/1 mile (2012)
Terrain
Tarmac, dirt tracks, wooden walkways, jumps
Field size
50
Website
www.valparaiso cerroabajo.cl
Contact
Via website

Competitors are faced with a multitude of jumps and obstacles

Spectators marvel as riders fly through the city ▶

Ten Minutes of Hell
United Kingdom
Road

Tunnel vision? There's a light at the end of this unique time trial

What do you get if you cross the Queensway tunnel under the Mersey with a bunch of time triallists, including the current men's and former women's national time trial champions Alex Dowsett and Julia Shaw? Ten Minutes of Hell – that's what. As bike races go, it's certainly on the unusual side, but the popularity of the inaugural time trial event in February 2012 has encouraged organisers Vita Cycles from the Wirral to go for it again in 2013.

A total of 58 other riders took on Sky's Dowsett and Shaw of Drag2Zero over the course that consisted of 3.2 km of tunnel from the south of the Mersey to central Liverpool where riders turned to ride the 3.2 km back again. The prizes on offer were unprecedented for what was a relatively low-key event, with £1,000 and a Swift aero frameset to the winner of both the men's and women's categories, which, sure enough, were won by Dowsett and Shaw. The Sky man also took home another £500 and a limited-edition TAG Heuer watch for posting the fastest mid-way split time of 4 minutes 8 seconds, with Dowsett beating the hell out of the event's title by screaming through the underworld in just 8 minutes 28 seconds in total. Shaw, meanwhile, dipped under the 10-minute mark with 9 minutes 59 seconds, earning her first place in the women's event and ninth overall.

Not a bad day's work at all – especially when your work day is less than 10 minutes long.

Statistics
Location
Merseyside
Distance
6.4 km/4 miles (2012)
Terrain
Tarmac
Field size
60
First event
2012
Website
www.vitacycles.co.uk
Contact
info@vitacycles.co.uk

Warming up before the impending sprint

Kuurne–Brussels–Kuurne voor Wielertoeristen Belgium

Road

The new sportive version of Belgian one-day Classic Kuurne–Brussels–Kuurne

As a new event, with a choice of three actually doable distances, compared to hellish days out on the bike at sportive versions of races like Paris–Roubaix or the Tour of Flanders, Kuurne voor Wielertoeristen – literally 'cycle tourists', but don't let the pedestrian-sounding moniker fool you – is a great introduction to riding in Belgium. The route may not follow the entire parcours of the pro event, but it takes on many of the same cobbles and climbs depending, of course, on whether you plump for the 85 km, 55 km or 35 km option. With all three distances starting and finishing at the official elite race gantry in Kuurne, you'll want to rest those tired legs afterwards by staying overnight and watching the pros race 'your' event the next day. You deserve it.

Statistics

Location
Kuurne

Distance
85/55/35 km
52.8/34.2/21.7 miles
(2012)

Terrain
Tarmac and cobbles

Field size
2,000

First event
2012

Website
www.kuurne-brussel-kuurne.be

Contact
informatie@odorncy.be

Kuurne

Omloop Het Nieuwsblad
Belgium
Pro one-day race

This mini Tour of Flanders is a good gauge of who might be approaching form for 'De Ronde'

The honour of kicking off the Belgian Classics season falls to the Omloop Het Nieuwsblad, but you won't hear many locals referring to it by its full name. Instead, they'll call it 'The Volk' when talking in English – a half-hearted translation of the newspaper Het Volk, meaning The People, which had given the event its name, but ceased publication in 2008. Historically its rival paper – but part of the same group since 2000 – Het Nieuwsblad now provides the event with its name, but it'll still take a few years yet before locals can get their heads around the change, if ever.

Short, sharp cobbled climbs characterise the race, which starts and finishes in Ghent these days, having gone through a number of route changes over the years. Ever present, however, is the passion, enthusiasm and encyclopaedic knowledge of Belgian cycling fans, as well as the threat of shocking weather: the race has occasionally had to be cancelled due to snow, with 2004 being the last time that happened, but cold, wind and rain comes as standard.

Belgians have historically dominated their home race, but the wins had dried up in recent years. In 2012, however, Garmin-Barracuda youngster Sep Vanmarcke scored the home nation's first win since Philippe Gilbert's 2008 victory by outsprinting none other than Belgium's Beckham, Tom Boonen. The new generation of Belgians might just have arrived...

Statistics

Location
Ghent

Distance
200 km/124.3 miles (2012)

Terrain
Tarmac and cobbles

Record wins
Joseph Bruyère (Bel), Ernest Sterckx (Bel), Peter Van Petegem (Bel) (all three wins)

Field size
200

First event
1945

Website
www.omloophet nieuwsblad.be

Contact
info@flanders classics.be

Ghent

Juan Antonio Flecha winning the event in 2010

Kuurne–Brussels–Kuurne
Belgium
Pro one-day race

The second race of the opening Belgian Classics weekend, geared very much towards the sprinters

Just as all the big races with 'Paris' in their name don't actually start or finish in the French capital, Kuurne-Brussels-Kuurne stops some way short of Brussels – about 20 km short, in fact, at the town of Ninove for its turnaround point.

Although the Het Nieuwsblad/Kuurne weekend heralds the beginning of the always-eagerly-awaited Classics season, Kuurne, in particular, is more one for the sprinters than the out-and-out one-day specialists. It's very much a strongman's race – one for hardy sprinter-types who can also get over a climb or two, such as the cobbled, two-kilometre-long Oude Kwaremont, with sections of up to 11 per cent. The winners' list reflects that, including as it does names such as Tom Boonen, Jaan Kirsipuu and Fred Moncassin, with the 2012 edition having been won by Sky's world champion, and the sprinting man of the moment, Mark Cavendish.

Statistics
Location
Kuurne, Ninove
Distance
195 km/121.2 miles (2012)
Terrain
Tarmac and cobbles
Field size
200
First event
1945
Website
www.kuurne-brussel-kuurne.be
Contact
info@kuurne-brussel-kuurne.be

Omloop Het Nieuwsblad Cyclo **Belgium**
Road

Think you can call yourself a Belgian cycling fan? Not until you've taken on the mighty Molenberg by bike!

Try to remember that you're supposed to be enjoying yourself and smile to the cameraman on the final climb of the Molenberg... The organisers place a photographer on this tough, cobbled obstacle, offering you the chance to take home a souvenir of your suffering. How kind. Choose the longer, 95 km version of the Het Nieuwsblad sportive and you'll have the Eikenberg, the Wolvenberg and the Leberg to take on in addition to the Molenberg. While the 65 km version might escape a bit of climbing, the shorter distance doesn't escape very many of the cobbled sections, so everyone needs to remember their double-wrapped handlebar tape – pro-style. The Ghent start/finish is handy for hotels and restaurants, while the 10 euro entry fee will leave you with enough money to reward yourself with a Belgian beer or two – after your ride.

Statistics
Location
Ghent
Distance
95/65 km
59/40.4 miles (2012)
Terrain
Tarmac and cobbles
Website
www.omloophet nieuwsblad-cyclo.be
Contact
cyclo@flanders classics.be

Hell of the Ashdown
United Kingdom
Road

A southeast, season-starting sportive that takes
no prisoners

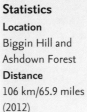

Often southeast-of-England-based riders'
first 'proper' outing of the new year, the Hell
of the Ashdown is a good gauge of how your
winter training has gone – or, if you're a real
masochist, is a good place to start riding your
bike again after an off-season of excesses.

Ride HQ is at Biggin Hill, Kent, but from
there it's out into the hell that is the Ashdown
Forest – which is in fact a really lovely place
in summer, and pretty stunning in winter,
too. So, why hell? It's the combination of the
very tough climbing and the fact that such
a hard route comes so early in the year, and
snow isn't uncommon, either. Hellishly hot, it
certainly isn't.

Introduced in 2009, the short 1-in-4
section on Cudham Test Hill is one way to
wake you up after an early start – riders
head off in groups every 2 minutes
from 8am – and from there this 65-mile
roller-coaster ride never lets up. Star Hill,
coming at the end of the ride, is the real
killer, but get over this in one piece, and
you'll be off to a flyer for the new season.

Marshalled by members of the Catford
Cycling Club, it's not only considered one
of the toughest sportives with its 2,000 m
of climbing, but one of the best organised,
marshalled and signposted ones, too.

Statistics
Location
Biggin Hill and
Ashdown Forest
Distance
106 km/65.9 miles
(2012)
Terrain
Tarmac
Field size
1,500
Website
www.hell.gb.com
Contact
hell.ashdown@
ntlworld.com

Winter in the Ashdown Forest

Yak Attack
Nepal
Mountain bike

High-altitude Himalayan madness at this international mountain-bike stage race

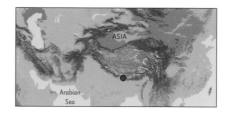

Mercifully, attacks by yaks are few and far between during this extreme mountain bike stage race in the Himalayas in Nepal. Over two weeks, competitors take on each other and, more importantly, the terrain between Kathmandu and Myagdi, which takes them up to an altitiude of 5,418 m (17,775 ft). Mountain biking doesn't get much more extreme than this, and those taking part need to bear in mind that there will be moments when they have to hike with their bike, so the comfort of full-suspension rigs is discouraged due to their extra weight.

The event may be organised by British company Extreme World Challenges, but its purpose is to promote Nepalese mountain biking and give local riders the opportunity to ride against an international field, as well as providing much-needed income to businesses on the Yak Attack route, such as the teahouses used for accommodation after each day's stage.

Statistics

Location
Kathmandu and Himalayas

Distance
400 km/248.5 miles over 10 stages (2012)

Highest point
5,418 m (2012)

Terrain
Off-road

Record wins
Ajay Pandit Chhetri (Nep) (three wins)

Field size
32

First event
2007

Website
http://yak-attack.co.uk

Contact
info@yak-attack.co.uk

Riders contend with Nepal's mighty Himalayas

Tour of Murcia
Spain
Pro stage race

Traditional Spanish stage race that has retained its excitement despite the economic downturn

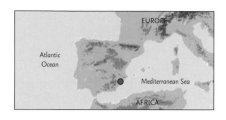

It was that man Jonathan Tiernan-Locke of the Endura Racing team again showing why he was the sensation of the 2012 early season, having already won the Tour of the Mediterranean and the Tour du Haut Var, by finishing third on the opening stage of the Tour of Murcia, 16 seconds down on Movistar's Nairo Quintana.

It was the Briton who attacked on the day's main climb, the Collado Bermejo, dropping big-name riders like Robert Gesink and Samuel Sanchez, but taking Quintana with him, and it was the Spanish rider who attacked again near the top and who got away alone to plunge down the descent to win in Sierra de Espuna.

The Spanish stage race was simplified to a two-day stage race for 2012, due to a lack of sponsors during a period of real crisis facing prestigious Spanish stage races, but it certainly didn't diminish any of the excitement.

The next day's concluding time trial stage – a flat 12 km around the streets of the city of Murcia – saw the British rider claw back 10 seconds on Quintana, but it wasn't enough, and Tiernan-Locke had to settle for second place overall, nevertheless proving once more to the top pro teams that he was a sure-fire bet for the future.

Statistics

Location
Murcia

Distance
210.5 km/130.8 miles over 2 stages (2012)

Terrain
Tarmac

Record wins
Alejandro Valverde (Spa) (three wins)

Field size
133

First event
1981

Website
www.vueltaciclista murcia.com

Contact
info@vueltaciclista murcia.com

Alejandro Valverde has won the Tour of Murcia three times

Strade Bianche
Italy
Pro one-day race

Italy's answer to Paris–Roubaix on the 'white roads' of Tuscany

There are very few events where the professional race has grown out of the amateur version, but that's what happened with the Strade Bianche. The sportive version – the Eroica – takes place over the same route in October each year, and celebrates bike racing of old by taking competitors – who all dress up in old woollen jerseys and ride old bicycles – over unmade roads.

In 2007, the pros decided they thought it looked like fun – or, at least, somebody at Giro d'Italia organisers RCS did – and the modern one-day Classic was born. Between Gaiole in Chianti and Siena, riders take on Tuscany's famous strade bianche – or 'white roads' – and the race winds its way through stunning countryside, past vineyards, farmhouses and olive groves, on the gravel roads.

It's often a gauge of who's coming into form nicely for Roubaix and the Tour of Flanders and, having also won the 2008 edition, Belgian Classics specialist Fabian Cancellara won the Strade Bianche again in 2012. Like at Roubaix, the less-than-ideal road surfaces mean punctures, and the Swiss rider fought his way back to the front despite suffering both a front and rear puncture in quick succession halfway through the 190 km race. Powering up the final hill into beautiful Siena, alone, he was the worthy winner of a race surely destined to become as prestigious as the oldest Classics in the not-too-distant future.

Statistics

Location
Gaiole in Chianti to Siena, Tuscany
Distance
190 km/118 miles (2012)
Terrain
Tarmac and gravel roads
Record wins
Fabian Cancellara (Swi) (two wins)
Field size
112
First event
2007
Website
www.gazzetta.it/ Speciali/Strade Bianche/en
Contact
marketing.sport@rcs.it

Riding on the meandering dirt roads of rural Tuscany

Maxim Iglinskiy (left) congratulates Fabian Cancellara on his win in Strade Bianche in 2012 ▶

Paris–Nice
France
Pro stage race

Tour de France contenders limber up on the Gallic roads between the capital and the Côte d'Azur

'The Race to the Sun' rarely disappoints, both in terms of the quality of the racing and the sun the riders are racing towards down on the Côte d'Azur.

However, almost without fail the peloton experiences freezing temperatures on some of the higher ground the race tackles on its journey south from just outside Paris to Nice on the south coast, but the promise of sunshine after a tough week of racing appears to appeal.

One look at the list of past winners demonstrates just how much of a 'mini Tour de France' this is, although you'll find the Tour contenders split pretty much between riding Paris-Nice and the Tirreno-Adriatico

stage race in Italy going on at the same time, with much depending on personal preference. In 2012, for example, Team Sky split their two Tour stars between the races, with their overall contender Bradley Wiggins preferring the route of the French race, while sprint star Mark Cavendish fancied his chances in Italy, where there tend to be more stages suited to bunch sprints.

French riders have dominated the race since its inception in 1933, but between 1982 and 1988, no one could touch Ireland's Sean Kelly, who still holds the record for the most editions of the race won, with an almost unbeatable seven straight victories.

Statistics

Location
Between Paris and Nice
Distance
1,155.5 km/718 miles over 8 stages (2012)
Highest point
1,149 m (2012)
Terrain
Tarmac
Record wins
Sean Kelly (Irl) (seven wins)
Field size
176
First event
1933
Website
www.letour.fr
Contact
cyclisme@aso.fr

Thomas De Gendt wins stage 1 of the 2011 edition

Sky's Bradley Wiggins on his way to overall victory in 2012 ▶

Tirreno–Adriatico
Italy
Pro stage race

The Italian alternative to Paris–Nice, which also helps get riders in the mood for Milan–San Remo

For riders targeting Milan–San Remo, Tirreno–Adriatico – 'the race of the two seas' between the Tyrrhenian and the Adriatic – tends to be the race of choice over Paris–Nice. This is mainly due to its closer proximity, days-wise, to Milan–San Remo, which comes four days later, so it's not as difficult to hold form, whereas there's almost a week between the finish of Paris–Nice and the start of the Italian one-day Classic – and what a difference even just a couple of days make, as any pro will tell you.

However, riders tend to chop and change and experiment from year to year depending on how their previous season has gone, or due to illness or a lack of fitness, as Tirreno always starts a few days after Paris–Nice. In 2011, for example, Matt Goss became the first rider since 1999 to win

Milan–San Remo having ridden Paris–Nice, but just a year later he was back with the tried-and-tested Tirreno route to trying to repeat his victory at San Remo.

In recent years, Tirreno has also often featured a team time trial, so any riders targeting that relatively unusual discipline at one of the Grand Tours – Italy, France or Spain – may also plump for Tirreno–Adriatico over Paris–Nice to get some practice in. Cadel Evans certainly got it right in 2011. Overall victory at Tirreno set him up nicely for his win at the Tour de France in July, and the Australian's BMC squad managed to learn from their mistakes and up the ante between sixth place in the TTT at Tirreno and then second place against the clock four months later.

Statistics

Location
The Tyrrhenian Sea to the Adriatic

Distance
1,063 km/660.5 miles over 7 stages (2012)

Highest point
1,450 m (2012)

Terrain
Tarmac

Record wins
Roger De Vlaeminck (Bel) (six wins)

Field size
176

First event
1966

Website
www.gazzetta.it/ Speciali/Tirreno Adriatico/en

Contact
marketing.sport@rcs.i

Mark Cavendish holds off stiff competition to win stage 2 of the 2012 race

Mark Cavendish celebrates his stage 2 win ▶

Cape Argus Pick n Pay Cycle Tour South Africa

Road

A huge, spectacular, must-ride bike ride in Cape Town, South Africa

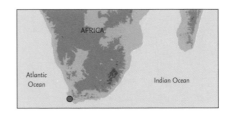

The largest mass-participation bike ride in the world, the Cape Argus may be 110 km long, but it brings out riders young and old – although everyone has to be capable of completing the course in under seven hours.

It's a truly international field that the Cape Argus attracts, and it has captured the imagination of local riders too, who are rightly proud of their race. It is a race up front: pro riders keep things flying along up at the sharp end, while things are a little more sedate further back.

In theory, this is a once-in-a-lifetime trip for people coming from outside South Africa, but the fact that participants tend to return time and again is testament to just how spectacular a ride it is.

The route heads south out of central Cape Town to the coast and down to Table Mountain National Park and Smitswinkel Bay. Here it heads west across to the other side of the Cape peninsula and the Atlantic coast, before heading back north for the uphill finish at Green Point. It's a truly breathtaking route – and arguably the most picturesque bike ride in the world, with Table Mountain always in view, watching over the whole course.

Spectators treat the ride as an excuse for a big party with plenty of families enjoying barbecues as the riders come through, often helping to cool hot and bothered riders down with garden hoses on hotter editions as the Argus passes through Cape Town's neighbourhoods.

Statistics

Location
Cape Town
Distance
110 km/68.4 miles (2012)
Terrain
Tarmac
Field size
35,000
First event
1978
Website
www.cycletour.co.za
Contact
info@cycletour.co.za

Towering Table Mountain can be seen throughout the course

Rugged route around the Cape peninsula ▶

Milan–San Remo
Italy

Pro one-day race

A sprinter's paradise where late attacks always threaten to spoil the party

Milan–San Remo is one of cycling's five 'Monuments' – along with the Tour of Lombardy, Liège–Bastogne–Liège, Paris–Roubaix and the Tour of Flanders – and the Italian Classic comes in around mid-way in the unofficial pecking order of greatness, just after Roubaix and Flanders.

While the latter two share a DNA of cobbles, inclement weather and boozed-up Belgian spectators, Milan–San Remo stands apart as a sun-soaked and frenetic speed fest, attended by the Italian Riviera's beautiful people.

As the first Monument of the year, Milan–San Remo signals that the season has really begun: that from here on in, the world's top riders need to start upping their game, and that there's no more hiding in the peloton as many have done through the earlier spring races.

The real iconic moment it all seems to kick off is when the peloton flick off the main road onto a side road for the start of the narrow, 4 km climb to the top of the Poggio, where the riders have little time to enjoy the stunning views over the Mediterranean. This is where the sprinters, in particular, have to be sure that they've included a few hill reps in their winter training. They've tended to dominate the race since its first edition in 1907, but they need to arrive at the start in Milan in close to top form if they want to be in the mix at the end, as while the speed of the race

slowly ramps up as the riders make their way to San Remo, it's on the Poggio that any potential race-winning move has the best chance of success and of avoiding a bunch gallop.

The breakneck descent down the other side with around 6 km left to the finish is always heart-in-mouth time, as riders either risk everything to escape the clutches of what's left of the peloton, or the bunch takes desperate measures to try to reel in any remnants of a breakaway move.

Sprint finish after a marathon 298 km

Statistics

Location
Between Milan and San Remo

Distance
298 km/185.2 miles (2012)

Highest point
532 m (2012)

Terrain
Tarmac

Record wins
Eddy Merckx (Bel) (seven wins)

Field size
200

First event
1907

Website
www.gazzetta.it/ Speciali/Milano Sanremo/en

Contact
marketing.sport@rcs.it

Matthew Goss of the HTC-Highroad team wins the 2011 edition of the Milan–San Remo ▶

Nokere Koerse
Belgium
Pro one-day race

A chance to see the emergence of the Classics stars of the future

The Nokere Koerse began life in 1944 as the Grand Prix Jules Lowie in response to the popularity of the Nokere native of the same name who had put the town on the map by winning the 1938 Paris–Nice.

In recent years it's been an opportunity for some of the sport's talented domestiques – who normally help their leaders to win – and up-and-coming young riders to shine, with many of the top sprinters and Classics riders heading to Milan–San Remo instead. Past winners include the emerging Belgian talent Jens Keukeleire, in 2010, and also the late Wouter Weylandt in 2008, who died in an accident at the 2011 Giro d'Italia.

The race finishes atop the Nokereberg, which also features in the Dwars Door Vlaanderen and its sportive.

Statistics

Location
Nokere
Distance
196 km/121.8 miles (2012)
Terrain
Tarmac
Record wins
Hendrik Van Dijck (Bel) (three wins)
Field size
200
First event
1944
Website
www.nokerekoerse.be
Contact
info@nokerekoerse.be

Cholet Pays de Loire
France
Pro one-day race

French stars come out to play at one of France's most popular one-day races

Cycling is hugely popular in the Loire, and cycling fans flock to Cholet in western France for the Cholet Pays de Loire each March, which attracts all the big French teams and their star riders, including Tour de France stage winners Thomas Voeckler and Pierrick Fedrigo, who have both won this race. Such is cycling's popularity that there's a whole weekend of events planned around the race, with a sportive taking place the day before and a women's race on the morning prior to the men's event.

The '10 Climb Challenge' – effectively a 'King of the Mountains' competition for this single-day race – helps spice things up further, with points awarded to the first three riders over each of the race's 10 climbs.

Statistics

Location
Cholet
Distance
199 km/123.7 miles (2012)
Terrain
Tarmac
Record wins
Jaan Kirsipuu (Est) (three wins)
Field size
128
First event
1978
Website
www.cholet-pdl.com
Contact
Via website

Dwars Door Vlaanderen Cyclo Belgium

Road

Take on the best of the Dwars Door Vlaanderen's cobbles and climbs in this mini Tour of Flanders

The 120 km sportive version of the Dwars Door Vlaanderen takes in all the race's major climbs. At just 400 m in length, the Paterberg is but a blip compared to some of the climbs around Flanders, but factor in that it's cobbled and maxes out at 20 per cent, and it's a climb that's going to plead with you to get off and walk it. The Oude Kwaremont, meanwhile – which, along with the Paterberg, now features prominently in the new finish of the Tour of Flanders – is a

much longer climb at almost 2,500 m, and is often where the first serious moves by the favourites go in the professional event, so consider turning the screw there if your friends look like they're flagging and you're feeling strong enough.

Statistics

Location
Waregem

Distance
120/90/60 km
74.6/55.9/37.3 miles
(2012)

Terrain
Tarmac and cobbles

First event
1973

Website
www.dwarsdoor
vlaanderen-cyclo.be

Contact
cyclo@flanders
classics.be

PROFESSIONAL RACE

Settimana Internazionale di Coppi e Bartali Italy

Pro stage race

Two of Italy's greats are remembered in this hard-fought stage race

This five-day, six-stage race's rather grand name – which translates as International Coppi and Bartali Week – remembers two of Italy's best-loved riders from the 1940s and 1950s, who managed to split the nation such was their popularity.

Despite not being a WorldTour-level race, like the Giro d'Italia and Tirreno-Adriatico, it nevertheless enjoys its status as one of Italy's most important stage races, welcoming many of the country's top pros

who use it as preparation for the Giro, which comes two months later. It's one of the few events to feature a team time trial, and there's an individual time trial, too, which means plenty of practice against the clock in what is a relatively short race so early in the season.

Statistics

Location
Emilia-Romagna

Distance
580 km/360.4 miles
over 6 stages (2012)

Terrain
Tarmac

Record wins
Moreno Argentin (Ita),
Damiano Cunego (Ita)
(both two wins)

First event
1984

Website
www.gsemilia.it

Contact
gsemiliaciclismo@tin.it

Tour of Catalonia
Spain
Pro stage race

The sport's third oldest stage race still attracts big-name riders

Coming after Paris–Nice and Tirreno–Adriatico, the normally pleasant weather down in Catalonia is a further opportunity for stage racers to hone their fitness as their big goals for the season approach. It is Spain's second biggest stage race after the Tour of Spain, and cycling's third oldest stage race behind the Tour de France and the Tour of Italy, having started in 1911.

Since then, its place on the calendar has constantly shifted from June to May to its current March slot, which allows it to fit in to the sport's top-tier WorldTour circuit, and its history makes this a prestigious race that consistently attracts big names. Past winners include Eddy Merckx, Francesco Moser, Miguel Indurain and Britain's Robert Millar, in 1985.

Statistics
Location
Catalonia
Distance
1,242.6 km/772.1 miles
over 7 stages (2012)
Terrain
Tarmac
Record wins
Mariano Cañardo (Spa)
(seven wins)
Field size
184
First event
1911
Website
www.voltacatalunya.cat
Contact
volta@volta
catalunya.cat

Spectacular Catalonia coastline

Alberto Contador (right
won the 2011 race
but was later stripped
of the title for
doping, forfeiting
victory to Michele
Scarponi (left) ▶

Dwars Door Vlaanderen
Belgium

Pro one-day race

The best of Flanders in a more relaxed atmosphere than the coming madness in the region it heralds

It's really at the Dwars Door Vlaanderen – the 'Across Flanders' – that the countdown to the Tour of Flanders truly begins, and in 2011 it gave the perfect indication of approaching form when Saxo Bank's Nick Nuyens and Sky's Geraint Thomas held off a speeding bunch behind them, led by Garmin sprinter Tyler Farrar, with Belgian Nuyens just pipping the Welshman to the win, much to the delight of the home crowd. Two weeks later, Nuyens sent his already delighted fans into overdrive when the Belgian bagged the big one at 'De Ronde'.

The Dwars Door would round off a perfect week away in Flanders, allowing fans to watch the nearby Nokere Koerse, followed a few days later by participating in the sportive version of the Dwars Door, and then the race proper that weekend.

Statistics

Location
Roeselare to Waregem

Distance
200 km/124.3 miles (2012)

Terrain
Tarmac and cobbles

Field size
200

First event
1945

Website
www.ddvl.eu

Contact
info@dwarsdoor
vlaanderen.be

Nick Nuyens winning the 2011 race

E3 Prijs Vlaanderen-Harelbeke Belgium

Pro one-day race

The Tour of Flanders' 'little brother' is all grown up

Quite understandably, the race formerly known as the E3 Prijs Vlaanderen-Harelbeke tended to be referred to simply as 'the E3', but the organisers eventually saw sense, and it's now simply the E3 Harelbeke. It's still quite superb that the event is named after a combination of a nearby motorway and the name of the town where the race starts and finishes, although even the E3 has had a name change. It's now the A14.

At this point in the season, the clock is ticking for the Tour of Flanders, which means whoever comes out on top at the E3 is a shoo-in for the list of favourites for its 'big brother' just over a week later.

It's very much a case of the same hallowed turf – or, rather, cobbles – as the Tour of Flanders, and for feverish Flandrian fans it's the ideal warm-up event to check that their air horns, vuvuzelas and comedy hats are working properly.

In 2012, having gained WorldTour status – cycling's top division of races – the E3 route inherited the famous Muur van Geraardsbergen from Flanders, which saw a change of route, and so it's a case of the little brother playing second fiddle even less than before as the cobbled climb to the chapel elevates the E3's status to bona-fide top-drawer Classic.

Tom Boonen has won the race five times

Statistics

Location
Harelbeke, Flanders

Distance
203 km/126.1 miles (2012)

Highest point
148 m (2012)

Terrain
Tarmac and cobbles

Record wins
Tom Boonen (Bel) (five wins)

Field size
200

First event
1958

Website
www.e3-harelbeke.be

Contact
info@e3-harelbeke.be

Red Hook Crit Brooklyn
USA
Night

Brakeless criterium racing, anyone? Get yourself to Brooklyn

Hold on tight – you're in for quite a ride... This anarchic, night-time criterium takes place in the Red Hook neighbourhood of Brooklyn, New York, with competitors racing on brakeless fixed-wheel bikes for 24 laps around a 1.25 km course at nine o'clock at night. It's not really the secret alley-cat race it was when organiser David Trimble first ran the event in 2008 (to celebrate his birthday), but the vibe is still the same, with every type of cycling tribe

coming together to race, cheer each other on, talk trash and then all enjoy the after-party together.

As of 2010, the Red Hook has also transplanted those same Brooklyn values to Milan, Italy, while a Berlin version is also in the pipeline to bring New York alley-cat cool to Germany.

Statistics

Location
Brooklyn, New York
Distance
30 km/18.6 miles
(24 laps of a 1.25 km
circuit) (2012)
Terrain
Tarmac
Field size
100
First event
2008
Website
http://redhookcrit.com
Contact
Via website

Ghent–Wevelgem Cyclo
Belgium
Road

Fancy your chances on the Kemmelberg? Come climb the cobbles in this tough sportive

Take on the fearsome cobbled Kemmelberg yourself in the sportive version of one-day Classic Ghent–Wevelgem. If it's windy and rainy – as it often is – the long, energy-sapping 180 km option, over much of the same route the pros will take the next day, will leave you with a new-found respect for what they go through. The shorter 127 km and 85 km versions are marginally less painful, but there's no way the organisers are going to spare you the

Kemmelberg – and all this for an entry fee of just 10 euros.

For the first time, in 2012, there was a ladies-only version of the sportive, ridden on the same day over a 45 km course, in aid of the Belgian campaign for the fight against breast cancer, Think Pink: www.think-pink.be.

Statistics

Location
Wevelgem
Distance
180/127/85 km (45 km
ladies only) (2012)
Terrain
Tarmac and cobbles
Field size
1,400
Website
www.gent-wevelgem-
cyclo.be
Contact
cyclo@flanders
classics.be

Ghent–Wevelgem
Belgium
Pro one-day race

The sprinters' Classic' is getting tougher by the year for sprinters to win

The E3 Harelbeke, two days prior to Ghent–Wevelgem, might better mimic the course of the one-day Classic every Belgian wants to win – the upcoming Tour of Flanders – but Ghent–Wevelgem is a prestigious race in its own right.

Since its beginnings in 1934, the race has catered for an eclectic mix of sprinters and Classics specialists, boasting past winners such as Eddy Merckx, Rik Van Looy, Mario Cipollini and Tom Boonen. It's a strong sprinter who is able to get over two ascents – and descents – of the bone-shaking, cobbled climb of the Kemmelberg, but the recent addition of even more climbing has made the race even more selective, and bunch gallops are becoming a rarity these days.

Statistics
Location
Between Deinze and Wevelgem
Distance
235 km/146 miles (2012)
Terrain
Tarmac and cobbles
Record wins
Tom Boonen (Bel),
Eddy Merckx (Bel),
Mario Cipollini (Ita),
Rik Van Looy (Bel),
Robert Van Eenaeme (Bel) (all three wins)
Field size
200
First event
1934
Website
www.gent-wevelgem.be
Contact
info@gent-wevelgem.be

Tom Boonen powering over the cobbles

Critérium International France

Pro stage race

A three-day 'Tour de France' on the stunning island of Corsica

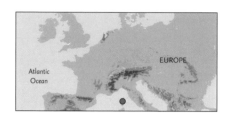

If Paris–Nice is a 'mini Tour de France', then Critérium International must be considered a 'mini-mini Tour', held as it is over just two days, but covering the whole gamut of what Tour riders experience over three weeks: namely, mountains, sprints and time trials.

The opening day's hilly stage sets the scene for the overall classification, quickly establishing who the main contenders are likely to be, as the sprinters keep their powder dry for the following morning's flat stage. The time trial stage that afternoon then tips things back in the favour of those going for the general classification, and the race is decided against the clock.

All this with Corsica as its backdrop, birthplace of Napoleon Bonaparte II, and popular holiday destination each summer for thousands of Frenchmen seeking sun, sea and, in some cases, cycling, perfect as it is for riding thanks to quiet roads and almost every imaginable type of terrain.

The race's significance becomes all the greater with the approach of the 2013 Tour, which starts on the Mediterranean island on June 29th, spending three days there before the race continues on the mainland, in Nice, with a team time trial. Participants in the last four editions of Critérium International ahead of the 2013 Tour will therefore be at a distinct advantage, having got to know the island ahead of time.

While at its previous home based around Charleville Mézières in the Champagne region of northeast France before it switched to Corsica in 2010, the race was dominated by Germany's Jens Voigt – a rider wellknown for his ability to work tirelessly for his team leaders, but strong as an ox allround, meaning that he could always be in the mix on the hilly stage that took riders into the Ardennes, hold his own on the flat stage, and then use his power to get a result in the time trial. As a five-time winner, Voigt shares the record number of wins with France's Emile Idée and Raymond Poulidor but, having turned 40 in 2011, the German turned helper for his team-mate, Frank Schleck, and helped secure a Leopard-Trek victory in Corsica, admitting that the toughness of the climbing there was too much even for him.

Sun, sea and cycling in Corsica

Statistics

Location
Corsica
Distance
280 km/174 miles over 3 stages (2012)
Highest point
956 m (2012)
Terrain
Tarmac
Record wins
Raymond Poulidor (Fra), Jens Voigt (Ger), Emile Idée (Fra) (five wins each)
Field size
128
First event
1932
Website
www.letour.fr
Contact
cyclisme@aso.fr

Frank Schleck (in yellow) en route to victory in 2011 ▶

Cheshire Cat
United Kingdom
Road

"Every adventure requires a first step." The Cheshire Cat, Alice's Adventures in Wonderland

You'll be grinning like one when you take part in the Cheshire Cat – considered the UK's real opener to the sportive season. In 2012, it also happens to fall on the start of British Summer Time, so there are multiple reasons to ride it with a smile. That might be hard when you hit the Mow Cop Killer Mile, but even then there are medals for those who make it to the top of this climb alone without walking or stopping for a rest. Gun Hill will also be familiar to fans of the Tour of Britain, which regularly features the climb on its route.

The full event is over 102 miles, but there's also a 76-mile option, taking in most of the same tough climbs, and then a slightly easier 47-mile option – ideal for sportive first-timers.

Statistics
Location
Crewe, Cheshire
Distance
164.2/122.4/75.7 km
102/76/47 miles (2012)
Terrain
Tarmac
Field size
3,000
Website
www.kilotogo.com
Contact
contact@kilotogo.com

Three Days of De Panne
Belgium
Pro stage race

A tough few days of stage racing on Flanders' famous cobbles

British fans already familiar with Koksijde for the round of the cyclo-cross World Cup and Ghent for the six-day track racing will have no problem getting across to De Panne in the corner of Belgium closest to the UK to watch some top-class pro racing, where there are four stages of racing squeezed into three days.

British fans attending in 2010 would have enjoyed the race's first ever British winner in David Millar, too, who put himself in the perfect position for victory prior to the race's final time trial, which he won to take the overall title.

Coming midweek in the few days before the Tour of Flanders, the stage race is a real gauge of who has timed their fitness peak just right, and since its first edition in 1977, 'double' winners of De Panne and Flanders include Peter Van Petegem (1999) and Alessandro Ballan (2007).

Statistics
Location
De Panne, Koksijde
Distance
544 km/338 miles
over 4 stages (2012)
Terrain
Tarmac and cobbles
Record wins
Eric Vanderaerden
(Bel) (five wins)
Field size
192
First event
1977
Website
www.veloclub-
depanne.be
Contact
veloclub.depanne@
skynet.be

Cape Epic
South Africa
Mountain bike

Mountain biking's Tour de France' – in South Africa's Western Cape

While riders converge on Cape Town at the start of March for the Cape Argus on the roads around Table Mountain, by the end of the month it's all about off-roading as the Cape Epic mountain-bike stage race gets under way.

It's been dubbed the Tour de France for mountain bikes, and certainly the stunning trails around the Western Cape between Durbansville and the Helderberg Mountains provide a stiff challenge to the two-man teams who take it on. Teams have to stay within 2 minutes of each other, strictly enforced thanks to timing mats; three strikes and you're out.

Current RadioShack-Nissan road-racing pro Jakob Fuglsang is one of a number of mountain bike stars who have taken on the Cape Epic – others include Bart Brentjens and Christoph Sauser – with Fuglsang winning the event in 2008 with his Cannondale-Vredestein partner Roel Paulissen before the Dane made the switch to road cycling, and is now a regular Tour de France rider and loyal team-mate to the Schleck brothers.

The amount of climbing facing competitors is up there with the Tour, too: 16,300 m of climbing faced the riders in the 2012 edition during the 780 km over eight days between the Meerendal Wine Estate and what has become the Cape Epic's own Champs-Elysées finale, the famous Lourensford Wine Estate – one of the Western Cape's best known wineries.

Statistics

Location
Cape Town
Distance
780 km/484.7 miles
over 7 stages (2012)
Terrain
Singletrack, jeep tracks
and gravel roads
Record wins
Karl Platt (Ger)
(four wins)
Field size
1,200 (600 pairs)
First event
2004
Website
www.cape-epic.com
Contact
registration@cape-epic.com

Swiss rider Ralf Naef takes on Tokai Forest

Tour of Flanders for cyclotourists Belgium
Road

The Tour of Flanders, just for people slightly slower than the pros

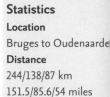

Along with Paris–Roubaix, the Tour of Flanders is the big one, and it's the sportive versions of those same two spring Classics that are the routes amateur riders want to test themselves on above all others, too. Only around a quarter of entrants take on the full route of Flanders, as it's widely believed to be about the toughest day on a bike, both physically and mentally, that you're ever going to experience.

The cobbled sections are brutal and energy-sapping; the cobbled climbs are simply horrible.

The one small mercy in 2012 was that the long route was 'only' 244 km against 260 km the year before due to a change to the pro race, and after that many hours on a bike, 16 km makes a huge difference. A shame, perhaps, that the famous climb of the Muur van Geraardsbergen has been removed from the route, but faced with the Koppenberg, the Oude Kwaremont and the Paterberg, it's hardly become a holiday.

Most popular is the 'medium' route of 138 km – which is still plenty, and still takes in most of the route's major climbs – while those looking for a slightly gentler introduction to the cobbles of Flanders might want to plump for the 87 km option first time round, although 'gentle' it certainly isn't, made up mainly of all the big climbs squeezed into a shorter distance.

Statistics
Location
Bruges to Oudenaarde
Distance
244/138/87 km
151.5/85.6/54 miles
(2012)
Terrain
Tarmac and cobbles
Field size
15,000
First event
1992
Website
www.rondevan
vlaanderen.com
Contact
info@golazo.com

Riding over Flanders' famous cobbled bergs

Route Adélie de Vitré
France
Pro one-day race
Breton one-day race that is part of the Coupe de France competition

This French one-day race based on a course around the town of Vitré, in Brittany, is run over a laps of a 21 km circuit around picturesque Breton countryside before returning to Vitré to complete eight laps of a smaller circuit around the town.

Cycling fans may remember it better by its previous name, the Tour d'Armorique, named after the Breton national park, but since 1997 it's been known by its somewhat prettier new name, which in fact comes

from local ice-cream manufacturer Adélie.

French riders have dominated the race, which began in 1980, and is part of the Coupe de France – the country's season-long competition of races for French riders, won overall in 2011 by Cofidis's Tony Gallopin.

Statistics
Location
Vitré
Distance
198 km/123 miles (2012)
Terrain
Tarmac
Record wins
Jaan Kirsipuu (Est) (two wins)
Field size
144
First event
1980
Website
www.routeadelievitre.fr
Contact
roland.montenat@ routeadelievitre.fr

Volta Limburg Classic
Netherlands
Pro one-day race
Holland's own 'Hell of the North' in Limburg

The Volta Limburg Classic is also known as the 'Hell of the Mergelland' – a nod to Paris–Roubaix's 'Hell of the North' nickname thanks to the cobblestones and hills covered on the route around Holland's Mergelland area of south Limburg.

With the UCI road cycling world championships taking place in Limburg in September, the 2012 Volta Limburg Classic welcomed an even more international field than normal, keen to take advantage of the

opportunity to scout out the region's roads.

From its first edition in 1973, the race was dominated by Dutch riders, but between 2000 and 2011, foreign riders, including Germany's Bert Grabsch and Tony Martin, kept the local riders at bay until Vacansoleil's Pim Ligthart broke the duck – and scored his first ever pro win – to bring the 'Hell of the Mergelland' back home.

Statistics
Location
Maastricht, Limburg
Distance
198 km/123 miles (2012)
Terrain
Tarmac and cobbles
Record wins
Raymond Meijs (Ned) (four wins)
Field size
200
First event
1973
Website
www.helvanhet mergelland.nl
Contact
info@ voltalimburgclassic.nl

GP Miguel Indurain
Spain
Pro one-day race

'Big Mig' immortalised forever in this hilly
Spanish one-day race

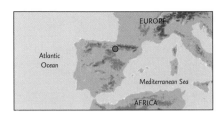

Starting out in 1951 as the Gran Premio
de Navarra, this Spanish one-day race
based around the city of Estella-Lizarra
in the Navarre region was renamed the
GP Miguel Indurain in 1998 in honour of
the Spanish rider who won the Tour five
times in succession, between 1991 and 1995.
However, rather than being a time trial –
which would have been a more appropriate
discipline to bear Indurain's name,
considering that it was against the clock

that 'Big Mig' would annihilate his
competition at the Tour – it is a hilly road
race. The 180 km route finishes atop the
Basilica del Puy, which looks out over the
city, and requires a strong finish, with
past winners including Samuel Sanchez,
Indurain's former team-mate Pedro Delgado
and, in 1987, Indurain himself, who comes
from nearby Villava, near Pamplona, in the
same region.

Statistics

Location
Navarre
Distance
180 km/111.8 miles
(2012)
Highest point
825 m (2012)
Terrain
Tarmac
Record wins
Juan Fernandez (Spa),
Miguel Maria
Lasa (Spa),
Hortensio
Vidaurreta (Spa)
(all three wins)
Field size
110
First event
1951
Website
www.clubciclista
estella.com
Contact
info@clubciclista
estella.com

Miguel Indurain

Tour of Flanders
Belgium
Pro one-day race

'De Ronde' does battle with Paris-Roubaix for 'best one-day race' honours

This is one of the really big ones – the must-ride-at-least-once for pros, the must-win for one-day Classics specialists, and the must-watch for cycling fans. To call it a must-ride for sportive riders depends on just how keen you are.

Putting the route aside for a moment, it's the sheer passion of the Flandrians that really helps to elevate the status of the race. It's Belgium's answer to the UK's Grand National or Boat Race, or the USA's Super Bowl. In Flanders, it's known simply as 'De Ronde' – 'The Tour' – which makes it necessary to refer to that other rather famous tour around France by its full name. A win in Flanders is a true 'never-buy-yourself-another-beer-in-Belgium again' experience. Victory here makes you the talk of Belgium for some time – especially if you're Belgian. Local knowledge of the brutal climbs and cobbles means that Belgian riders have prevailed considerably more often on home 'turf' than any other nation: after ninety-five editions of the race they had sixty-seven wins, against the next most successful nation, Italy, with ten.

Like Roubaix, the race also tends to favour older riders, who use their strength over longer distances, and their knowledge of how to ride the cobbles no matter what the weather conditions, to good advantage against young pretenders.

One exception to that rule is Belgium's own David Beckham, Tom Boonen, who won in 2005 and 2006, and for the first time aged just 24. That first time, he showed his strength and skill across the cobbles by accomplishing the rare feat of winning both Flanders and Paris–Roubaix a week later – an achievement repeated by Switzerland's Fabian Cancellara in 2010.

For 2012, Boonen, Cancellara et al were up against some major changes to the Flanders route with the addition of three laps of a finishing circuit that included climbs of the Oude Kwaremont and the Paterberg, replacing the finale of the iconic Muur van Geraardsbergen and the Bosberg. Instead of finishing in Meerbeke, the town of Oudenaarde celebrated the 'Ronde' champion in 2012.

However, Flanders' loss is the Eneco Tour stage race and the one-day E3 Harelbeke's gain, as both events added the Muur van Geraardsbergen to their routes in 2012. Who's to say that the Muur might not one day return to the Flanders course?

Nick Nuyens wins the 2011 sprint

Statistics

Location
Bruges to Oudenaarde
Distance
257 km/159.7 miles
(2012)
Terrain
Tarmac and cobbles
Record wins
Tom Boonen (Bel),
Eric Leman (Bel),
Fiorenzo Magni (Ita),
Achiel Buysse (Bel),
Johan Museeuw (Bel)
(all three wins)
Field size
200
First event
1913
Website
www.rvv.be
Contact
info@flanders
classics.be

Nick Nuyens celebrates his victory in 2011 with Sylvain Chavanel and Fabian Cancellara, who finished second and third respectively ▶

KBC

PRIMUS
HAACHT

QUICK·STEP
floors

innergetic
Sleep better

SAXO
BANK
SUNGARD

SAXO
BANK
SUNGARD®

CRAFT
TREK

Dengie Marshes Tour
United Kingdom
Pro one-day race
The UK's Paris–Roubaix

The Dengie Marshes Tour included more off-road farm tracks than ever for the 2012 edition – a popular British race that, like more than a few others around the world, borrows its 'Hell of the East' nickname from the original 'Hell of the North', France's Paris–Roubaix cobbled Classic.

Dengie also became part of the UK's Premier Calendar series in 2012 – recognition of its popularity with both spectators and the riders taking part. Like the cobbles of Roubaix, the bumpy, dusty farm tracks – which become mud baths in wet weather – cause havoc once the riders hit them in the latter stages of the race, having spent the majority of the race on smooth Essex tarmac.

Statistics
Location
Burnham-on-Crouch, Essex
Distance
167.4 km/104 miles (2012)
Terrain
Tarmac and unmade farm tracks
Field size
124
First event
2008
Website
www.dengie marshestour.com
Contact
alan@arosner. orangehome.co.uk

Riders compete against uneven tracks, as well as each other

Volta Limburg Classic
Toertocht Netherlands
Road

Holland's 'Hell' the day after the pros have
shown you how it's done

Check out the Limburg region of the
Netherlands for yourself – site of the 2012
world championships – in this, the sportive
version of the Volta Limburg Classic.
Holland's own 'Hell' of a race includes
a combination of Paris–Roubaix-esque
cobbles and tough climbs. Although the pro
race has been going since 1973, the sportive
only started in 2011, with Limburg taking
advantage of the increasing interest from
amateurs wishing to ride the same roads
as the pros to promote the area. Although,
whereas many sportive versions of major
races take place the day before the pros
ride, the Volta Limburg's unusual in that
it's the other way round: scare yourself by
witnessing just how much the pros suffer
during the race before doing your level
best to emulate them the next day – ideally
without quite as much pain!

Statistics
Location
Limburg
Distance
150/120/85 km
93.2/74.6/52.8 miles
(2012)
Terrain
Tarmac and cobbles
First event
2011
Website
www.helvanhet
mergelland.nl
Contact
info@voltalimburg
classic.nl

2012 winner, Pavel Brutt

Tour of the Basque Country Spain

Pro stage race

Mountainous stage race that brings out the Spanish big guns

This well-loved stage race in the Basque Country – the area of northeast Spain that borders France, and which has long fought for independence from Spain – has been up against it, financially, for the past few years due to the economic climate in Europe, prompting cycling's governing body, the UCI, to consider stepping in to help fund its survival in 2012.

However, at the eleventh hour, Basque bank Sabadell Guipuzcoano came in with a two-year sponsorship deal for both the stage race and August's one-day race, the San Sebastian Classic, which had also been in trouble. It guaranteed the continuation of a tough, mountainous, week-long race that attracts star riders – and especially Spanish climbers – looking to test themselves ahead of their Giro or Tour goals.

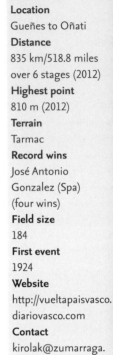

Statistics

Location
Gueñes to Oñati

Distance
835 km/518.8 miles over 6 stages (2012)

Highest point
810 m (2012)

Terrain
Tarmac

Record wins
José Antonio Gonzalez (Spa) (four wins)

Field size
184

First event
1924

Website
http://vueltapaisvasco.diariovasco.com

Contact
kirolak@zumarraga.net

Mountainous Basque Country

Circuit de la Sarthe
France
Pro stage race

A tradition-rich French stage race in the Loire

For what's a relatively small French stage race, the Circuit de la Sarthe – not to be confused with the motor racing circuit of the same name, which is home to the Le Mans 24 Hour – boasts some illustrious past winners. They include Bernard Hinault, Britain's David Millar and an up-and-coming Greg LeMond, who took his first ever European stage race victory there in 1980.

The 'Circuit Cycliste' uses narrow, undulating roads; it's a real racer's race, and one almost any rider is capable of winning if he can get into the right breakaway on the right day. April in northwest France can bring with it almost any type of weather, and it's a lottery as to whether this is a beautiful, sun-soaked event or a miserable grimace-inducing slog through rain and battering winds.

Statistics
Location
Sarthe, Loire
Distance
635 km/394.3 miles over 5 stages (2012)
Terrain
Tarmac
Record wins
Jean-Pierre Danguillaume (Fra) (three wins)
Field size
108
First event
1953
Website
www.circuitcycliste. sarthe.com
Contact
Via website

Scenic Sarthe

Scheldeprijs
Belgium
Pro one-day race

*A midweek Belgian one-dayer that favours
the sprinters*

You might expect this midweek Belgian one-day semi-Classic, which comes slap-bang in between the Tour of Flanders and Paris–Roubaix, to draw the same kind of rider as those two events that sandwich it, but it's a race that, on the flat roads of northeast Belgium, tends to favour the sprinters – albeit those capable of suffering across the sections of heavily cobbled Flandrian roads.

Those riders looking ahead to 'The Hell of the North' tend to either roll around it – figuratively speaking – to keep the legs ticking over, or rest up and give Scheldeprijs a miss completely.

Despite these days being outshone by the Tour of Flanders, Scheldeprijs is nevertheless the oldest race in Flanders, holding its first edition in 1907. A hundred years later, it was where sprinter of the moment, Britain's Mark Cavendish, took his first pro win, riding for the T-Mobile team and, in 2011, Cavendish was still at it, winning his third Scheldeprijs title, outsprinting rising sprint star Denis Galimzyanov and Yauheni Hutarovich.

If you're already in Belgium for Flanders or Roubaix, it's well worth extending your trip for a few more days to catch Scheldeprijs, too, but its accessibility from the UK, and the chances of a British winner, make it a decent race to get over to watch in its own right.

Statistics

Location
Antwerp to Schoten
Distance
202 km/125.5 miles
(2012)
Terrain
Tarmac and cobbles
Record wins
Piet Oellibrandt (Bel),
Mark Cavendish (Gbr)
(both three wins)
Field size
200
First event
1907
Website
www.scheldeprijs.be
Contact
info@scheldeprijs.be

Antwerp, Belgium

Record holder
Mark Cavendish

GP Pino Cerami
Belgium
Pro one-day race

Flemish-style cobbles and climbing in French-speaking Belgium

While most of the cycling world's attention is turned to Flanders during the months of March and April, the Grand Prix Pino Cerami heralds the return of the sport – albeit temporarily – to French-speaking Belgium, before France proper takes up the reins for Paris–Roubaix just a few days later.

Ask the riders, though, and they'll say that only the language has changed; the route of Pino Cerami is almost indistinguishable from those races just a little further north over the Wallonia/Flanders border.

The race starts in Saint Ghislain, and meanders through Wallonia's Hainaut region over tough cobbled climbs before finishing in Frameries.

The first edition of the race was in 1964, and was named after Giuseppe 'Pino' Cerami, a naturalised Belgian as of 1956, having been born in Italy. Cerami won the 1960 Paris–Roubaix, and is also the oldest ever winner of a stage of the Tour de France, in 1963, aged 41.

Statistics

Location
Saint Ghislain to Frameries

Distance
200 km/124.3 miles (2012)

Terrain
Tarmac and cobbles

Record wins
Marco Serpellini (Ita), Joop Zoetemelk (Ned) Gerrie Knetemann (Ned) (all two wins)

Field size
128

First event
1964

Website
www.grandprix cerami.be

Contact
info@grandprix cerami.be

Saint Ghislain, Belgium

Brabantse Pijl Cyclo
Belgium
Road

Sportive version of the Brabantse Pijl, in the heart of Belgium

Take to the roads of the 'Brabant Arrow' yourself, and follow in the tyre tracks of past winners such as Merckx, Maertens, Bartoli and Boogerd. Like the pro event, both distance-choices of the Brabantse Pijl Cyclo – 130 km and 65 km – start in Leuven, but whereas the pros make their way to Overijse, the sportive is far more convenient in that it loops you all the way back to Leuven and your waiting car and/or family. Both distances present riders with more than enough short, sharp climbs to test the legs, and both include the cobbled climb of the Hertstraat, just outside Overijse, where Philippe Gilbert jumped away from the peloton to set himself up for his 2011 victory in the pro event.

Statistics
Location
Leuven to Overijse
Distance
130/65 km
80.8/40.3 miles (2012)
Terrain
Tarmac and cobbles
Website
www.debrabantse
pijl-cyclo.be
Contact
cyclo@flanders
classics.be

Leuven, Belgium

Good Friday Track Meeting
United Kingdom

Track
Iconic Herne Hill track hosts Easter race action

Statistics
Location
Herne Hill, London
Terrain
Track
First event
1903
Website
www.bristowevents.
co.uk
Contact
graham@
bristowevents.co.uk

The London Olympics' new indoor velodrome in Stratford threatened to consign the Herne Hill outdoor cycle track to history. However, together with hard work from the Velo Club de Londres cycling club, the south London velodrome has been given a new lease of life, and has been resurfaced in time to be used as a training venue for national teams coming to the UK capital for the Games. Perhaps even more importantly, it will continue to provide track riders in southeast England with a safe, fun venue at which to race.

In recent years, and despite its popularity, the venue for the track cycling events at the 1948 Olympics has had to fight for its survival in the face of funding and leasing troubles. The track's regeneration has also seen the Good Friday Meeting – run at Herne Hill for the first time in 1903 – return to its proper home for 2012 after a year at the Manchester Velodrome due to the necessary resurfacing. The meet has always attracted big-name riders from abroad, as well as a regular stream of well known 'home' riders to SE24, including Graeme Obree, Rob Hayles and Bradley Wiggins, who rode his first races at Burbage Road as a youngster. Club riders can also enter, giving them the chance to race against some top names. It's a special place, and riders who race there are proud of the track, and are keen to see its continued use and survival in an age of more modern, indoor facilities.

Herne Hill is the last surviving venue of the 1948 Olympics

Cyclists lined up for the start of the sprint race in 1937

Gran Fondo Las Vegas
USA
Road

Try your luck at this spectacular sportive

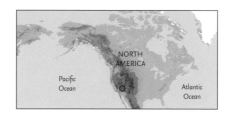

Statistics
Location
Las Vegas
Distance
160.1 km/100 miles
(2012)
Terrain
Tarmac
Website
www.granfondo
lasvegas.com
Contact
Via website

With Las Vegas being one of those 'must visit' destinations, then for cyclists visiting Las Vegas, the Gran Fondo Las Vegas is a 'must ride' event. The absolutely spectacular Red Rock Canyon becomes your playground after you've rolled out from the western suburbs of Vegas, and it's there you're faced with your first climb of the day. The amazing views help, though, and after reaching the gypsum-mining village of Blue Diamond, south of Red Rock, the climbing's over for those riding the 70-mile 'Mini Fondo', as it's the turnaround point. However, the climbing's only just getting started for those doing the full Fondo, who have 100 miles on the menu, and 8,000 feet of climbing. Much of that comes on the Lovell Canyon Road where, after refuelling at the top of the climb, you turn around to retrace your tyre tracks back to town – and most of it's downhill.

Red Rock Canyon National Conservation Area, Nevada

Tour DoonHame
United Kingdom
Pro stage race

Previously known as 'The Girvan', this Scottish stage race consistently helps shape British road stars

The Tour DoonHame stage race – part of the UK's elite Premier Calendar series – might be better known to many as the Girvan Three-Day, or even simply 'The Girvan'. Although the race moved from the southwestern Scottish town just a little further south to Dumfries in 2010, in order to find extra accommodation for the race's entourage, in 2012 it headed back to Girvan for the finish of the first stage from Castle Douglas. It remained in Girvan for stage two later the same day – a circuit race on the roads around Victory Park, bringing back a stage that had been a popular part of the Girvan since 1971.

The race has hosted British cycling's biggest names over the years, many of whom went on to even bigger things on the European stage. They include Sean Yates, Mark Cavendish, Chris Boardman, and Scotland's own Robert Millar and Brian Smith. Cavendish briefly led the race having won the opening stage way back in 2004.

The organisers have fought hard against the economic climate, and although the race was reduced to two days for the 2012 event, they were still able to squeeze three stages of racing in across the Easter weekend's Sunday and Monday, the final stage – having left Girvan behind – being a tough, hilly stage between Moffat and Annan to help decide a worthy winner.

As for the name: 'Doon hame' means 'down home' due to Dumfries's southern location in relation to the rest of Scotland, and in addition to the town being known as 'Queen of the South', those who hail from Dumfries are known as 'doonhamers'.

Statistics
Location
Dumfries
Distance
326.7 km/203 miles
over 3 stages (2012)
Terrain
Tarmac
Record wins
Paul Curran (Gbr)
(three wins)
Field size
143
First event
1968
Website
www.tourdoon
hame.info
Contact
event.organiser@
tourdoonhame.info

Some of cycling's biggest names race through southern Scotland

Paris–Roubaix
France
Pro one-day race

The must-see cobbled Classic known as 'The Hell of the North'

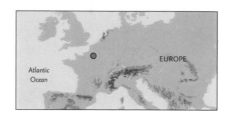

For many, it's a toss-up between the Tour of Flanders and Paris–Roubaix as to which is the greatest one-day race in cycling. Flanders has the history, the cobbled climbs and, perhaps most importantly, the passion of a partisan Belgian crowd. Roubaix, though, you could argue, has even more to offer: that same partisan Belgian crowd, despite the fact that it's a French race, who travel to the race in their thousands, an even longer history, more severe cobbles, the dust in the dry, the mud in the wet, the finish on the velodrome, the iconic photos of blackened faces peering through the steam in the famous velodrome shower block...

As for spectating, at Roubaix it's like nowhere else; it's arguably more exciting than standing at the roadside at the Tour de France. In northern France, on an often freezing April afternoon, no matter whether it's a wet or dry edition of the race, you feel like you've stepped back in time; that you could just as easily be standing at the edge of those horrific cobbled roads back at the turn of the twentieth century when the race was in its infancy.

If you're lucky enough to be able to make it to see the finish, and nab a spot at the side railings overlooking the Roubaix velodrome or, even better, a seat in the grandstand, or – even better again, and only the preserve of the lucky few – a spot in the centre of the track, then you're in for a real treat. It's the noise or, rather, the lack of it that really

gets you – the calm before the storm. You think you can almost make out the rattle of man and machine over the final section of cobbles coming into town before realising that it's the approaching TV helicopter, and then the riders – or lone rider if someone's on a particularly good day – burst onto the track, accompanied by a feverish eruption of noise from the crowd. A lap-and-a-half still awaits, and there's joyous confusion as more and more dazed riders join the track in threes, fours and fives, everyone relieved to have finally found a smooth surface to ride on after a long day on the cobbles of the 'The Hell of the North'.

Outsider Johan Van Summeren upset the odds when he won in 2011

Statistics
Location
Compiègne to Roubaix
Distance
257.5 km/160 miles (2012)
Terrain
Tarmac and cobbles
Record wins
Roger De Vlaeminck (Bel)
Tom Boonen (Bel) (both four wins)
Field size
200
First event
1896
Website
www.letour.fr
Contact
cyclisme@aso.fr

Competitors traverse Paris–Roubaix's infamous cobbles ▶

Tour of Cologne
Germany
Pro one-day race
A German single-dayer for the sprinters

Held on Easter Monday each year, the Rund um Köln is the second oldest bike race in Germany, having started in 1908. The country's oldest race, the Rund um die Hainleite, first held in 1907, however, is now only kept alive as a stage of the Internationale Thüringen Rundfahrt stage race.

From the start in Hückeswagen, north-east of the city, the 196.7 km race quickly gets into a lumpy 170-odd-kilometres to soften everyone's legs before a flat run into central Cologne for three laps of a 6.6 km circuit, meaning that the race has favoured sprinters in recent years. A separate mountains classification, however, encourages breakaways in the first half of the race before the fast men's teams reel them in and all hell breaks loose in the sprint for the line in Cologne's Bayenstrasse.

Wilfried Trott holds the record for the most wins, triumphing in 1972, 1976 and 1979

Statistics
Location
Cologne
Distance
196.7 km/122.2 miles (2012)
Highest point
367 m (2012)
Terrain
Tarmac
Record wins
Wilfried Trott (Ger) (three wins)
Field size
168
First event
1908
Website
www.arturtabat.online.de
Contact
info@rundumkoeln-challenge.de

Skoda Velodom Cologne
Germany
Road

Enjoy beautiful Cologne by bike just hours ahead
of the pros

The Skoda Velodom Cologne is the sportive
version of the Tour of Cologne, taking place
on the same day as the one-day pro event.
Cologne is a city easily accessible by train,
plane or automobile, and so a trip to enjoy
the ride around the beautiful city, and then
watch the top pros come home, makes for a
great day.

Starting on Bayenstrasse in the centre of
Cologne, the main, 126.4 km event picks up
the last 110 km of the pro event at Odenthal,
albeit without the three laps of the finishing
circuit. Odenthal's where the climbing starts,
too, but don't think you're going to get
away without any climbing by plumping for
the 69.3 km version; it's still plenty lumpy
enough to provide a challenge.

Statistics

Location
Cologne
Distance
126.4/69.3 km
78.5/43.1 miles (2012)
Highest point
250 m (2012)
Terrain
Tarmac
Website
www.arturtabat.online.
de
Contact
info@rundumkoeln-
challenge.de

Cologne, Germany

Cotswold Spring Classic
United Kingdom
Road

Stunning scenery helps the miles fly by in this Cotswolds sportive

Anyone who has never ridden their bike in the Cotswolds is truly missing out: quiet, challenging roads seem almost as though they were made for cycling. The Cotswold Spring Classic, held on Easter Monday, provides the perfect opportunity to see what the fuss is all about – a sportive renowned for impeccable organisation, and which includes motorbike outriders help to ensure participants' safety. Perfectly showcasing the area by way of a tough, circular route around Cirencester, taking in Fairford and Stroud on either a 105 km or 105 mile (169 km) route. Plus you don't even have to decide which route you wish to do until the course splits after 100 km. Cirencester College, just outside the market town, is the start and finish venue for both distances.

Statistics

Location
Cotswolds

Distance
169/105 km
105/65.2 miles (2012)

Terrain
Tarmac

Field size
750

First event
2009

Website
www.
cotswoldspringclassic.
co.uk

Contact
Via website

Scenic Stroud is the most westerly point of the route

Paris–Camembert
France
Pro one-day race

It's all about wheels of cheese at this one-day semi-Classic

Those riders who don't like cheese need not apply: the winner of Paris–Camembert – and, in fact, second and third places on the podium, too – receives a huge wheel of the local creamy, soft cheese for their efforts. Starting in Magnanville, 60 km northwest of Paris, Paris–Camembert's hilly 'parcours' is taken advantage of by many riders to ready themselves for the upcoming Ardennes Classics in Holland and Belgium. In the same way as it doesn't actually start in Paris, the race finishes in Vimoutiers near, rather than in, the tiny town of Camembert, in the Normandy department of Orne, making catching some of the sport's top names in action easily accessible from the UK.

Statistics

Location
Magnanville to Vimoutiers

Distance
206.5 km/128.3 miles (2012)

Terrain
Tarmac

Record wins
Laurent Brochard (Fra) (three wins)

Field size
120

First event
1934

Website
www.paris-camembert.fr

Contact
copc61@orange.fr

Jimmy Casper triumphed at the 70th edition of Paris–Camembert

Brabantse Pijl
Belgium
Pro one-day race

An Ardennes-style one-day race in Flanders

Just to confuse matters, Pino Cerami, who gives his name to the GP Pino Cerami, taking place just down the road, only a few days before the Brabantse Pijl, was the race's first winner in 1961. It used to take place a week ahead of the Tour of Flanders, but today, the race is a key warm-up event in the build-up to the three Ardennes Classics: Amstel Gold, Flèche Wallonne and Liège–Bastogne–Liège. The province of Brabant straddles both Flanders and Wallonia, with bilingual Brussels at its heart, but the Brabantse Pijl enjoys a very similar topography to the Ardennes races, and indeed its hilly 'parcours' makes it perfect for riders preparing for Amstel Gold just a few days later.

Statistics

Location
Leuven to Overijse
Distance
195 km/121.2 miles
(2012)
Terrain
Tarmac and cobbles
Record wins
Edwig Van Hooydonck
(Bel) (four wins)
Field size
184
First event
1961
Website
www.debrabantse
pijl.be
Contact
info@flanders
classics.be

Philippe Gilbert celebrates victory in 2011, finishing ahead of Björn Leukemans and Anthony Geslin

Vuelta Ciclista Castilla y Leon Spain

Pro stage race

A mini, five-day Tour of Spain to test both sprinters and climbers

British team Sky struck gold at the 2011 edition with up-and-coming young British sprinter Ben Swift winning the final stage of the race, while Spain's Xavier Tondo, of the Movistar team, was crowned overall race winner. However, just a month later, Tondo was tragically killed in a horrific freak accident when he was crushed by his electric garage door. He will be remembered in future editions of the race.

The five-day stage race, around the northwestern region of Castile and Leon, offers a variety of stunning terrain and therefore a range of stages, from time trials to flat sprinters' stages to mountain stages. It's a veritable mini Tour of Spain, and gives teams the chance to take a mixed squad of riders with chances for everyone.

Statistics

Location
Castile and Leon

Distance
491 km/305.1 miles
over 3 stages (2012)

Terrain
Tarmac

Record wins
Alberto Contador (Spa)
(three wins)

Field size
156

First event
1985

Website
www.vueltacastilla
yleon.com

Contact
cadalsa@cadala
eventos.com

Spain's Alberto Contador is the race's most prolific winner

Scheldeprijs Cyclo
Belgium
Road

Sportive riders' opportunity to take on the Scheldeprijs route – spaghetti included

The Scheldeprijs Cyclo is one of the newer events on the sportive calendar but, following the route of the pro event, which was first run in 1907, it feels every bit as 'classic' as the better known Flanders or Roubaix sportives. As you toil across cobbles towards the finish, be buoyed by the thought of the opportunity to take a shower at the event headquarters in Schoten, just outside Antwerp, where the event starts and finishes, and then sit down to a well-deserved spaghetti dinner, which is included in your 10-euro entry fee – and which outside of 'European Sportive World' would have cost you at least 10 euros on its own. Bon appétit!

Statistics

Location
Schoten

Distance
150/100 km
93.2/62.1 miles (2012)

Terrain
Tarmac and cobbles

First event
2011

Website
www.scheldeprijs-cyclo.be

Contact
cyclo@flanders classics.be

Tro Bro Cyclo
France
Road

Follow the pros off-road in this Breton sportive

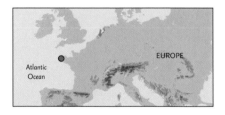

Like the Tro Bro Léon pro event that comes the day after, the Tro Bro Cyclo takes riders across Brittany's rough-and-tumble farm tracks, harking back to that age when all bike racing was like this. With its start and finish in Lannilis, just north of Brest, this is an event easily accessible from the UK, and a sportive that riders who have ridden the Eroica on Tuscany's 'white roads', the Flanders sportive or the Paris–Roubaix sportive will have to add to their list of achievements. Riders have the option of a 60 or 120 km route.

Statistics

Location
Lannilis, Brittany

Distance
120/60 km
74.6/37.3 miles (2012)

Terrain
Tarmac and dirt roads

Website
www.tro-bro-leon.com

Contact
jp.mellouet@tro-bro-leon.com

Amstel Gold Race
Toerversie Netherlands
Road

Take on the Amstel Gold route in the sportive version of the race

The day before the pros, take on the best climbs Holland's Limburg region has to offer in the Amstel Gold Toerversie, or 'tour version'. It's an extremely well-run event and so popular is it, in fact, that organisers have had to cap the field at 12,000, and entry is by way of a London Marathon-style lottery.

The start and finish are both in Valkenburg, making it an ideal base for the weekend to participate and then spectate, while the choice of ride routes is huge, with six options between 65 km and the full 250 km, ensuring there's an Amstel Gold for every ability.

Statistics

Location
Limburg
Distance
65–250 km
40.4–155.3 miles (2012)
Terrain
Tarmac
Field size
12,000
Website
www.amstegoldrace.nl
Contact
info@amstel
goldrace.nl

 RACE AGAINST THE PROS

Tour of the Battenkill
Pro/Am USA
Road

New York state's family-friendly weekend of riding

The ominous-sounding Battenkill Valley, New York, is the battleground for riders of the Tour of the Battenkill Pro/Am races. Of course, only the higher-category amateur riders will face off against the pros, but for everyone taking part in their own race category, the thrill is in covering the same roads – and lack of them – as the pros themselves. The next day's race is pro only, but pros without a spot there compete with the best of US amateurs for bragging rights on the dirt roads around Cambridge, New York, in the Pro/Am. There's plenty more going on at Battenkill, with kids' rides, a bike expo and, in 2012, the presence of three-time Tour de France winner Greg LeMond, no less.

Statistics

Location
Cambridge, New York
Distance
128.7/100 km
80/62 miles (2012)
Terrain
Tarmac and dirt roads
Field size
3,000
Website
http://battenkill,
squarespace.com
Contact
Via website

Mallorca Classic
Spain
Road

A major Mallorcan sportive event for
warm-weather hunters

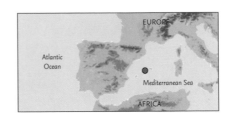

This is the official sportive event of the
Tour of Mallorca, organised by Swiss
Mallorcan holiday specialists Max Hürzeler.
Stick around for another week, though,
and you almost get two for the price of
one as the two-day Duva International
sportive takes place six days later. If you're
in Mallorca for a week of training, then
two sportives – or, rather, three – in quick
succession are going to push your fitness
levels along a lot faster than pootling
along at your own pace for a week. The
Mallorca Classic has routes starting from
Playa de Palma or Playa de Mura, which
then converge at Inca to tackle a timed
section over the climbs of the Puig Major
and Soller – both tough, well-known climbs
to those regular visitors to Mallorca, and an
excellent way to build fitness.

Statistics
Location
Mallorca
Distance
135/124 km
83.9/77.1 miles (2012)
Highest point
920 m (2012)
Terrain
Tarmac
Website
www.vuelta
mallorca.com
Contact
info@unisport
consulting.com

Playa de Palma, Mallorca

Granfondo Golfe de Saint Tropez France

Road

Springtime sportive in sunny Saint Tropez

The sportive rolls out of opulent Saint Tropez and finishes in the surrounding hills of Gassin, overlooking Saint Tropez. The circular route takes in a number of climbs, the highlight of which is the Notre Dame des Anges, 80 km into the full 179 km route. It features on the 'medium' 136 km route option, too, while the shorter 59 km version – which accepts entries from school children   follows the first 50 km of the longer event before doubling back to Gassin.

The sportive is also the opening European event in the UCI World Cycling Tour calendar, made up of fifteen international events through which riders can qualify for the 'final' in Pietermaritzburg, South Africa, at the end of the season.

Statistics

Location
Saint Tropez
Distance
179/136/59 km
111.2/84.5/36.6 miles
(2012)
Highest point
680 m (2012)
Terrain
Tarmac
Field size
1,000
First event
1987
Website
www.sport
communication.com
Contact
Via website

Grandiose Saint Tropez, France

Amstel Gold Race
Netherlands

Pro one-day race

Holland's biggest and best bike race kicks off the Ardennes Classics

Amstel Gold is the first in the series of the three races that make up the so-called Ardennes Classics, the other two being Flèche Wallonne and Liège–Bastogne–Liège, which tend to attract the grand tour riders as much as the Classics specialists. Amstel rolls out of Maastricht, but the only rolling the riders will do after that is down the other side of a number of tough climbs around the region of Limburg. The race finishes at the top of the Cauberg near Valkenburg, having climbed it twice already along the way.

With five wins, Dutch cycling legend

Jan Raas holds the record for the number of victories at Amstel, which has been run only since 1966, making it one of the newer Classics. It's one of the longest, too, at over 250 km. The race has always attracted the big names, and Amstel can boast four Tour de France winners as its past champions: Eddy Merckx, Bernard Hinault, Joop Zoetemelk and Bjarne Riis.

The 2012 world championships road race follows a very similar route to Amstel Gold, using the Cauberg as its final climb, although the finish line is a couple of kilometres further on past the summit.

Statistics

Location
Limburg
Distance
256.5 km/159.4 miles (2012)
Terrain
Tarmac
Record wins
Jan Raas (Ned) (five wins)
Field size
192
First event
1966
Website
www.amstel
goldrace.nl
Contact
info@amstel
goldrace.nl

Whoever said Holland was flat?

The race passes a mill in Beek ▶

Tour of the Battenkill
Professional USA

Pro one-day race

America's answer to the European spring classics

'America's toughest one-day race' might be self-styled, but it isn't far from the mark, as the US gets in on the 'Hell of the North'/Roubaix action with its own pro race featuring long off-road sections to test the very best American and international pro teams in this UCI-ranked one-day event. Unlike the pro/am races the day before, this is the big one, and invite-only, and closes a weekend programme of cycling races and activities in Cambridge, New York. In 2012, UK squads Team IG-Sigma Sport and Team Raleigh made the trip across the pond. The 124-mile (200 km) course is punctuated by short climbs, and when these climbs are on the dusty, sandy off-road sections, the treacherous descents down again require the utmost bike-handling skill and concentration.

Statistics

Location
Cambridge, New York
Distance
199.6 km/124 miles
(2012)
Terrain
Tarmac and dirt roads
Field size
174
Website
http://battenkill.
squarespace.com
Contact
Via website

The USA's own Paris–Roubaix

Tro Bro Léon
France
Pro one-day race

Brittany's Paris–Roubaix

Tro Bro Léon is yet another of those March/April events with off-road sections that gets compared to Paris–Roubaix, but this is a race that can that bit more legitimately be referred to as 'Brittany's Paris–Roubaix', sharing its French heritage as it does, and neither does it try to steal its big brother's thunder, respectfully coming after Roubaix on the calendar.

The race takes in a number of sections of ribinou – farm tracks – as it makes its way around the northwestern tip of France, near Brest, and it's these dirt roads which earn it its 'Petit Paris–Roubaix' moniker in French. It started as an amateur event in 1984, but quickly caught the attention of the bigger teams, and is today part of the UCI Europe Tour series.

Statistics

Location
Lannilis, Brittany
Distance
206.4 km/128.3 miles (2012)
Terrain
Tarmac and dirt roads
Record wins
Philippe Dalibard (Fra) (three wins)
Field size
136
First event
1984
Website
www.tro-bro-leon.com
Contact
jp.mellouet@tro-bro-leon.com

The peloton makes its way around Brittany

Giro del Trentino
Italy
Pro stage race

The Dolomites are the riders' playground at this Italian four-day stage race

The Tour of Trentino makes good use of the Dolomites on its doorstep, and as a result is a stage race often used by riders for last-minute tuning for the Tour of Italy, which normally falls a week or so after Trentino.

The record for Trentino wins stands at three, held by Damiano Cunego, who hails from the Veneto – the province next door – so the Dolomite climbs are well known to the Italian. 'The Little Prince' used his first Trentino victory, in 2004, as a springboard for his first – and still only – overall Tour of Italy success.

In 2012, the race was set to finish, and no doubt be decided, atop the famous Passo Pordoi, known to many thanks to its regular appearances in the Giro d'Italia.

Statistics
Location
Trentino
Distance
511 km/317.7 miles
over 4 stages (2012)
Highest point
2,239 m (2012)
Terrain
Tarmac
Record wins
Damiano Cunego (Ita)
(three wins)
Field size
136
First event
1962
Website
www.girodel
trentino.com
Contact
info@girodel
trentino.com

Battling against the testing gradients of the Dolomites

Flèche Wallonne
Belgium
Pro one-day race

The climb of the Mur de Huy provides an exciting finale to 'The Walloon Arrow'

Flèche Wallonne is a monstrous, edge-of-your-seat race to watch on the television, with everything building towards the final climb of the Mur de Huy to the finish. Visiting the race in person makes this the vantage point of choice to watch the race from too, especially as the riders tackle it three times.

'The Walloon Arrow', which starts in Charleroi, is the second of the three Ardennes Classics, but is perhaps the lesser of its two weekend cousins, falling as it does midweek. It's certainly no less exciting a race, though, and has produced winners of the highest calibre over the years – often big-name climbers and grand tour riders

who are able to survive the bumping and elbows on the narrow roads that define traditional springtime Belgian racing, combined with the ability to climb like an angel once the race hits the Mur, which is not to be confused with the Muur van Geraardsbergen, used for so long at the Tour of Flanders. Eddy Merckx, Bernard Hinault, Lance Armstrong and Cadel Evans have all won here, while it was the halfway point of Philippe Gilbert's Ardennes treble in 2011, making him only the second rider in history, after Davide Rebellin in 2004, to have won Amstel Gold, Flèche and Liège–Bastogne–Liège in the same season.

Statistics

Location
Charleroi to Mur de Huy, Wallonia
Distance
200 km/124.3 miles (2012)
Terrain
Tarmac
Record wins
Eddy Merckx (Bel), Marcel Kint (Bel), Moreno Argentin (Ita), Davide Rebellin (Ita) (all three wins)
Field size
200
First event
1936
Website
www.letour.fr
Contact
cyclisme@aso.fr

Charleroi, Belgium

Philippe Gilbert triumphs atop the Mur de Huy in 2011 ▶

Duva International
Spain
Road

A challenging, two-day sportive taking in Mallorca's major climbs

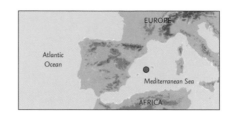

This two-day, British-organised sportive in Mallorca enjoys rolling road closures, almost guaranteed sunshine and offers a real challenge to club cyclists keen to push themselves and discover the best of what the Balearic biking island has to offer. Day one's 135 km route takes you over the Orient, followed by Soller and then the big one – the Puig Major. Day two's flatter 95 km route is that bit more sedate by default, and it is also possible to just ride one day or the other if it all seems a bit too much. Organisers Wheels In Wheels, who organise a number of UK sportive events, also offer a training camp week in the run-up to the Duva sportive, so you've got no excuses not to fly up the climbs.

Statistics
Location
Mallorca
Distance
230 km/143 miles
over 2 days (2012)
Terrain
Tarmac
First event
2008
Website
www.wheelsin
wheels.com
Contact
info@wheelsin
wheels.com

Orient, Mallorca

Liège–Bastogne–Liège Challenge Belgium

Road

Think you've got what it takes to take on La Redoute?

Tackling the climbs of La Redoute, the Roche aux Faucons and the Côte de Saint-Nicolas is not for the faint of heart, so it's a good job that the Liège–Bastogne–Liège Challenge offers alternative, shorter distances to the full 271 km experience. Not that either of them get you out of climbing the triumvirate: all roads lead to Ans, and the climbs feature on all three route choices, albeit with fewer kilometres to soften your legs – and your resolve – before you tackle them. While this is the official Liège–Bastogne–Liège sportive, taking place the day before the real deal, May's Tilff–Bastogne–Tilff is also worth a look, and tends to enjoy even better weather.

Statistics

Location
Liège and Bastogne

Distance
271/155/80 km
168.4/96.2/49.7 miles
(2012)

Terrain
Tarmac

First event
2011

Website
http://sport.be.msn.com/lblcyclo

Contact
info@golazo.com

The Côte de la Redoute is the race's most famous climb

Presidential Cycling Tour of Turkey Turkey

Pro stage race

Turkey benefits from the internationalization of professional cycling

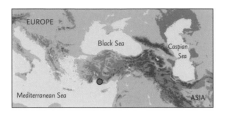

EUROPE

Black Sea

Caspian Sea

Mediterranean Sea

ASIA

Unfairly, many will remember the Tour of Turkey from 2009 when Holland's Theo Bos forced South African Daryl Impey into the barriers at the end of stage eight. The result was that Impey still took the overall title that year, but walked away – or was taken away, at least – with two cracked vertebrae and some significant dental work to look forward to. Bos claimed it was unintentional, and crashed himself, too, but Impey's injuries put him out of action for four months, while Bos received a month ban from the UCI.

However, there's a lot more to the Presidential Cycling Tour of Turkey. The race began life in 1968, but remained relatively low key until 2008 when the UCI's bid to further 'internationalise' the sport led to the race being upgraded on the international calendar, leading to piqued interest from the top pro teams. Since then, the race's mix of flat sprinters' stages and tough days in the mountains has kept big-name riders and their teams coming.

Statistics

Location
Alanya to Istanbul
Distance
1,174 km/729.5 miles
over 8 stages (2012)
Highest point
1,850 m (2012)
Terrain
Tarmac
Field size
200
First event
1968
Website
www.tourofturkey.org
Contact
aacikalin@
tourofturkey.org

President Abdullah Gul attends the podium presentation

Andrea Guardini celebrates his stage-one victory in 2011 ▶

Liège–Bastogne–Liège
Belgium

Pro one-day race

'La Doyenne' attracts cycling's biggest stars

Statistics
Location
Liège and Bastogne
Distance
255.5 km/158.8 miles
(2012)
Terrain
Tarmac
Record wins
Eddy Merckx (Bel)
(five wins)
Field size
200
First event
1892
Website
www.letour.fr
Contact
cyclisme@aso.fr

Of all the three Ardennes Classics, Liège–Bastogne–Liège is arguably the one that the grand tour contenders who come to test their legs in the Ardennes would most dearly love to win. Liège is one of the sport's five 'Monuments' – the oldest, greatest one-day races on the calendar – and its hilly route gives the stage-race riders a better chance of success than the cobbled Monuments such as the Tour of Flanders and Paris–Roubaix.

The race is affectionately known as 'La Doyenne', meaning 'The Old Lady' – albeit in a respectful tone – due to the first edition having taken place way back in 1892. Of the climbs, La Redoute is arguably the best known and toughest of them all, at over 2 km in length and with an average gradient of 8.4 per cent. It's narrow, too, so the spectators can really feel as though they're suffering along with the passing riders. Like the two Ardennes Classics before it – Amstel the previous weekend and the midweek Flèche Wallonne – Liège's uphill finish to Ans, a northwestern suburb of the city, provides excitement to the last.

Despite its late-April slot, Liège has sometimes been affected by freezing weather – most famously in 1980, when Bernard Hinault helped establish his 'hard-man' persona by all but ignoring the heavy snowfall and destroying his opponents, many of whom pulled out because of the conditions.

City of Liège on the river Meuse, Belgium

Philippe Gilbert completed a hat-trick of wins in 2011, becoming only the second man to win all three of the Ardennes Classics in a single year ▶

Mount Laguna Bicycle Classic USA

Road

Stunning, traffic-free roads, and more than a little climbing in Southern California

Mount Laguna, in San Diego County, Southern California, is climbed three times via three different routes as part of the main 101-mile route for a total of 10,000 feet of climbing, although 75- and 45-mile options are also available, still climbing 7,000 and 4,000 feet, respectively.

The real selling point, climbing aside, is the rest of the stunning scenery you'll enjoy as part of what is a generally traffic-free part of the world, just 70 km east of San Diego itself. At 6,000 feet, Mount Laguna rewards riders with jaw-dropping views, although you need your wits about you again for the fast descent off the climb back to the Pine Valley start/finish area.

Statistics

Location
San Diego County
Distance
162.5/120.7/72.4 km
101/75/45 miles (2012)
Terrain
Tarmac
Field size
350
First event
2010
Website
www.adventurecorps.com/mlbc
Contact
Via website

Twilight Gambler Bike Ride USA

Road

Join in the Twilight fun with this ride around northeast Georgia

This ride, along with the famous Twilight Criterium pro race, is part of a weekend programme in central Athens, Georgia, simply called Twilight, featuring other bike races, a running and walking event, a 'twiathlon', music, food and even trapeze artists. Join in the fun on what is a daytime bike ride, despite the name, over your choice of 50 km or 100 km around the hilly roads of northeast Georgia. The 'Gambler' aspect of the ride's name alludes to the playing cards you're given at the start, at the three checkpoints/refreshment stops on the route, and at the finish. The riders with the best poker hands win prizes.

Statistics

Location
Athens, Georgia
Distance
100/50 km
62.1/31.1 miles (2012)
Terrain
Tarmac
Website
www.athenstwilight.com
Contact
Via website

Tour of Romandy
Switzerland
Pro stage race

The 'other Tour of Switzerland' that showcases
French-speaking Romandy

The Tour of Romandy is one of two major
stage races in Switzerland – the other
being the Tour of Switzerland – and neither
ever disappoints thanks to the plethora
of stunning mountain views, lush green
meadows and the tinkling of cow bells
on offer, just as you imagine Switzerland
should be. The Tour de Romandie, as it's
called locally, centres on French-speaking
Switzerland, with the race based around
Geneva and Lausanne.

The race is often the next port of call
for those who have ridden the Ardennes
Classics, which means the presence of Tour
de France stars keen to at last enjoy some
sunnier spring weather and test each other
out on the various climbing and time trial
stages that make up the race.

**Sky's Ben Swift won a stage of
the 2011 Tour of Romandy**

Statistics
Location
Lausanne to
Crans-Montana (2012)
Distance
694.8 km/431.7 miles
over 6 stages (2012)
Terrain
Tarmac
Record wins
Stephen Roche (Irl)
(three wins)
Field size
152
First event
1947
Website
www.tourde
romandie.ch
Contact
info@tourde
romandie.ch

Athens Twilight Criterium
USA

Pro one-day race

Crazy American-style circuit racing in downtown Athens, Georgia

American bike fans hold the Athens Twilight Criterium up as one of the most fun and enjoyable races on the calendar, although competitors might disagree in the heat of battle when they're getting beer sprayed all over them, but such is the appeal of a race taking place at twilight in a town populated by overly-excited and possibly over-fuelled students, home as it is to the University of Georgia.

Twilight is a race, and carnival, for everyone, with 30,000 spectators estimated to line the 1 km route in central Athens. The men compete over 80 laps, with past winners including such illustrious names as road stars Steve Bauer, Malcolm Elliott and Chris Horner, while the 40 km women's event, which takes place just beforehand, is held on the same course.

Statistics

Location
Athens, Georgia

Distance
80 km/49.7 miles
(2012)

Terrain
Tarmac

First event
1980

Website
www.athens
twilight.com

Contact
Via website

Cyclists complete laps around a city-centre course

Spectators enjoy the beer and bicycles on offer

Rutland–Melton International CiCLE Classic
United Kingdom
Pro one-day race

A little piece of Belgium in the East Midlands

The CiCLE Classic brings Belgian-style Classics racing to the UK, with sections of this one-day race on dirt roads, reminiscent of Paris–Roubaix, while the undulating course throws in a bit of Flanders. The race attracts an international field as part of the UCI Europe Tour, and attracts squads from as far away as Africa and the US, but British winners since its first edition in 2005 remain in the majority – for now.

Starting in Oakham town centre,

the race takes the peloton on a 168 km journey through the East Midlands' most challenging terrain, with a finish in Melton Mowbray.

Setting up shop in Owston gives spectators the possibility of seeing the race six times, while new for 2012 was an additional 15 km loop at the finish giving spectators at the finish in Melton Mowbray the opportunity of seeing the riders twice.

Statistics

Location
Oakham to Melton Mowbray

Distance
168 km/104.4 miles (2012)

Terrain
Tarmac and dirt roads

Field size
180

First event
2005

Website
www.cicle classic.co.uk

Contact
colin.l.clews@ btinternet.com

Riders race across the varied terrain of the East Midlands

Rund um den Finanzplatz Eschborn-Frankfurt Germany

Pro one-day race

German one-day 'semi-Classic' that attracts the top pro teams

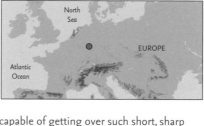

There really are some great bike race names out there, and the 'Tour of the Eschborn-Frankfurt Financial District' ranks right up there with the best of them. The race's previous incarnation as the Rund um den Henninger Turm – the Tour of the Henninger Tower – wasn't much catchier, either.

Despite the 26 per cent section of the Mammolshain, the race tends to nevertheless favour sprinters who are capable of getting over such short, sharp climbs, and central Frankfurt spectators are normally greeted by the sight of a hard-fought sprint finish. With that city-centre finale, and a supporting 'jedermann' sportive race for the public taking place the same day, the organisers seem to have got the recipe right for a great day's cycling.

Statistics

Location
Frankfurt

Distance
200 km/124.3 miles (2012)

Terrain
Tarmac

Record wins
Erik Zabel (Ger) (three wins)

Field size
192

First event
1962

Website
www.eschborn-frankfurt.de

Contact
AmueMedien@aol.com

Professional riders race through the city

Skoda Velotour Eschborn-Frankfurt Germany

Road

Join in the Frankfurt fun in the sportive version of the Frankfurt pro race

The Skoda-sponsored Velotour Frankfurt is a 'jedermann' (everybody) event taking place on the same day, and over a similar course, as the pro Rund um den Finanzplatz Eschborn race. It really is for everyone, welcoming tandems, handbikes, tricycles and even penny farthings and scooters

for the shorter-distance options. Those options are a 42 km or 70 km ride, while the longest version is 103 km, with all distances starting and finishing in Eschborn, located just a few kilometres northwest of Frankfurt.

Statistics

Location
Frankfurt
Distance
103/70/42 km
64/43.5/26.1 miles
(2012)
Terrain
Tarmac
Website
www.eschborn-frankfurt.de
Contact
velotour@macona.de

Frankfurt, Germany

Tour of the Gila
USA
Pro stage race

US stage race gains UCI America Tour status

For 2012, the Tour of the Gila acquired UCI America Tour status, which meant that top professional teams were able to compete there, which hadn't been the case while it had been a national-level race. Exceptions had been made in the past, such as when Lance Armstrong took part in the 2009 edition as part of a special three-man team with regular team-mates Levi Leipheimer and Chris Horner, and again in 2010 with Leipheimer and Jason McCartney. Leipheimer won the race overall on both occasions. Although the race overlaps with the start of the Giro in 2012, and so misses out on welcoming some big names, the Tour of the Gila does fall just ahead of the Tour of California, so serves as an excellent warm-up event.

Statistics

Location
Silver City, New Mexico

Distance
477 km/296.4 miles over 5 stages (2012)

Highest point
2,284 m (2012)

Terrain
Tarmac

Record wins
Burke Swindlehurst (USA) (three wins)

Field size
152

First event
1987

Website
www.tourofthegila.com

Contact
Via website

Riders feel the heat in New Mexico's premier road race

Four Days of Dunkirk
France

Pro stage race

A French five-day stage race definitely in need of a name change...

Another northern French stage race easily accessible to British fans from across the Channel, the Four Days of Dunkirk nevertheless threatens to cause confusion and play havoc with your hotel booking and return ticket by being staged over five days. The race has grown and added the extra day, of course, but there's still a small, traditional feel to the race which stays faithful to its name in one respect and always starts and finishes in Dunkirk. In 2012, the race made a small detour into West Flanders in Belgium for stage three, but was soon back in France and its familiar hilly circuit around Cassel, serving to break the race apart and find its worthy winner before another flat sprinters' stage back to Dunkirk on the final day.

Statistics

Location
Dunkirk

Distance
887.5 km/551.5 miles over 5 stages (2012)

Terrain
Tarmac

Record wins
Freddy Maertens (Bel) (four wins)

Field size
160

First event
1955

Website
www.4joursde
dunkerque.org

Contact
Via website

Dunkirk harbour

The peloton fights out the last stage by Dunkirk's historic beaches ▶

Giro d'Italia
Italy
Pro stage race

The world's second biggest race is every bit as exciting as its French cousin

More often than not referred to as the Giro d'Italia, the Tour of Italy is second in importance only to the Tour de France. Almost everything to do with the event is pink, and it's also known in Italian as La Corsa Rosa – simply, the pink race. In place of that iconic yellow leader's jersey at the Tour is a pale pink one for the Giro: easily as iconic on Italian soil, if not more so.

The first Giro took place in 1909, its organisers inspired by the French grand tour, which had seen the light of day just a few years earlier. The Tour's yellow jersey first appeared in 1919, while the first pink Giro leader's jersey was worn in 1931 – its colour taken from the colour of the pages of race sponsor La Gazzetta dello Sport, an Italian sports newspaper much like L'Equipe in France.

Statistics

Location
Herning, Denmark to Milan, Italy (2012)

Distance
3,476 km/2159.8 miles over 21 stages (2012)

Highest point
2,757 m (2012)

Terrain
Tarmac

Record wins
Fausto Coppi (Ita), Alfredo Binda (Ita), Eddy Merckx (Bel) (all five wins)

Field size
198

First event
1909

Website
www.gazzetta.it/ Speciali/Giroditalia/ 2012/en

Contact
marketing.sport@rcs.i

Pink is the Giro's signature colour

While the Tour de France has mass appeal, the Giro has carved itself a nice niche among cycling fans as the connoisseur's three-week stage race – a secret to study and covet away from the popularity of the Tour, and which in recent years has become as innovative and exciting as any Tour de

France, and some would say even more so. It is the Giro, more than the play-it-safe Tour, that has regularly taken riders out of their comfort zones, with ever higher and tougher mountains, off-road sections and foreign starts in the Netherlands and, in 2012, Denmark.

The jagged Dolomites are an integral part of the race ▲

In addition to the pink leader's jersey, the race now awards a blue mountains jersey (replacing the traditional green), a white best-young-rider jersey and a red points jersey. Prior to 2012 the three jerseys combined – bar the pink leader's jersey – to form the green, white and red of the Italian tricolore flag.

While the world's best cyclist, Eddy Merckx, triumphed five times at the Giro, the race has mainly served to make names and careers out of Italian riders, including Alfredo Binda (five wins), Felice Gimondi (three wins), Gilberto Simoni (two wins), Fausto Coppi (five wins) and Gino Bartali (three wins). The latter two enjoyed a period in the Forties and Fifties when Italy was truly split in its support between the fiercely Catholic Bartali and the non-religious 'man of the people' Coppi. Such loyalty to individuals and teams is still evident at today's Giro, where the passion of the tifosi tends to far outweigh that of roadside spectators at the Tour de France who are there simply to enjoy the spectacle.

The Tour is an institution in France; in Italy, it is accurate to say the Giro runs through people's veins.

Alberto Contador lifts the winner's trophy in front of the Duomo, Milan in 2011 ▶

Breathtaking views are all in the Giro rider's day's work

North Pennine Sportive
United Kingdom
Road

Northumberland sportive that includes a 12-mile family ride

Organised, like the Premier Calendar Tour of the Reservoir, by the Tyne Valley Cycling Club, the North Pennine Sportive takes place the day before the pro race, and starts and finishes in Blanchland. Unusually for a pro-race-accompanying sportive, the longest, 100-mile distance option is in fact a touch longer than the 96-mile pro race, which for once gives the amateurs bragging rights. However, while the Tour of the Reservoir is based on multiple laps of Derwent Reservoir, the shortest sportive option – 12 miles, for families and riders new to the sport – is the distance that most faithfully follows the pro route, with the 100-mile and 42-mile options heading out west to Allendale and Rookhope before their return to the buffet in Blanchland.

Statistics
Location
Blanchland,
Derwent Reservoir
Distance
160.9/67.6/19.3 km
100/42/12 miles (2012)
Terrain
Tarmac
Website
www.tynevalley
cycling.co.uk
Contact
david@chain-events.
co.uk

There's always time for a breather and a photo

Tour of the Reservoir
United Kingdom
Pro one-day race

Premier Calendar event on a spectacular and spectator-friendly course

For a long time the opening round of the Premier Calendar series, these days new events and some changes see the Tour of the Reservoir as the third event of the six-race series. Just like the Tour of Lombardy, the Tour of the Reservoir, despite sounding like a stage race, is just a one-day race. While Lombardy takes place in Lombardy, the 'Reservoir' of this UK Premier Calendar event refers to Derwent Reservoir. Race HQ is Blanchland, near Hexham in Northumberland, from where the peloton rolls out for eight laps of the 12-mile circuit around the large body of water – a true tour of the reservoir. A rolling, rather than particularly hilly parcours means that the sprinters' teams have their work cut out keeping it all together.

Statistics

Location
Blanchland,
Derwent Reservoir

Distance
154.5 km/96 miles
(2012)

Terrain
Tarmac

Website
www.tynevalley
cycling.co.uk

Contact
jimkennedy@talktalk.
net

Derwent Reservoir

Five Boro Bike Tour
USA

Road

*Cruise the neighbourhood on two wheels
– New York style*

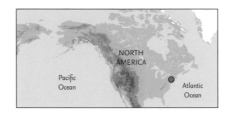

With 32,000 participants, the Five Boro Bike Tour is the USA's biggest cycling event. However, rather than trying to compete with pro races such as the Tour of California, this is a far more sedate affair. Starting near Battery Park, riders head up through Manhattan to Central Park. If the famous Manhattan greenspace is busy on normal weekday lunchtimes with riders getting their training miles in on what is a tough, hilly circuit, come the Five Boro Tour,

it's really something else again entirely. Enjoying the fully closed roads for the event, riders head on up to the Bronx before looping back down to cross into Queens via the Queensboro Bridge. From there, it's a straight run down to Brooklyn and then the Verrazano Bridge to Staten Island, where the ferry awaits riders to return them to Battery Park to complete the loop. What a way to see a city.

Statistics

Location
New York City
Distance
64.4 km/40 miles
(2012)
Terrain
Tarmac
Field size
32,000
First event
1977
Website
www.bikenewyork.org
Contact
Via website

New York's busy streets are closed to traffic

Tick off all five of NYC's boroughs by bike

Tour de Picardie
France

Pro stage race
Picardy plays host to the sprinters over three days

This three-day race in the Picardy region of northern France is considered to herald the start of summer, often attracting sprinting's big names, keen to polish their technique ahead of the Tour de France, which, like Picardie, is also organised by ASO. It's relatively unique in being nigh-on a sprinter's stage race, with very few serious climbs, but Britain's David Millar—more time triallist than fast finisher – got the better of them to become the first British winner in 2003, while compatriot Ben Swift demonstrated his development as a sprinter to win the 2010 edition – which was also his British team Sky's first-ever stage race victory.

Statistics
Location
Abbeville to Péronne
Distance
514 km/319.4 miles
over 3 stages (2012)
Terrain
Tarmac
Record wins
Willy Teirlinck (Bel),
Gilbert Duclos-Lassalle
(Fra),
Michael Sandstød (Den)
(all two wins)
Field size
144
First event
1936
Website
www.letour.fr
Contact
cyclisme@aso.fr

Coastal Abbeville, Picardy

Lincoln Grand Prix Sportive
United Kingdom
Road

Take on the Lincoln GP's Michaelgate climb

Arguably Britain's prettiest race has also had the 'sportive treatment', allowing mere mortals the opportunity to enjoy the delights of the scenic Lincolnshire countryside. Like the Lincoln Grand Prix, participants get the opportunity to tackle the 1-in-6 cobbled climb of Michaelgate, right in the centre of Lincoln, although they only have to climb it once, unlike the pros who have to struggle over it 11 times.

All the rides start at the Yarborough Leisure Centre, with a choice between a challenging 55-mile route, a tougher 77-miler and the longest 94-mile option, which takes riders out towards Grimsby before looping back round for the finish that all three rides share on Michaelgate. There's also a 22-mile family ride, taking participants north of Lincoln on a course that is only slightly flatter, and returning to the leisure centre start, missing out Michaelgate.

Statistics
Location
Lincoln
Distance
151.3/123.9/88.5/35.4 km
94/77/55/22 miles
(2012)
Terrain
Tarmac and cobbles
Website
www.itpevents.co.uk
Contact
Via website

Imposing Lincoln Cathedral dominates the course skyline

Etape Caledonia
United Kingdom
Road

'Scottish Etape' riders can enjoy completely closed roads and epic climbs

The year 2012 marked the fourth edition of the Etape Caledonia, which takes place in and around Pitlochry in the Scottish Highlands. Although only an 'etape' in name rather than actually being a stage of the Tour de France, participants can nevertheless enjoy the experience of life as a pro thanks to fully closed roads. The Etape Caledonia organisers have worked hard with locals to demonstrate to them the economic benefits such an event brings to the area, while simultaneously raising large amounts of money for charity.

In 2012, the organisers decided to incorporate the 'stage of the Tour de France' idea even more by making two sections of the course timed: the first a kilometre-long sprint and the second a 2 km climb, with a winner announced for each section.

Statistics

Location
Pitlochry, Highland Perthshire, Scotland
Distance
130 km/81 miles (2012)
Terrain
Tarmac
Field size
5,000
First event
2007
Website
www.etape caledonia.co.uk
Contact
info@etape caledonia.co.uk

Highland Perthshire belongs to cyclists for a day

Pitlochry's main street hosts the start ▶

Lincoln Grand Prix
United Kingdom

Pro one-day race

Cobbled climbing in Lincoln's Premier Calendar pro event

The Lincoln Grand Prix combines a spectator-friendly circuit with tough, spirited racing to make this race the British Premier Calendar series' flagship event. While the glorious Lincolnshire countryside makes a real impression on those visiting the race, it's Lincoln itself that packs the real punch, both in terms of the town's stunning architecture, dominated by the towering Lincoln Cathedral, and the punishing ascent of the cobbled climb of Michaelgate the riders face each lap, the top of which is also where the race finishes ominously on the thirteenth time through. The leg-sapping 1-in-6 climb also affords the race's best vantage point, with the town's plethora of pubs and tearooms all within easy reach. The race also welcomed Olympics officials in 2012, observing policing and marshalling protocols ahead of the Olympic road races.

Statistics

Location
Lincoln

Distance
163 km/101 miles
(2012)

Terrain
Tarmac roads, cobbles and rolling hills

Record wins
Paul Curran (Gbr)
(four wins)

Field size
160

First event
1956

Website
www.lincolngrand
prix.org.uk

Contact
Via website

Competitors have no time to be awed by Lincoln's architecture

Riders bounce
along the cobbles
of Michaelgate ▶

Fred Whitton Challenge
United Kingdom
Road
The Lake District is your playground at this popular, and hilly, sportive

'The Fred Whitton', as it's popularly known, is an extremely challenging 112-mile ride through the best the Lake District has to offer, held in memory of Lakes Road Club's club secretary Fred Whitton. It's a tough, mountainous course, starting and finishing in Coniston, taking in mighty climbs along the way such as Kirkstone, Hardknott and Wrynose passes. The ascents are not so much short and sharp as relatively long, sharp climbs. Such steep ascents need to come with a warning, too: what goes up must come down, and all that, and so descending during the Fred Whitton needs to be carried out with the utmost care.

Always oversubscribed, this is an event that showcases the Lake District like no other.

Statistics
Location
Coniston, Lake District
Distance
180.2 km/112 miles (2012)
Terrain
Tarmac
Field size
1,400
First event
1999
Website
www.fredwhitton challenge.org.uk
Contact
Via website

Lakeland passes after strenuous climbing and super-fast descending

Cycletta
United Kingdom
Road

Women-only events to inspire confidence and unearth hidden talent

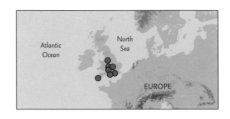

As cycling has grown in popularity, so has the demand for women-only events, mirroring running. Cycletta events span the country and, in 2012, seven venues – including Cheshire, Wiltshire and Warwickshire – offered the choice of a 40 km ride or a longer ride for those who are more experienced, with distances up to 80 km, as offered at the Brighton and New Forest events.

All days offer advice, mechanical assistance, goody bags and even 'helmet-hair remedy centres' to riders of all ages and abilities. Meanwhile, support for the timed events – allowing you to push yourself as hard as you like – comes from Olympic and world champion Victoria Pendleton, helping to inspire a new generation of top female cyclists.

Statistics
Location
Woburn Abbey, Bedfordshire;
Lydiard Park, Wiltshire;
Ragley Hall, Warwickshire;
Brighton, East Sussex;
Tatton Park, Cheshire;
New Forest, Hampshire;
St Michael's Mount, Cornwall
Distance
40 km or longer choice (up to 80 km)
Terrain
Tarmac
Field size
1,000
First event
2011
Website
www.cycletta.co.uk
Contact
info@cycletta.co.uk

Girl power propels the Cycletta series

Victoria Pendleton champions the women-only event ▶

Felice Gimondi
Italy

Road

Italian legend lends his name to one of Italy's biggest gran fondos

What reverence three-time Giro d'Italia champion Felice Gimondi was, and still is, held in is evident by the fact that this gran fondo is known simply by the Italian former pro's name. Based on the climbs around Bergamo, in Lombardy, the event is one of the biggest of its kind in Italy, and regularly attracts big-name pro riders of yesteryear such as Eddy Merckx, Gianni Bugno, Francesco Moser and Claudio Chiappucci. They, like everyone else, then have to choose between the 162 km Gran Fondo, the 129 km Medio Fondo and the 89 km Fondo. All end back in Bergamo, where the obligatory 'pasta party' ensures everything is right with the world.

Statistics

Location
Bergamo
Distance
162/129/89 km
100.7/80.2/55.3 miles
(2012)
Highest point
1,036 m
Terrain
Tarmac
First event
1996
Website
www.felicegimondi.it
Contact
info@felicegimondi.it

Experience Bergamo's chiseled hillsides

Tour of Chongming Island World Cup China

Pro one-day race

Chinese one-day race makes up part of the UCI Women's World Cup

The UCI Women's World Cup is made up of eight events, starting with the Ronde van Drenthe in Holland in mid-March and culminating with the GP de Plouay-Bretagne in France at the end of August. Chongming Island, near the city of Shanghai, hosts both a round of the World Cup and a three-day stage race.

In 2011 it was German sprinter Ina-Yoko Teutenberg who outgunned Britain's Lizzie Armitstead to win the of Chongming Island World Cup, having also been victorious in the stage race three days previously. Might a Teutenberg versus Armitstead duel also be on the cards at the Olympic road race?

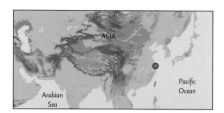

Ina-Yoko Teutenberg has won the event twice

Statistics

Location
Chongming
Distance
136.3 km/84.7 miles (2012)
Terrain
Tarmac
Record wins
Ina-Yoko Teutenberg (Ger) (two wins)
First event
2010
Website
www.shcmty.net
Contact
shcmhds@vip.163.com

Stephen Roche Tour de Cure Ireland

Road

A ride that bears the name of Ireland's Tour de France winner

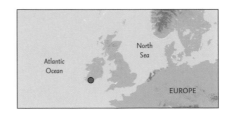

Ireland's Stephen Roche is rightly held up as one of the country's greatest-ever sportsmen. In 2012, Ireland celebrated 25 years since Roche 'did the treble', winning the Giro d'Italia, the Tour de France and the world championships in the same season. It is Roche who lends his name to, and is the ambassador for, this sportive that takes place in Midleton, County Cork. There's something for everyone, with routes taking in the beautiful – and undulating – roads around east Cork, with distance options of a family-friendly 15 km, a 50 km 'Novice' route, the 100 km Challenge and the 165 km Expert option, with all routes starting and finishing at the same place.

Statistics

Location
County Cork
Distance
165/100/50/15 km
102.5/62.1/31.1/9.3 mile
(2012)
Terrain
Tarmac
First event
2009
Website
www.stephenroche
tourdecure.com
Contact
Via website

Stephen Roche in his pomp

DIVA 100
United Kingdom
Road
Davina McCall's call to arms – on bikes!

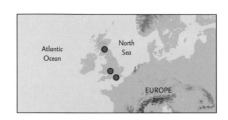

TV presenter Davina McCall fronts the nationwide three-event DIVA 100 series of women-only rides in Sussex, Scotland and Warwickshire, all raising money for Action Medical Research. McCall has become an avid fan of road cycling, and rode the opening Sussex event in 2012 on 13 May in Cowdray Park, Midhurst.

The Scottish event, in Fife, takes place the following week, with the Stratford-upon-Avon, Warwickshire, event another week after that. All three feature both a 100 km option and a 50 km ride, all with chip timing, mechanical assistance, massage and medals included in the entry fee.

Davina McCall

Statistics
Location
Sussex, Scotland, Warwickshire
Distance
100/50 km
62.1/31.1 miles (2012)
Terrain
Tarmac
First event
2011
Website
www.action.org.uk/diva
Contact
Via website

Mount Lemmon Time Trial USA

Road

A long 10 mile time trial up one of Tucson's toughest climbs

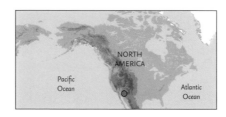

In the UK, club time triallists enjoy their 'evening tens' in the summer months. It's a chance to better your personal best of the season before, or go head-to-head with the club-mate who always beats you, but isn't going to this week because you've been training hard. In Tucson, USA, they do things a little differently – bigger and better, obviously. Again, it's a 10-mile time trial but, horrifically, it's all up a hill: Mount Lemmon, to be precise – a climb that gains around 3,000 feet from start to finish. British riders are used to the end-of-season hill-climbs, which, hard as they are, tend to take a matter of minutes to get up but, in the US, its geography is put to good use, and longer uphill TTs are the norm.

No prizes on offer here, but bragging rights for holding the record are worth so much more.

Statistics

Location
Tucson, Arizona

Distance
16.1 km/10 miles (2012)

Terrain
Tarmac

Website
www.saguarovelo.org/infolemmon.htm

Contact
info@saguarovelo.org

Tucson, Arizona

Squeeze out every last drop of energy on Mount Lemmon ▶

Tour of California
USA

Pro stage race

The USA's biggest stage race that attracts Tour de France stars

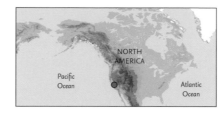

The Tour of California is arguably the USA's biggest and best-loved stage race, although its crown is perhaps under threat from the newest kid on the block, the USA Pro Cycling Challenge that, to all extents and purposes, is a Tour of Colorado. However, for a country that has had its fair share of races disappear due to lack of sponsorship, new events must be welcomed as a sign that either the economy, or American cycling, is on the up.

Statistics

Location
California

Distance
1,180.5 km/733.5 miles over 8 stages (2012)

Terrain
Tarmac

Record wins
Levi Leipheimer (USA) (three wins)

Field size
144

First event
2006

Website
www.amgentourof california.com

Contact
ATOCGeneralinfo@ amgentourofcalifornia. com

American squads mix with the top European teams

The irony of the Tour of California being sponsored by Amgen – a pharmaceutical company that manufactures EPO – was quickly got over, and quite rightly, too, as the addition of a big-name sponsor has helped stabilize the race, and prevent it going the way of now defunct US stage races like the Tour de Georgia.

A stage finish on ▲
Mount Baldy, at
10,000 ft is a feature
of the race

The race started life in 2006 as a February stage race, but even the consistently pleasant California weather couldn't absolutely guarantee that it was going to behave itself, and in 2010 was given a calendar-slot swap to May, putting it up against the Giro d'Italia for attracting big-name riders. While that may have at first appeared a little unfair against the Giro behemoth, the fact that the Italian grand tour has become such a tough race in recent years means that there are relatively few riders with their eye on Tour de France success who want to take on the Giro, and so the likes of the Schleck brothers – Frank and Andy – often plump for the good life in California.

That's not to say that the race is easy – far from it. Rather, the difficult climbs help hone Tour riders' fitness with France's premier event barely two months away. Organisers try to visit and revisit different pockets of California, with a lot of new venues keen to be a part of the race each year, too. Old favourites such as San Francisco, Los Angeles and the lesser known Solvang tend to feature regularly, as does the climb of Mount Baldy as a fitting finale to the race's 'queen stage', with 2012 being no exception.

The individual time trial at Solvang is a challenging test ▶

2011 champion Chris Horner wears the golden leader's jersey after stage seven

Oxygen Challenge VTT
France

Mountain bike

Join trail runners for this three-day mountain-bike festival in France's Auvergne

Stunning Auvergne scenery greets participants in France's Oxygen Challenge VTT – VTT standing for *Vélo Tout Terrain*, meaning mountain bike in French. Mountain bikers join trail runners for this multi-sport festival held at Le Lioran ski resort in the Cantal department – famed for its cheese. The main mountain-bike event is made up of a series of three races – one on each day: a short, 2.7 km prologue time trial, a 55 km cross-country race and a 24 km 'rally', made up of three separate timed sections. Beyond the race series, there are also a number of single off-road events across the three days, including a 24 km *randonnée* – a non-timed off-road sportive that takes you down the mountain where you can taste local Auvergne products to fuel you for the return journey back up the climb.

Statistics

Location
Cantal, Auvergne

Distance
82 km/51 miles
over 3 stages (2012)

Terrain
Off-road

First event
2008

Website
www.oxygen
challenge.com

Contact
oxygenchallenge@
aso.fr

Cantal's lush landscapes await

London Revolution
United Kingdom
Road

Celebrating the Olympics with a two-day ride around London

The London Revolution serves to celebrate the 2012 Olympics by leading riders on a two-day, London-discovery tour around the capital's Games hotspots. Day one starts at the ExCeL exhibition centre in the Docklands and takes in Epping Forest and Lee Valley Park before heading into the Chilterns and a finish at Windsor Castle via the Olympic rowing venue at Eton, making 101 miles in all. Those who have taken the overnight option can then enjoy a bit of rest and recovery before turning in for the night in their tent, ready for day two. The 84 miles takes riders down to Box Hill – which features on the 2012 cycling road race route – and on to the Herne Hill velodrome for a lap of the 1948 Olympics venue. From there, it's just a short ride across Tower Bridge to home.

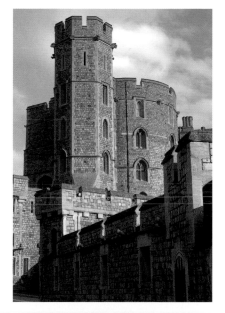

Statistics
Location
London
Distance
298 km/185 miles over 2 days (2012)
Terrain
Tarmac
Field size
2,000
First event
2012
Website
www.london-revolution.com
Contact
info@london-revolution.com

The route takes in London's iconic landmarks, including Windsor Castle and Tower Bridge

Silk Route
Asia
Long distance

Retrace the steps of the ancient trade
route – by bike

The Silk Route – also known as the Silk
Road – is an ancient trade route connecting
the great civilisations, and is in fact still in
use today. The Silk Route retraces its steps
from Shanghai in China to Istanbul in
Turkey, via Kyrgyzstan, Tajikistan, Uzbekistan,
Turkmenistan and Iran – 12,160 km, with
104 days of riding, but twenty-five rest days
along the way to enjoy the spectacular
sights, sceneries and cultures you'll
encounter. Although organised by the same
team behind the Tour d'Afrique, this is more
of an expedition rather than a race, but
averaging 125 km each day of cycling, this is
nevertheless an extremely tough challenge.

Statistics
Location
Shanghai, China
to Istanbul, Turkey
via Kyrgyzstan,
Tajikistan, Uzbekistan,
Turkmenistan and Iran
Distance
12,160 km/7,555.9 miles
over 129 days
Highest point
Over 3,600 m
Terrain
Tarmac, deserts and
mountains
Field size
13 full-tour riders,
18 'sectional' riders
First event
2008
Website
www.tourdafrique.com
Contact
info@tourdafrique.
com

Riding the Silk Road is a journey of discovery

**The Hindu Kush
is one of many
epic obtacles** ▶

La Look
France
Road

La Look sportive celebrates the Nevers-based company's achievements

Nevers, two hours south of Paris, is home to Look – the French company most famous for inventing the 'clipless' pedal in the mid-1980s, but now just as well known for its high-end carbon racing frames. Although the event takes place in one of the flatter parts of France, far away from the Alps and Pyrenees, it is nevertheless a far from flat

parcours. The famous Magny-Cours motor-racing circuit is the start point for all three distances on offer: a 'full' 156 km, a 89 km option and a non-timed 57 km *randonnée* aimed at encouraging younger riders to take part. All three options finish in Nevers town centre.

Statistics

Location
Nevers

Distance
156/89/57 km
96.9/55.3/35.4 miles
(2012)

Highest point
254 m

Terrain
Tarmac

Field size
Over 1,000

First event
2004

Website
www.sport
communication.com

Contact
Via website

Magny-Cours motor-racing circuit hosts the start

An Post Rás
Ireland
Pro stage race
Ireland's toughest stage race

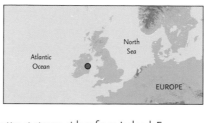

The An Post Rás celebrated its sixtieth edition of the race in 2012. Previously known as the Rás Tailteann and the FBD Milk Rás, it's often simply known as the Rás, and is known as Ireland's toughest stage race.

"It's really only been exceeded in that hierarchy of difficulty by the Nissan Classic and its later incarnation, the Tour of Ireland, yet it has outlived both and continues to attract strong riders from Ireland, Europe and beyond," explains Irish cycling journalist Shane Stokes.

"It's a race that has been won in the past by young riders such as Stephen Roche and Tony Martin, who highlighted their talent by coping best with the aggressive racing, convoluted tactics and general unpredictability of the event."

Statistics
Location
Dunboyne to Skerries
Distance
1,168 km/725.8 miles
over 8 stages (2012)
Terrain
Tarmac
Record wins
Shay O'Hanlon (Ire)
(four wins)
Field size
175
First event
1953
Website
www.anpost.ie/AnPost/
IrishCyclingRas
Contact
dermotdignam@
anpostras.com

The seaside town of Skerries is journey's end for the Rás

Gran Fondo New York
USA

Road

Italian gran fondo riding has arrived in the Big Apple

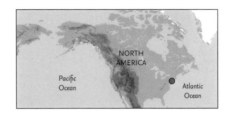

In contrast to the Five Boros Bike Tour, which takes over Manhattan a couple of weeks previously, the Gran Fondo brings with it a racier type of rider, recreating as it does an Italian gran fondo, although anyone over the age of 18 is able to take part, regardless of ability. The Gran Fondo New York is not a timed event as such, but the four major climbs out on the beautiful New Jersey roads are each timed from start to finish, establishing a King of the Mountains, and a Queen of the Mountains, at the end of the 177 km event. The shorter Medio Fondo is not timed at all, but is a better introduction to sportive riding, held over 100 km.

Statistics

Location
New York City
Distance
177/100 km
110/61 miles (2012)
Terrain
Tarmac
First event
2011
Website
www.granfondony.com
Contact
info@granfondony.com

The city gives way to the scenic, rural roads of New Jersey

The start is on the famous George Washington Bridge ▶

Etape du Dales
United Kingdom
Road

Yorkshire's finest scenery doubles up as this sportive's difficult route

The Etape du Dales takes in the very best of the Yorkshire Dales – 'best' if climbing is your thing, that is. The terrain is truly relentless from start to finish – leaving from Wharfedale Rugby Club in Grassington and returning 112 difficult miles later – but you couldn't ask for a better showcase of the Dales. At once both beautiful and monstrous, much depends on your mood, fitness and the wholly uncontrollable variable that is the weather, ranging from beautifully sunny to wet, windy and misty – often in the space of just a couple of hours. The climbs will be well known to long-time admirers of the Tour of Britain or the Milk Race as it used to be known: Fleet Moss, Buttertubs, Coal Road and the always windswept climb of Tan Hill, tempered somewhat by being the location of Britain's highest pub, should you feel the need to stop – which you might.

The mixture of shorter, sharper climbs coupled with longer, ever so slightly less steep ascents means that there's an equal amount of difficult descending, made all the more dangerous in inclement weather, so care is needed. All proceeds go to the Dave Rayner Fund, supporting young up-and-coming riders to take the next step up the ladder to turning professional.

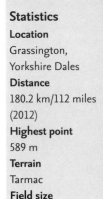

Statistics
Location
Grassington,
Yorkshire Dales
Distance
180.2 km/112 miles
(2012)
Highest point
589 m
Terrain
Tarmac
Field size
1,000
First event
2005
Website
www.etapedu
dales.co.uk
Contact
Martyn.Bolt@kirklees.
gov.uk

Thirsty riders can take a break from the punishing route at Britain's highest pub

Wild and beautiful
Yorkshire is super
cycling country ▶

Wight Riviera Sportive
United Kingdom
Road

It's no holiday on the Isle of Wight for this tough sportive

The atmosphere and scenery on the Isle of Wight might tease you into thinking you're on holiday, but the tough riding will soon banish such thoughts. Heading off from Yarmouth, the Needles, Freshwater Bay and Carisbrooke Castle in Newport, not to mention the stunning seaviews, will all nevertheless help to alleviate the pain. Three distance options are offered – 154 km, 110 km or 62 km – and for all of them the Wight Riviera Sportive uses what is called the Sportive Avantage format – a closed-road 25 km loop to start the event, allowing spectators at the start to enjoy the atmosphere, for riders to settle into the event, and for a pecking order of ability to safely form without the danger of other road users before the participants head out onto the open road. The Wight Riviera Ride is a fun, family event that starts at the same time as the sportives, albeit just behind them, using the same Avant loop, making for a safe, traffic-free riding experience. Both the Ride and the Sportive form part of the 2012 Cycle Wight weekend, which also includes mountain bike events and family rides on the island.

Statistics

Location
Isle of Wight
Distance
154/110/62 km
95.7/68.4/38.5 miles
(2012)
Highest point
174 m
Terrain
Tarmac
First event
2012
Website
www.southern
sportive.com
Contact
info@southern
sportive.com

Carisbrooke Castle

The Needles,
Isle of Wight

Montmartre Downtown
France
Mountain bike

Almost surreal MTB action in front of one of Paris's most iconic tourist attractions

Here's an idea: why not take the normally genteel and touristy area of Montmartre in the north of Paris, put down a load of ramps and 'North Shore' boardwalks on those famous steps leading down from the Sacré-Coeur to the Place Saint Pierre, then invite a load of pro downhill mountain bikers to ride down it as fast as they can – pulling some tricks on the way, of course – in front of a crowd of thousands?

The Montmartre Downtown is as 'simple' as that, but such an amazing backdrop has made it an attractive event for both riders and spectators alike. For its third edition in 2012, France's best up-and-coming downhillers were also invited to show what they could do against the elite athletes.

Statistics

Location
Montmartre, Paris
Terrain
Tarmac and wooden boardwalks
Field size
21
First event
2010
Website
www.montmartre-downtown.com
Contact
hexagonal@lhexagonal.com

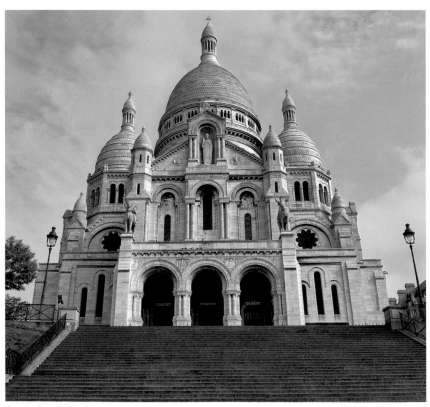

Sacré-Coeur, Paris

The basilica steps are converted into an urban downhill course with a difference ▶

Nove Colli
Italy
Road

Take on the nine hills in one of Italy's toughest gran fondos

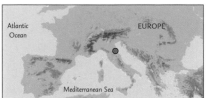

The 'Nine Hills' is one of Italy's best known gran fondos, starting and finishing in the Adriatic coastal town of Cesenatico. The locals' passion for cycling is big here, and even more so compared to the rest of Italy due to the fact that the late Marco Pantani – the flawed but loved Italian climber, who died in 2004 – lived here. In fact, the race is also known as the Nove Colli Marco Pantani.

The first edition of the event was back in 1971 – before the term 'gran fondo' or 'sportive' had even been invented. Back then, it was much simpler: it was either a bike ride, training or a race. The seventeen riders taking part in that first edition through the Apennines covered 200 km,

and it's that same distance that those doing the full route do, although today there's also a 130 km option. However, distance aside, the longer option is far tougher when it comes to the number of climbs on its route – all nine of them. Distance and climbs aside, what really marks the Nove Colli out as such a great event is the almost unbelievable support from the side of the road. It's almost enough to think that those watching aren't watching a bunch of amateur riders of various degrees of fitness, and that instead they're witnessing something really special – which, in a way, they are.

Statistics

Location
Cesenatico
Distance
200/130 km
124.3/80.8 miles (2012)
Highest point
791 m
Terrain
Tarmac
First event
1971
Website
www.novecolli.it
Contact
spada@novecolli.it

Eager riders await the gruelling gran fondo

The Italian coastal town of Cesenatico hosts Nove Colli ▶

Tour of Belgium
Belgium
Pro stage race

Springtime stage racing in the land of
the Classics

For a country that is supposedly no great fan of stage racing – here, the tough, one-day spring Classics like the Tour of Flanders are king – the Tour of Belgium has nevertheless captured the imagination of the home fans since 1908, albeit with a decade-long hiatus in the 1990s. Perhaps the fact that it takes place in May, not long after the spring Classics have finished, is part of the appeal – that, rather than the height of summer, there's still that spring-like feel to things, and riders like Belgian favourites Tom Boonen and Philippe Gilbert tend to take part, too. Both, in fact, are former winners of the five-day race.

Statistics

Location
Mechelen to Engis
Distance
727 km/451.7 miles
over 5 stages (2012)
Terrain
Tarmac
Record wins
Mottiat, Masson,
Vermandel, Van
Kerckhove, Foré,
Merckx, Swerts,
Devolder (all Bel),
Maassen (Ned)
(all two wins)
Field size
168
First event
1908
Website
www.rondevan
belgie.be
Contact
chris.vannoppen@
golazo.com

City of Mechelen

Local hero Philippe Gilbert at the Tour of Belgium in 2010 ▶

Bayern Rundfahrt
Germany
Pro stage race
German stage race around stunning Bavaria

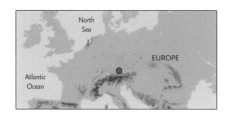

The Tour of Bavaria is a German five-day race, where in 2011 Sky's Geraint Thomas took his first overall pro stage race victory. It was a successful trip to Germany all round for the British squad, as Edvald Boasson Hagen won the opening stage and took the first yellow leader's jersey before Bradley Wiggins showed superb form to win the time trial on stage four by more than 30 seconds from then time trial world champion Fabian Cancellara. Thomas's fourth place on the TT stage netted him the race lead, which he held on to for the remainder of the race. It's a race that tends to be won on the time trial stage, but it's a popular proving ground for big teams as the build-up to the Tour de France begins in earnest.

Statistics

Location
Traunstein to Bamberg
Distance
802 km/498.3 miles
over 5 stages (2012)
Terrain
Tarmac
Record wins
Michael Rich (Ger),
Jens Voigt (Ger)
(both three wins)
Field size
133
First event
1980
Website
www.bayern-rundfahrt.com
Contact
info@bayern-rundfahrt.com

The Bavarian town of Traunstein hosts the start

La Tropicale Amissa Bongo
Gabon

Pro stage race

Gabon stage race tests home riders against top French pros

The event is named in memory of Albertine Amissa Bongo, who died in 1993, daughter of former president Omar Bongo, and sister of the current president, Ali Bongo, who took over the presidency following his father's death in 2009. Gabon may have gained independence from France in 1960, but top French pro outfits FDJ and Europcar regularly make their way to the west-central African country to test themselves against local teams from Gabon and nearby Eritrea and Cameroon. The race, which was first held in 2006, takes place over six stages, and is essentially a Tour of Gabon.

Statistics

Location
Fougamou to Libreville

Distance
659 km/409.5 miles
over 6 stages (2012)

Terrain
Tarmac

Record wins
Anthony Charteau
(Fra) (two wins)

Field size
90

First event
2006

Website
www.tropicale
amissabongo.com

Contact
presse.tropicale@
gmail.com

Frenchman Yohann Gène won two stages in the 2011 race

Iron Horse Bicycle Classic USA

Road

Racing the train in Durango, Colorado

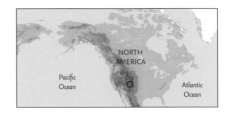

Few things in life get the blood pumping faster than racing against a steam train by bike, and that's exactly what Durango's Iron Horse Bicycle Classic is all about. Local brothers Jim and Tom Mayer are credited with establishing the first rider-train rivalry. Tom, on his bike, would take on elder sibling Jim, an engineer on the train, across the 50 miles to Silverton, although things always seemed to go in the train's favour. The day Tom was there waiting for Jim and his train, however, was the day the event was really conceived and, as of the following year – 1972 – riders haven't stopped racing the Durango-Silverton locomotive between the two Colorado towns.

Once out of Durango, the train takes a longer, easier route, while the riders pile straight on – onwards and upwards, over lung-busting high altitude climbs, so it's well worth out-of-towners considering arriving ahead of the race to acclimatise to the altitude. The two main obstacles – Coal Bank Pass and Molas Pass – take riders up and over 10,500 ft before a long descent to finish in the old mining town of Silverton after a tough 50-mile ride.

This original ride is known as the Citizen Tour, while the Iron Horse Bicycle Classic is more of an umbrella moniker for a whole programme of events, including road races, kids' races and mountain bike races.

Statistics
Location
Durango, Colorado
Distance
80.5 km/50 miles
(2012)
Highest point
3,312 m/10,867 ft
Terrain
Tarmac
Field size
1,300
First event
1972
Website
www.
ironhorsebicycleclassic.
com
Contact
director@
ironhorsebicycleclassic
com

You need pistons for legs to beat the train

The riders take
the high road
to Silverton ▶

BHF London to Brighton Night Ride United Kingdom
Night
The world-famous bike ride – with a twist

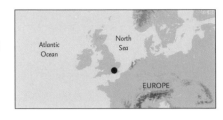

This may not be the London to Brighton, but there'd be an argument for saying that this is a step up once more from the traditional capital-to-coast ride. It is, too, the British Heart Foundation organising it – the same charity team behind the original and best London–Brighton bike ride, which after 30 years has grown enormously in popularity, hence the growth of an off-road London–Brighton and this challenge, lit only by the moonlight and your own bike lights.

Statistics
Location
London to Brighton
Distance
96.6 km/60 miles
(2012)
Terrain
Tarmac
First event
2012
Website
www.bhf.org.uk
Contact
Via website

Ride the London to Brighton Night Ride by moonlight

Robert Millar Sportive
United Kingdom
Road

British cycling hero puts his name to challenging Scottish sportive

As the organisers of this new-for-2012 sportive point out, it is the first time that Robert Millar has lent his name to such an event. Arguably the UK's greatest-ever stage racer – fourth overall at the 1984 Tour de France and winner of the polka-dot jersey competition that year – the Glasgow-born rider's climbing abilities are recognised and celebrated by the sportive with a couple of extremely tough course options, over 95 miles or 46 miles, with the longer option taking in central Scotland's most challenging climbs, such as Tak Me Doon Road and the Crow Road. Money raised will go to both the Braveheart Fund and Millar's old club, Glasgow Wheelers, to help nurture young talent. With medals to all finishers, and with Glasgow preparing to host the 2014 Commonwealth Games, it seems everyone's a winner.

Statistics

Location
Kirkintilloch, Scotland

Distance
152.9/74 km
95/46 miles (2012)

Terrain
Tarmac

Field size
750

First event
2012

Website
www.robertmillar
sportive.com

Contact
info@maximise
sport.com

Robert Millar in his pro years

Trans-Sylvania Epic
USA

Mountain bike

A seven-day mountain bike stage race – and not a vampire in sight

Central Pennsylvania is the venue for this week-long mountain bike adventure, but you've got to admire what the Trans-Sylvania Epic organisers have done with the event's name. Using the Seven Mountains Scout Camp in Spring Mills, close to State College, as its base, this mountain bike stage race is made up of seven stages, starting with an 11-mile prologue time trial. After that, stage distances are around 40 miles a day, and so manageable by all abilities, who are very much encouraged to take part. The social aspect of bringing like-minded bike racers together is also important, and there's even a childcare service available,

so there's no reason not to bring the whole family along to enjoy the event. Enter as a solo rider riding every day, or as part of a team of between two and five riders, taking it in turns to ride the stages if you're not up for the full week of riding. Feed stations en route ensure everyone's fed and watered.

The event also serves to raise funds for the Outdoor Experience Organization – a non-profit organisation that raises money to help look after the Pennsylvania trails for walkers, cyclists, horse riders and anyone who wants to take advantage of an outdoor lifestyle to improve their health, fitness and wellbeing.

Statistics

Location
Pennsylvania
Distance
322 km/200 miles
over 7 stages (2012)
Terrain
Single-track and
gravel roads
First event
2010
Website
www.tsepic.com
Contact
Via website

Whether its boulders or branches, it's all smiles in the Epic

Tilff–Bastogne–Tilff
Belgium
Road
An alternative Liège-Bastogne-Liège sportive

While the Ardennes Classic Liège–Bastogne–Liège these days has its own official sportive event, which takes place the day before the pro event, since 2005 Tiff–Bastogne–Tilff has played the role of unofficial Liège sportive. In the same way that the pro race actually finishes in Ans rather than Liège, Tilff starts and finishes in Angleur – near to Tilff, in turn near to Liège.

Basically, all these events are on the same page, based in the same area, and taking on the same climbs, like the redoubtable La Redoute. Three distance options go from the very long to the frankly ridiculous: 87 km, 147 km or the breakfast-missing 242 km, which starts at 5.30am, but luckily has five feed stations on its route to help you push through.

Statistics

Location
Angleur, Liège

Distance
242/143/83 km
150.4/88.9/51.6 miles
(2012)

Terrain
Tarmac

Website
http://sport.be.msn.com/cyclingtour/tilffbastognetilff

Contact
info@golazo.com

Cyclists take on the same climbs as Liège–Bastogne–Liège

Liège is the spiritual if not actual home of the event

Tour of Luxembourg
Luxembourg
Pro stage race

The Schleck brothers' home race attracts plenty of other Tour de France stars, too

The tiny duchy of Luxembourg gets some love in May from the cycling world with a major competition for the pros and spectators alike to get their teeth into. The five-day stage race features something for everyone, opening with a prologue time trial, and is used by a number of riders to test their form as they build towards July's Tour de France.

Charly Gaul really put the nation on the cycling map in the Fifties, winning the 1958 Tour de France, and today it is the Schleck brothers – Frank and Andy – flying the flag for Luxembourg, with Andy having recently been retrospectively awarded the 2010 Tour title following Alberto Contador's doping ban. The Schlecks are regular competitors at their home tour, and Frank won the title in 2009. It's no great surprise that they know the roads like the backs of their hands; the brothers have always lived in Luxembourg, in close proximity to their family, never having felt the lure of Italy or Spain to train in the mountains. As they say themselves, their country has everything they need to train effectively: quiet roads, plenty of hills... It doesn't seem to have done them much harm, anyway.

Statistics
Location
Luxembourg
Distance
726.5 km/451.4 miles over 4 stages (2012)
Terrain
Tarmac
Record wins
Mathias Clemens (Lux) (five wins)
Field size
136
First event
1935
Website
www.aotdl.com
Contact
press@aotdl.com

City of Luxembourg

Home rider
Frank Schleck ▶

La Ventoux Beaumes de Venise France
Road

Take on the mythical Mont Ventoux and the stunning surrounding roads in this superb sportive

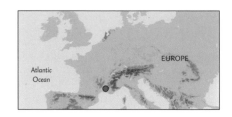

The stunning Provençal village of Beaumes-de-Venise plays host to this must-ride French sportive. Its main draw, of course, is that it includes Mont Ventoux on its route – in fact, one-and-a-half climbs of the Ventoux. Rolling out of Beaumes-de-Venise takes you to Bédoin, and the start of the 'traditional' route up the Ventoux – at least, the one the Tour de France tends to favour. Once you've struggled up to above the treeline, you see for the first time what a truly mythical place the mountain is, with its almost lunar landscape and virtually its own microclimate. The observatory at the very top slowly gets closer, but with around 1.5 km to go, there is on the right-hand side of the road the memorial to British rider Tom Simpson, who died right there during the 1967 Tour de France due to a combination of amphetamines and that day's extreme heat on the climb. Those that keep riding doff imaginary caps, while those that stop often leave a token offering: a water bottle or even an inner tube that is placed next to the stone.

The sportive course drops you down the other side to Malaucène, and shortly afterwards riders have the option of heading straight back to Beaumes-de-Venise for the 102 km version. Those doing the 170 km head on eastwards, north now of the Ventoux, on arguably some of the most fantastic roads for riding in the world: quiet, undulating, surrounded by nature, and with villages cut out of the rock to your left. Eventually, you get to Sault, which indicates the start of the third, 'easy' side of the Ventoux. Easy it isn't, but it is much shallower than the other two ascent options. At the café-restaurant Chalet Reynard halfway up the Ventoux, the route then takes a left back down the descent to Bédoin – down the way you'd come up earlier – and you retrace your steps back to Beaumes-de-Venise for a well-deserved pastis.

Rustic Beaumes-de-Venise

Statistics
Location
Beaumes-de-Venise
Distance
170 km/102 km
105.6/63.4 miles (2012)
Highest point
1,912 m (2012)
Terrain
Tarmac
Website
www.sport
communication.com
Contact
Via website

Mont Ventoux's infamous moonscape summit ▶

Bethany Sportive
United Kingdom
Road

The beauty of Scotland unfolds on the quiet roads
of this Scottish Borders sportive

Midlothian town Bonnyrigg provides the
start and finish of this sportive offering
both a 102- and 72-mile option. The Etape
Caledonia, in the Grampians, is already on
many cyclists' radar, but cycling's growth
has seen a real boom in the number of
Scottish sportives being organised, and the
challenging and spectacular terrain only
help to make them more attractive to riders
from all over the UK.

The Bethany Trust Edinburgh Sportive
is in easy reach of competitors arriving in
Edinburgh, and showcases the tough climbs
and virtually traffic-free roads around this
areas of the Scottish Borders.

Money raised by riders taking part
goes to the Bethany Christian Trust,
helping homeless and vulnerable people
across Scotland.

Statistics
Location
Bonnyrigg, Midlothian
Distance
164.2/115.9 km
102/72 miles (2012)
Terrain
Tarmac
Field size
700
First event
2009
Website
www.edinburgh
sportive.btck.co.uk
Contact
sportive@bethany
christiantrust.com

Challenging climbs and quiet roads of the Borders

**It's tough, but it's
for a good cause so
keep smiling** ▶

Tour of Wessex
United Kingdom
Road
The UK's only multi-stage sportive

The Tour of Wessex is the UK's only multi-day/multi-stage sportive event, taking place, as its name suggests, around the former kingdom of Wessex, which today includes Somerset, Devon and Dorset. Somerton, in Somerset, is the race headquarters, and it's from here that each of the three stages starts and finishes. Despite the multi-stage format, and the timing chips that each rider is given to record a time each day, the Tour of Wessex is not a race, and is simply a multi-day sportive. However, riding in a bunch over such landmarks and areas as Cheddar Gorge, Exmoor and the Jurassic Coast – all familiar to those who've watched the Tour of Britain in recent years – certainly helps foster that 'pro' feeling, as does needing to recover quickly for the next day's stage.

Statistics
Location
Somerton, Somerset
Distance
527 km/327.5 miles over 3 stages (2012)
Terrain
Tarmac
Field size
2,300
Website
info@pendragon-sports.com
Contact
www.pendragon-sports.com

Stage one skirts Glastonbury Tor

Best of the west: winding ascents and pretty villages are on the menu ▶

Bergen–Voss
Norway
Road

Norwegian sportive with the kind of amazing scenery you might expect

Bergen-Voss is one of Norway's biggest cyclosportive events, and takes place each year between the pretty west-coast town and inland ski resort. Over the 170 km route, riders will encounter seriously jaw-dropping scenery, ride past countless fjords and take on roads cut out of rock faces. However, the constant climbing and descending will take its toll on the field that numbers well over 5,000 riders. The first major climb is Gullfjellet, but from there it gets tougher, and the Kvamskogen takes you to the highest point on the route, while descending off it takes you to the halfway point of the ride. The hairpin bends of Skjervet provide the final sting in the tail, but from there it's all downhill to Voss. Getting back to Bergen is a breeze, too, as the race organisers charter trains on the direct line from Voss. In turn, Bergen is easy to get to from a number of UK airports.

Statistics

Location
Bergen to Voss

Distance
170 km/105.6 miles (2012)

Highest point
464 m (2012)

Terrain
Tarmac

Field size
Over 5,000

First event
1977

Website
http://bergenck.no

Contact
bergenvoss2012@
bergenck.no

Coastal Bergen

Philadelphia International Cycling Championship USA

Pro one-day race

The pros take on 'The Wall' – and you get your chance, too

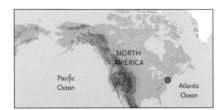

The Manayunk Wall is the highlight of the Philadelphia International Cycling Championship, and don't the spectators know it? Huge crowds throng the sidewalks of 'The Wall', which is tackled by the pros on no fewer than seven occasions. Previously the USPRO Championships, the race is famed for Lance Armstrong pocketing a cool $1 million in 1993, when the Texan used the climb to launch his race-winning attack and win the third race in the Triple Crown series and with it the insane bonus for taking all three events.

The women's Liberty Classic takes place on a similar course, and also takes in four ascents of The Wall, while prior to it all, amateur enthusiasts get their chance to test themselves on the climb as part of the Bicycling Open – a sportive held on the pro course and sponsored by the American cycling magazine.

The Manayunk Wall rears up at a leg-breaking 17 per cent (top), and after the wall comes the fall (right)

Statistics

Location
Philadelphia

Distance
199.6 km/124 miles (2012)

Terrain
Tarmac

Field size
168

First event
1985

Website
www.procyclingtour.com

Contact
pr@procyclingtour.com

Critérium du Dauphiné
France
Pro stage race

The mini Tour de France that gives riders a chance to ride in the Alps ahead of July's main event

The Critérium du Dauphiné competes with the Tour of Switzerland as the warm-up race of choice ahead of the Tour de France. Both races share the roads around the Alps, but the Dauphiné is organised by Tour de France organisers ASO, and as a result often tests out roads and climbs either due to feature, or which ASO is considering featuring, in the Tour. However, teams often feature squads in both the Dauphiné and the Tour of Switzerland, which gives them a chance to cover both bases and take a squad to the Tour in July with slightly different efforts in their legs, rather than having put all their eggs in one basket.

The French race started life in 1947 as the Critérium du Dauphiné Libéré, organised by the Dauphiné Libéré newspaper, but ASO took over the running of the race in 2010. Great Britain's Brian Robinson won the race in 1961, while Robert Millar scored another GB win in 1990. Bradley Wiggins then showed Tour form as the third Briton to win by taking the 2011 edition, only for his July campaign to hit the buffers when he broke his collarbone in a crash.

All five riders who have won the Tour de France five times or more have also won the Dauphiné, which indicates just how important a race it is, with one of those riders – Lance Armstrong – the rider to have most recently done the Dauphiné-Tour double in both 2002 and 2003.

Statistics
Location
Geneva and the French Alps
Distance
1,052 km/653.7 miles over 8 stages (2012)
Highest point
1,691 m (2012)
Terrain
Tarmac
Record wins
Nello Lauredi (Fra), Luis Ocaña (Spa), Charly Mottet (Fra), Bernard Hinault (Fra) (all three wins)
Field size
176
First event
1947
Website
www.letour.fr
Contact
cyclisme@aso.fr

The perfect leg-stretcher before the big one

Magnificat
United Kingdom
Road

Choose the 'cat sportive that's right for you

Statistics

Location
Newbury, Berkshire
Distance
204.4/130.4/82.1 km
127/81/51 miles (2012)
Terrain
Tarmac
First event
2008
Website
www.cyclegb.co.uk
Contact
Via website

The Magnificat is a 127-mile sportive starting and finishing at the Newbury Racecourse in Berkshire – a well-organised spring event used by many to ease themselves into a summer of riding, competition and bigger sportives such as the Marmotte or the Etape. The course takes in some fantastic roads around Hampshire and the South Downs, but if it's too much too soon, there's also the 81-mile InterCat or the 51-mile CommuniCat, or the 26-mile LadyCat – a women-only ride over a running marathon distance. Thanks to shorter circuits back at the racecourse for kids, much of the Magnificat's appeal lies in the fact that there's something for everyone here; it's truly an event to bring the whole family to.

Get ready for the bunch gallop . . .

Les 3 Ballons
France
Road

France's Vosges mountains provide the challenge in this sportive

The Vosges mountains of eastern France are certainly not as celebrated as the climbs in the Alps or the Pyrenees, yet it was the Ballon d'Alsace that was the first mountain ever to be included in the Tour de France, in 1905. The 3 Ballons sportive tackles the Alsace as the third ballon – literally, a balloon, named for the way the mountains tower over the landscape – following first the Ballon de Servance not long after the start in Champagney, and then the monstrous Grand Ballon, a giant in these parts at 1,325 m. The final climb, however, isn't a ballon at all: La Planche des Belles Filles also featured on the 2012 Tour de France route, providing a stiff finish to stage seven from Tomblaine with sections on its lower slopes of 14 per cent.

Statistics

Location
Champagney to La Planche des Belles Filles

Distance
205/104 km
127.4/64.6 miles (2012)

Highest point
1,325 m (2012)

Terrain
Tarmac

Website
www.sport
communication.com

Contact
Via website

Vosges mountains tower above the villages

Castelli 24H
Italy
Night

A 24-hour road race against Italian pro riders

Band together with a group of mates and head over to Feltre in northern Italy for this unique 24-hour road-race experience. Night-riding has never been so much fun as you take on a 1.9 km floodlit circuit through Feltre's old town that has it all, from a lung-busting climb to a corkscrew descent to a section of cobbles to organised chaos at the changeover point, where experienced pros battle it out with keen amateurs to complete the most number of laps as a team. Teams must consist of between eight and twelve members, who take to the course one at a time, while changeovers consist of craning your neck to see when your team-mate is heading into the pits and across the timing mat while you head out across the timing mat at the other end of the pits (there is a small 'grace period' to allow for botched swaps) and try to latch on to the back of the same group your team-mate was in. With 100 teams doing the same thing, it does get a little complicated, although it's all slightly staggered in that most riders tend to change over every few laps rather than each lap. Italian pros, retired or otherwise – past participants have included Paolo Bettini, Filippo Pozzato and the late Franco Ballerini – help out friends' or sponsors' teams, and 'help' everyone else by keeping the speeds high. The trick, though, is to find a group that suits you, speed-wise, and enjoy the franetic, but fun, ride.

Statistics
Location
Feltre
Distance
Laps of a
1.9-km/1.2-mile circuit
(2012)
Terrain
Tarmac and a section
of cobbles
Field size
100 teams of 8–12
riders
Website
www.24orefeltre.it
Contact
info@gfsportful.it

Atmospheric Feltre old town

Former world champion Paolo Bettini is one of a host of professionals who have guested

Tour de Suisse
Switzerland
Pro stage race

Tour de France 'preparation race' with a great history of its own

Overlapping as it does with the Critérium du Dauphiné stage race, the week-long Tour de Suisse faces stiff competition for drawing in the best Tour de France contenders for its race. Switzerland is up against it, too, when you consider that Tour de France organiser ASO also owns the Dauphiné, but the Tour de Suisse remains a big race on the international calendar, borne out by the illustrious names who have triumphed in the Swiss Alps since the race's inception in 1933: Bartali, Koblet, Merckx, De Vlaeminck, Kelly, Hampsten and home hero Fabian Cancellara.

In the same way Lance Armstrong is the last Tour de France winner to have won the Dauphiné in the same year – both in 2002 and 2003 – the American is also the last rider to have won the Tour of Switzerland and the Tour de France in the same year, in 2001. Proof, then, of how riders see the Dauphiné and Switzerland as being interchangeable: they are swapped, chopped and changed depending on factors such as route profiles, number of kilometres of time trials, climbs covered or indeed where rivals are racing – in order to either avoid them or test each other's legs.

Statistics

Location
Lugano to Sörenberg
Distance
1,399 km/869.3 miles over 9 stages (2012)
Highest point
2,005 m (2012)
Terrain
Tarmac
Record wins
Pasquale Fornara (Ita) (four wins)
Field size
152
First event
1933
Website
www.tourde
suisse.ch/en
Contact
Via website

Adoring fans give plenty of encouragement to Fabian Cancellara

Riders are dwarfed by mountains along the Alpine route ▶

London Nocturne
United Kingdom
Night

Night-riding in the UK capital where there's an event for everyone

Since 2007, the Smithfield Market area of London has been brought alive on a June evening each year by the sights and sounds of high-octane bike racing. It's a far cry from the early morning noise of the meat market, but with a menu that features a pro criterium, a folding bike race, a longest skid competition and a penny farthing race, the London Nocturne is very tasty indeed.

The pro race – lit up in the dark – is always the last event of the evening, and in 2011 Team Sky neo-pro Alex Dowsett did the unthinkable and lapped the field to take what turned out to be an easy victory. Earlier, a women's race and the spectacular penny farthing race had taken

place on the same circuit, while one of the most enjoyable races of the evening, for both competitors and spectators, is always the folding bike race, which requires competitors – dressed as commuters – to run to their bikes and unfold them before going on their way. In recent years, the folding bike race has become so popular that the Nocturne organisers have had to put on two heats with riders qualifying for a grand final. With plenty of food and drink venues surrounding the Smithfield circuit and helping to draw a large crowd, it's a fantastic evening out for spectators and competitors alike.

Statistics

Location
London

Distance
Laps of a
1.1-km/0.68-mile circui
(2012)

Terrain
Tarmac

Field size
500

First event
2007

Website
www.london
nocturne.com

Contact
info@nocturne
series.com

'Commuters' scrambling to unfold their bikes in a Le Mans-style start

Alex Dowsett cruising
to victory in 2011 ▶

World Naked Bike Ride
Worldwide
Road

People in various cities around the world embrace nudity and ride their bikes together

The World Naked Bike Ride movement is now present in most major cities, with June tending to be the preferred month to strip off and ride around with like-minded others. The reason? The sun's often out, which helps everyone, but despite all the fun everyone appears to have – except taxi drivers, who tend to get mightily upset – there are some serious messages that some naked bike riders want to get out there: to draw attention to vehicle emissions, and to encourage more people to join them and ride their bikes (you're free to 'dare to bare' as much as you feel comfortable with; there are no hard and fast rules), but also to demonstrate to other traffic users the vulnerability of the human form when on a bicycle.

A cheeky way to campaign against vehicle pollution

Statistics

Location
Various locations worldwide including: Argentina, Australia, Austria, Belgium, Brazil, Canada, Chile, Czech Republic, Denmark, France, Germany, Greece, Hungary, Ireland, Israel, Italy, Japan, Latvia, Mexico, Netherlands, New Zealand, Paraguay, Peru, Poland, Portugal, Russia, South Africa, Spain, Sweden, Switzerland, United Kingdom and United States

Terrain
Tarmac

First event
2004

Website
www.worldnaked bikeride.org/uk

Contact
londonpress@wnbr.org.uk

Cyclists bare all as they make their way around bemused London ▶

Dragon Ride
United Kingdom
Road

The UK's biggest sportive event sells out quickly

Margam Park in Wales hosts the UK's largest sportive event, with 4,500 riders taking part – and it's an event for which you have to be swift to enter each year if you want to pick up a place, as entries sell out very quickly. In addition, for the first time in 2012 it's also part of cycling governing body the UCI's Golden Bike series, giving it an added boost. It's an event used by many UK riders as preparation for the Etape du Tour, which takes place just a few weeks later, and Etape-bound riders will feel at home, too, thanks to the iconic yellow Mavic 'neutral support' mechanics' cars that are out on the course offering assistance to anyone in need.

Statistics

Location
Margam Park, near Port Talbot, Wales

Distance
206/125/40 km
128/77.7/24.9 miles
(2012)

Terrain
Tarmac

Field size
4,500

First event
2004

Website
www.wiggle dragonride.com

Contact
info@participate sport.com

The route profile resembles the teeth of a dragon

Granfondo Milan–San Remo Italy

Road

'La Classicissima' for amateurs takes in the full March pro route

The official Milan–San Remo gran fondo may come three months after the real thing, but following the same 290 km course as the pro event in virtually guaranteed pleasant, sunny Italian weather appears to be a much better option than the unpredictability of March. Cresting the iconic Cipressa and Poggio climbs in the final 30 km of the race means doing so with the most fantastic backdrop of the Mediterranean before dropping down into San Remo on the Italian Riviera and enjoying the virtually compulsory pasta party and a reviving coffee or two before the event buses are ready to take you and your bike back to Milan.

Statistics

Location
Milan to San Remo

Distance
290 km/180.2 miles (2012)

Highest point
346 m (2012)

Terrain
Tarmac

First event
1969

Website
www.milano-sanremo.org

Contact
Via website

San Remo, Italy

Maraton Franja
Slovenia
Road

Slovenian sportive in the fantastic countryside around beautiful capital Ljubljana

Slovenia is often unjustly overlooked as a choice of country in which to ride a sportive, yet the Maraton Franja is up there with the best of them. Locals and mainland Europeans certainly know about it, though, and the sportive that starts and finishes in cobbled capital city Ljubljana welcomes riders to soak up the stunning surrounding countryside on the 156 km ride. Things are neutralised for the first 25 km, at which point

the flag drops, and the race is on – for those at the front anyway. There are always plenty of fast riders taking part, but also plenty happy to just enjoy the ride, so you're free to make things as difficult as you like. Or make things a little easier again by plumping for the 'Little Marathon' over a slightly easier 97 km course. There are also family and kids' races, so something for the whole clan.

Statistics
Location
Ljubljana
Distance
156/97 km
96.9/60.3 miles (2012)
Terrain
Tarmac
First event
1982
Website
www.franja.org
Contact
info@franja.org

The race is neutralised for its urban start

ProRace Berlin
Germany
Pro one-day race

The German capital enjoys a high-end
one-day race

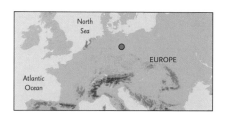

It was all about bringing professional
racing back to Berlin after an absence of
far too long, said the organisers, and it was
true that a major city of Berlin's stature
ought to show off the way its history meets
modernity: a hip young city with a memory.
It seemed suitable, then, to see up-and-
coming young German sprinter Marcel
Kittel winning the inaugural ProRace Berlin
in 2011 in a bunch gallop. It was a sprint up
what organisers described as "the longest
final straight in the world": the Strasse des
17. Juni, on which stands the Brandenburg
Gate. Currently ranked as a UCI category
1.1 event, the ProRace organisers hope to
graduate to UCI WorldTour status for 2013,
which would really put Berlin back on the
cycling map.

**Germany's promising Marcel Kittel won
the 1st edition of ProRace Berlin in 2011**

Statistics
Location
Berlin
Distance
182.9 km/113.6 miles
(2012)
Terrain
Tarmac
Field size
152
First event
2011
Website
www.skoda-
velothon-berlin.de
Contact
Via website

Paris–Roubaix Cyclo
France
Road

The classic cobbled sportive that will put hairs on your chest

There have been a couple of pretenders to the Paris–Roubaix sportive throne of late, but this one, organised by the Vélo Club de Roubaix Cyclotourisme, falls into that 'original and best' category. The fact that it only takes place every two years – in even years – helps to make it that bit more special, and gives you the extra time to find yourself the most shockingly surfaced section of road in your area to train on.

The biggest attraction of it all after 210 km – bar actually finishing – is finishing with a lap and a half of the iconic Roubaix velodrome, just like the pros in April, and unlike some rival events.

"Riding this proved to be the hardest single day I've ever had on a bike," says journalist Lionel Birnie. "You really have to see – and ride – the cobbles to believe it. The surface is so bad. The first few sections seem okay, fooling you into thinking that it's going to be all right, but then it hits you. It's almost like a video game, whereby your energy bar depletes as you ride across the cobbled sections, and then fills up again on the tarmac sections. It's such a brutal course. I saw one guy ride by with no saddle, and on another section of cobbles both my contact lenses fell out due to the jarring. Later in the ride, my friend stopped for a toilet break at a feed station, and in the meantime I decided to have a sit-down on a plastic chair. He came back to find me fast asleep.

"More than anything, it gives you a real

appreciation of what the pros go through," he continues. "When you watch them in the mountains, you can understand how tough what they're doing is – you can really see it and appreciate it. But until you experience the cobbles for yourself, it's difficult to appreciate how hard they are. There are no climbs – it's just a flat course – and yet it's so tough. Reaching the velodrome at the end is awesome, and just such a relief after what for me was almost eleven hours of riding."

The infamous cobbles of the Arenberg Forest

Statistics
Location
Troisvilles to Roubaix
Distance
210/120 km
130.5/74.6 miles (2012)
Terrain
Tarmac and cobbles
Field size
3,000
Website
www.vc-roubaix-cyclo.f
Contact
vcroubaix@vc-roubaix-cyclo.fr

The iconic Roubaix velodrome, where the pro race and the sportive finish ▶

Time Megève Mont-Blanc
France
Road

Epic Alpine sportive that takes in five mountain passes

If June's Paris–Roubaix Cyclo is one of the hardest days you'll ever have on a bike on the flat, the Time Megève Mont-Blanc, also in June, has to be up there among the hardest days in the mountains you'll ever have. It really is an epic, taking you over five tough climbs in the longest version over 148 km, forcing you to battle over the Col des Aravis, the Col de la Croix Fry, back over the Aravis, and the Col des Saisies twice before the finish back in Megève. To make matters worse, it's all too easy to plump for the longest version after the first ascent of

the Saisies, where the turn-off for the 118 km route is – there's also a 88 km route, which still takes in three climbs – but the kilometres really begin to take their toll after that. The last time up the Saisies with 120 km already in the legs, and the broom wagon nipping at your heels indicating the cut-off time, is quite the experience. The full version of the Time Megève Mont-Blanc requires nothing short of race fitness, and is right up there with the Etape du Tour for recreating that genuine 'stage of the Tour de France' feeling.

Statistics
Location
Megève
Distance
148/118/88 km
92/73.3/54.7 miles
(2012)
Highest point
1,657 m (2012)
Terrain
Tarmac
Field size
2,000
Website
www.csports
megeve.com
Contact
Via website

Col des Aravis

Town of Megève, the start/finish

Skoda Velothon Berlin
Germany
Road

Take to the streets of Berlin in the super-popular Velothon sportive

While the ProRace Berlin is a new pro one-day race in Germany's capital city, the Skoda Velothon Berlin sportive has been going since 2008, and is now one of the biggest sportives in Europe, regularly attracting 13,000 participants. Riders can choose between 60 or 120 km, and enjoy riding on roads closed completely to traffic.

Many of Berlin's major sights are included on the route, including the Brandenburg Gate and Potsdamer Platz, plus the big finish on the Strasse des 17. Juni, just like the elite riders. There's also a 'Kids' Velothon' organised the day before, giving youngsters the opportunity to ride on the same roads as their heroes, albeit on a shorter lap.

Statistics
Location
Berlin
Distance
120/60 km
74.6/37.3 miles
(2012)
Terrain
Tarmac
Field size
13,000
First event
2008
Website
www.skoda-velothon-berlin.de
Contact
Via website

Brandenburg Gate

Wet and windswept riders make their way around the German capital

Wicklow 200
Ireland
Road

Stunning scenery and tough climbs at the
Wicklow 200 challenge ride

The Wicklow Mountains, just south of
Dublin, provide the superb setting for the
Wicklow 200 and Wicklow 100 challenge
rides – and they are certainly challenging.
Both distances start and finish at Shoreline
leisure centre in Greystones, and little
has changed when it comes to the route
for the main event over 200 km other
than a change of checkpoint location to
ease congestion. Otherwise it's a relentlessly
hilly parcours, with a mix of longer, gradual
climbs and short, sharp shockers to keep
you on your toes. Like most northern
hemisphere sportives, the weather can, and
has, made a tough course all the harder, so
arrive at Wicklow ready for the worst the
weather can throw at you.

Statistics
Location
County Wicklow
Distance
200/100 km
124.3/62.1 miles (2012)
Highest point
528 m (2012)
Terrain
Tarmac
Field size
Over 2,000
First event
1981
Website
www.wicklow200.ie
Contact
admin@Wicklow200.
ie.

Wild country of the Wicklow Mountains

Race Across America (RAAM) USA

Long distance

One of the greatest races of them all – coast-to-coast across the USA

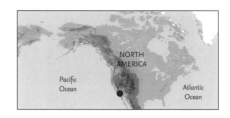

NORTH AMERICA

Pacific Ocean

Atlantic Ocean

'The Great American Bike Race', as its first edition was called in 1982, is well known to people these days as the RAAM – the Race Across America. From west coast to east coast, over 3,000 miles, the clock is ticking from the very first pedal stroke to the moment riders virtually fall off their bikes at the finish.

With the stopwatch always running, the biggest battle for participants is trying to balance getting enough sleep with getting the miles under their belt, and it's not unheard of for riders to actually fall asleep while still riding their bikes.

The first edition was raced by just four men, from Santa Monica Pier in Los Angeles to the Empire State Building in New York, but it took until 1992 for the race to be opened up to teams.

In 2012, the race started from Oceanside in Southern California, and made its way east to finish in Annapolis, Maryland, as has been the case for the past few years. Category competitions include fastest individual, pair, four-person and eight-person teams, with male, female and mixed categories in each. The fastest solo riders take eight days to reach the east coast.

Statistics

Location
Oceanside, California to Annapolis, Maryland

Distance
4,828 km/3,000 miles (2012)

Terrain
Tarmac

Record wins
Jure Robic (Slo) (five wins)

Field size
35+ solo, 300 team riders

First event
1982

Website
www.raceacross america.org

Contact
director@raceacross america.org

Riders of the first Race Across America in 1982, receive rewards of recognition in 2011

A sleep-deprived rider battles through pain and tiredness as he races through the night ▶

Race Across Europe
Europe
Long distance

The European version of the Race Across America

As its name suggests, the Race Across Europe is very much built on the back of the success of the Race Across America (RAAM), with a similar total distance – 2,933 miles – and the same solo and team competitions set-up. The European route starts in Calais and heads into Germany, continuing on into Austria. From there it heads south into Slovenia, and then westwards through Italy and back into France – where riders have to tackle the fearsome Mont Ventoux. Then it's on into Spain and the long ride down to Tarifa – Spain's southernmost point. Again, like at the RAAM, riders at the Race Across Europe have to provide their own support crews and try to decide between them the best strategy for moving as quickly and efficiently through Europe as possible.

Statistics
Location
Calais, France to Gibraltar, Spain
Distance
4,720 km/2,933 miles (2012)
Terrain
Tarmac
First event
2011
Website
www.theraceacross europe.com
Contact
info@greenrock.co.uk

Tarifa, Spain – journey's end

Tour de Beauce
Canada

Pro stage race

The Quebec race boasts the cream of North American bike racing

The Tour de Beauce is a Canadian stage race that takes place in the Beauce region just south of Quebec City. It attracts the top North American teams, giving them the chance to showcase their talents to a wider audience over the six stages. A young Levi Leipheimer – now with Omega Pharma-Quick Step – holds the record for most overall wins with two, victorious in both 1998 and 1999, while riding for the modest Saturn outfit. It was enough to secure him a contract with Lance Armstrong's US Postal squad for the 2000 season, and the Californian never looked back.

A sportive ride also takes place a couple of days before the start of the pro event.

Statistics

Location
Quebec

Distance
790 km/490.5 miles
over 6 stages (2012)

Terrain
Tarmac

Record wins
Levi Leipheimer (USA)
(two wins)

Field size
119

First event
1986

Website
www.tourde
beauce.com

Contact
info@tourde
beauce.com

Quebec City, Canada

Ster ZLM Toer
Netherlands
Pro stage race

Five-day Dutch stage race that favours the sprinters and Classics specialists

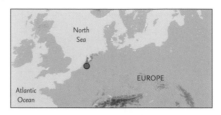

While the overall Tour contenders are fine-tuning their form at the Critérium du Dauphiné or the Tour of Switzerland, the sprinters get a chance to stretch their legs a bit more at this stage race. In 2011, in a desperate bid to garner some form ahead of the Tour de France, Garmin sprinter Tyler Farrar went straight to the Ster ZLM Toer from the Dauphiné, where things hadn't gone well. However, he won stage two in Holland and finished the race with the points jersey as best sprinter, and then went to the Tour and won stage three – his first ever.

The 2011 Ster ZLM Toer, though, was won overall by Philippe Gilbert by three seconds from Niki Terpstra, making the Belgian the only rider to have won the event twice since it began in 1987.

Statistics
Location
Eindhoven to Boxtel
Distance
684 km/425 miles over 4 stages (2012)
Terrain
Tarmac
Record wins
Philippe Gilbert (Bel) (two wins)
Field size
136
First event
1987
Website
www.sterzlmtoer.nl
Contact
janlivius@planet.nl

Philippe Gilbert was the overall winner in 2011, becoming the first to win the event twice

Tour of Slovenia
Slovenia
Pro stage race
A nice alternative to the Tour de France

Janez 'Jani' Brajkovic has arguably done more than most to put Slovenian cycling on the map, but the Tour of Slovenia doesn't do a bad job, either. If they could join forces, Slovenian cycling could perhaps get the attention it deserves, but Brajkovic has skipped the race in recent years due to Tour de France commitments; the race tends to fall too close to the Tour. However, it's a race taken very seriously by riders who aren't Tour-bound, such as 2009 overall winner Jakob Fuglsang, who had yet to make his Tour debut, and 2010 winner Vincenzo Nibali, who skipped the Tour that year to concentrate on the Giro.

However, having been in existence since 1993, and by managing to attract a decent field of riders despite its calendar slot, the relaxed atmosphere at Slovenia is something of a hidden gem for riders, journalists and fans.

Statistics
Location
Celje to Ljubljana
Distance
578 km/359 miles over 4 stages (2012)
Terrain
Tarmac
Record wins
Jure Golčer (Slo), Mitja Mahoric (Slo) (both two wins)
Field size
120
First event
1993
Website
www.posloveniji.si/si
Contact
cycling@adria-mobil.com

2010 winner Vincenzo Nibali

Route du Sud
France
Pro stage race
Traditional and much-loved stage race in the south of France

The Route du Sud is a race Tour de France director Christian Prudhomme says he loves, and always loved when working on it as a journalist, being able to enjoy the intimacy of the race just before many of the riders headed to the national championships and the Tour de France.

These days, very few Tour riders ride the Route du Sud as training for 'La Grande Boucle', coming as it does directly before the start of the Tour. Although, since 1977, back when it was known as the Tour du Tarn, it has played a vital role in riders' career development, boasting past winners such as Stephen Roche, Jonathan Vaughters, Laurent Jalabert and Levi Leipheimer. It's a race that, wrongly, has had to fight for survival in the face of newer, less traditional and moneyed races, yet in the past it has often served as a testing ground for Pyrenean climbs that the Tour has then taken on. Having Prudhomme on their side helps, but these smaller races remain in danger.

Statistics
Location
Southwest France
Distance
733.5 km/455.8 miles over 4 stages (2012)
Highest point
2,114 m (2012)
Terrain
Tarmac
Record wins
Gilbert Duclos-Lassalle (Fra) (three wins)
Field size
120
First event
1977
Website
www.routedusud.fr
Contact
contact@routedusud.fr

The Lapébie family are Pyrenean cycling royalty

Vätternrundan
Sweden
Night

Short Swedish nights, you, your bike and a very big lake...

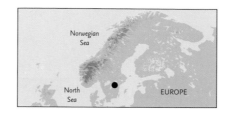

Three hundred kilometres around the periphery of Sweden's stunning Lake Vättern, 250 km west of Stockholm, is a proper bike ride. It sets off from Motala at 7.30pm, but the summer sun only setting late and rising again as early as 3am means that there's a only a short period of the night during which you'll need lights. This really is just a ride to enjoy, and not a race, but if the distance still sounds off-putting, other options include the Halvättern, over half the distance, and a 100 km women-only event (the Tjejättern). There are also two children's rides – one for 6–7 year olds and one for 8–10 year olds.

Statistics

Location
Motala

Distance
300 km/186.4 miles
(2012)

Terrain
Tarmac

Field size
23,000

First event
1966

Website
www.vatternrundan.se

Contact
info@vatternrundan.se

Lake Vättern, Sweden

L'Ardéchoise
France
Road

Huge Massif Central sportive with ten mountain passes on the menu

L'Ardéchoise celebrated its twenty-first edition in 2012 and, as ever, attracted a field from far and wide, with foreign riders given a particularly warm welcome. As well as the one-day event, riders can also get to know the Ardèche region, which is part of the Massif Central, even better thanks to two-, three- or four-day tours, all of which use the one-day event as their final day. The one-day event has a number of different distance choices, and riders don't have to make a decision about which to go for until out on the road, but the traditional Ardéchoise is over 220 km, and provides the challenge of ten mountain passes to get over.

Statistics
Location
Ardèche
Distance
220 km/136.7 miles (2012)
Terrain
Tarmac
Field size
15,000
First event
1992
Website
www.ardechoise.com
Contact
Via website

A tough day in beautiful countryside

Flatout in the Fens
United Kingdom
Road

Get some miles under your belt at this fast, flat and scenic sportive through Britain's lowest point

Flatout in the Fens is an unusual UK sportive in that it's almost entirely flat, with no climbs of note at all. Whereas most sportives boast about how hilly they are, or how many mountains you're going to have to go over, and basically gloat about how much it's going to hurt, Flatout in the Fens is all about getting a big number of miles in the bag and enjoying the wide-open scenery of the Fens themselves. In light of sprinting making something of a comeback thanks in no small part to a certain Mark Cavendish,

it makes sense that not every amateur rider fancies themselves as a stick-thin climbing type, and that some prefer instead to get up to speed and try to keep it there on the flat. One quirky fact about the sportive is that by taking you through the Fens, you'll be going beyond 'flat out' and will actually pass through the UK's lowest point of elevation at -4 m. The sportive starts and finishes at Peterborough Regional College and the longest distance option is a huge 154 miles, but there's also the choice of 112 or 77 miles.

Statistics
Location
Fens, Lincolnshire and Cambridgeshire
Distance
247.8/180.2/123.9 km
154/112/77 miles
(2012)
Terrain
Tarmac
Website
www.kilotogo.com
Contact
contact@kilotogo.com

The Fens of East Anglia are home to the lowest point in the United Kingdom

London to Brighton
United Kingdom

Road

The fun 50-miler from the capital to 'London-by-the-Sea'

This is the original London to Brighton and, by default, the best of them all. Start early on if you want to miss the mad crowds in the climbs, where the sudden decrease of speed causes everyone to bunch up and, eventually, stop. Ditchling Beacon, in particular, coming towards the end of the 54-mile ride, can take hours to get over, but as long as you're in no great hurry it's all good fun, whether you're with friends or making new ones.

Things get under way from Clapham Common in South London and, other than the general chaos that is getting out of London, quiet, stunning roads lead to Sussex and the south coast.

Reaching the top of Ditchling Beacon, which takes a Herculean effort no matter who you are – it didn't appear on the route of the 1994 Tour de France stage between Rochester and Brighton for nothing – is just reward with the spectacular views it affords: back north across the fields from whence you came and south to the shimmering sea where a well deserved ice-cream and fish 'n' chips awaits, although not necessarily in that order.

Statistics

Location
London to Brighton
Distance
86.9 km/54 miles
(2012)
Terrain
Tarmac
Field size
27,000
First event
1976
Website
www.bhf.org.uk
Contact
Via website

The cycle ride that non-cyclists do for charity

Gran Fondo Sportful
Italy
Road

Take to the Dolomites and experience a bit of cycling history

Italian clothing manufacturer Sportful is based right near the foot of the famed Croce d'Aune climb, so it seems only appropriate that it sponsors this classic gran fondo in the Dolomites.

The Croce d'Aune might only top out at 1,015 m, compared to the 2,000 m Passo di Valles, but whereas the Valles comes 135 km into the 215 km course, the Croce d'Aune has to be tackled with just 20 km left to go to the finish in Feltre. A perfect excuse, then, to stop at the top of the climb before the descent for home to pay homage to Tullio Campagnolo at the memorial. It was here that Campagnolo first had the idea for the quick-release wheel skewer when struggling to remove his rear wheel. Campagnolo also later invented the derailleur gear.

Statistics
Location
Feltre
Distance
216/122 km
134.2/75.8 miles (2012)
Terrain
Tarmac
Highest point
2,002 m (2012)
First event
1995
Website
www.gfsportful.it
Contact
info@gfsportful.it

Dolomites, Italy

RIDE24
United Kingdom
Night

Give it some gas at Goodwood

Speed demons fed up with having to toil up hills in almost every other sportive get the opportunity to really open it up on a real-life race track. The famous Goodwood motor circuit plays host to RIDE24, an Action Medical Research event in which teams or brave solo riders compete to complete as many laps of the circuit as possible during a 24-hour period.

A rider village ensures you and your team-mates are kept on the straight and narrow when it comes to equipment and nutrition, while physios and mechanics keep the engines ticking over, helping to ensure that your next stint out on the track is your best yet.

There are various prizes for different age groups in the solo and team categories, but the winning four-rider team will win a place at the French Le Mans 24 Hour bike race at the end of August, which winners should have just about recovered in time for.

Statistics

Location
Goodwood,
West Sussex

Distance
Laps of a
3.9-km/2.4-mile circuit
(2012)

Terrain
Tarmac

First event
2011

Website
www.action.org.uk/
ride24

Contact
Via website

Goodwood motor-racing circuit

London–Paris
United Kingdom and France
Road

The HotChillee-organised London to Paris takes
a three-day route between the two cities

London to Paris organisers HotChillee
welcome everyone on their city-to-city
ride, from top-notch pros to retired sports
personalities to keen amateur riders, thanks
to a unique format allowing you to be as
competitive as you like across the three-day
event. Those in the mix up front can indulge
in some full-on racing, with timed sections
of the course serving to find an overall race
leader who gets to wear the leader's yellow
jersey on the next stage. Clearly taking
its cue from the Tour de France, similarly
there's a green points jersey for the best
riders across the sprint sections, while a red
mountains jersey is awarded to the best
rider after each day's climbing section, again
with points on offer so as to end up with an
overall winner at the finish line in Paris.

The rolling road closures for the duration
of the ride are ably taken care of by no
fewer than forty-five outriders. Day one
takes participants the 170 km from London
to Dover, with much of the competitive
element of the day happening in the
morning before lunch – all participants
have a timing chip, but it's up to them
whether they wish to mix it with the faster
riders – with everyone then reconvening for
the more sedate ride to Dover and the ferry
to Calais.

After spending the night in a hotel, the
riders wake to the prospect of 176 km to
Amiens, again with the afternoon giving
riders an opportunity for a more sedate chat

with celebrity guests, which in the past have
included former footballers Geoff Thomas
and Lee Dixon, Formula One legend Nigel
Mansell, former England rugby captain Will
Carling and 1987 Tour de France champion
Stephen Roche.

The third day takes the riders from
Amiens to central Paris – just under 170 km
this time – culminating in a ride across the
normally crazy roundabout at the Arc de
Triomphe, with the traffic held back on this
occasion to let the 'L2P' riders pass through
safely, with the big finish in the shadow of
the Eiffel Tower.

En route to Amiens

Statistics
Location
London to Paris
Distance
550 km/341.8 miles
over 3 days (2012)
Terrain
Tarmac
Field size
365
First event
2003
Website
www.londres-paris.com
Contact
Via website

The route finishes
at the iconic Arc
de Triomphe ▶

Mountain Mayhem
United Kingdom

Mountain bike

Unruly weather – hot or cold – and a challenging course combine at this tough 24-hour race

As 'must ride' British mountain bike events go, Mountain Mayhem is it. The world's biggest 24-hour MTB race, it's an event that regularly attracts more than 2,500 participants, some racing as teams, some as individuals, but all racing against the clock to complete as many of the nine-mile laps around Eastnor Castle Deer Park in the Malvern Hills as they can. Weather-wise, the event has had it all, and although regular competitors might feel like it always seems to take place in pouring rain, there have been plenty of editions in boiling hot, dry conditions, too, so come expecting anything in what is, after all, a British summertime event. As of 2011, organisers also introduced a number of other events built around the main MTB race. Runners are catered for with a race on the evening before – Midsummer Madness – while a series of running and riding events make up the Mini Mayhem for little ones. There's a sportive on the road around the Malverns on the Sunday, the day after the MTB event, while even man's best friend gets a look-in thanks to Barking Mad – an off-road run for pooches and their masters on the Friday evening. Bring your tent, and camp out for a few days at what has become a true cycling – and running – festival.

Statistics

Location
Eastnor Castle Deer Park, Herefordshire

Distance
Laps of a 14.5 km/9-mile circuit (2012)

Terrain
Off-road

Field size
2,500

First event
1998

Website
www.wigglemountainmayhem.com

Contact
Via website

Riding up a dust storm round Eastnor Castle Deer Park

Quebrantahuesos
Spain
Road

'The Spanish Etape' that is a real bone-breaker

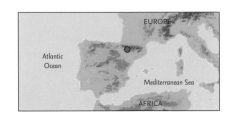

The Quebrantahuesos is a bird of prey that drops the small animals it's caught from a great height onto rocks in order to break the bones and get to the juicy marrow inside. The Quebrantahuesos bike ride, then, very loosely translates as 'The Bone Breaker', and certainly those that have ridden it can attest to its difficulty.

"This is pretty much the Spanish version of the Etape du Tour," explains cycling journalist Peter Cossins.

"Like its French cousin, it's very well run, attracts a large field, and is an extremely challenging event. After setting off from the start in Sabiñanigo, with everyone going like the clappers, the first climb, the Alto de Somport, drops you down into France. Next on the agenda is the Col du Marie Blanque,

from the steep side. The road is absolutely packed with riders here, yet there is no sound at all save for some puffing and the trickle of the stream alongside us."

"After this, in the valley, the road splits between the Col d'Aubisque and the Col de Portalet," Cossins continues, "and it's the Portalet the route takes. It's such a long climb – 28 km – and although it's not that steep at the bottom, it gets steeper as you go, and nearing the top is the hardest part of the ride, with almost 150 km covered. Going over the top takes you back into Spain, and some really pretty roads, but there's one more sting in the tail before the end, and that's the Alto de Hoz, which is only short at 2 km, but is a real killer before the finish back in Sabiñanigo."

Statistics

Location
Sabiñanigo
Distance
205 km/127.4 miles
(2012)
Highest point
1,795 m (2012)
Terrain
Tarmac
Field size
Over 10,000
First event
1991
Website
www.quebrantahuesos.
com
Contact
info@
quebrantahuesos.com

Preparing to set off from Sabiñanigo

The super-tough course draws thousands of keen cyclists ▶

Whisky Trail Sportive
United Kingdom
Road

Follow northeast Scotland's famous Whisky Trail at this new sportive

Cooper Park in Elgin, Morayshire, is the start and finish venue of this new sportive, which is part of the Scottish Sportive Series, with a choice of an 80- or 40-mile route, or a 10-mile family ride. The famous malt whisky distilleries are well worth a visit, although obviously not while riding the sportive... Instead, make time to savour the whiskies either before or, preferably, after your riding, and enjoy the area at a slower pace than on the bike.

Cooper Park, Elgin

Statistics
Location
Elgin, Scotland
Distance
128.7/64.4/16.1 km
80/40/10 miles
(2012)
Terrain
Tarmac
First event
2012
Website
www.thewhisky
trailsportive.com
Contact
charlie@maximise
sport.com

Moonriders London to
Brighton United Kingdom
Night

Central London by night, and on down to Brighton by moonlight and bike light

The Moonriders London to Brighton is a 100 km bike ride in aid of an Action Challenge charity partner of your choice, with participants each pledging to raise £300. The ride starts at the historic Alexandra Palace – or 'Ally Pally', as it's affectionately known – and makes its way, under cover of darkness, of course, down through central London, including Westminster Abbey and the Houses of Parliament. Chelsea Bridge takes riders over the Thames, and from there it's off out into the country and a date with the climb of Ditchling Beacon. A hot meal is provided en route, as is a hot breakfast on arrival at Brighton Race Course, while mechanics and medics ensure everyone is well looked after during the ride.

Statistics
Location
London to Brighton
Distance
100 km/62.1 miles
(2012)
Terrain
Tarmac
First event
2011
Website
www.moonriders.co.uk
Contact
info@moonriders.
co.uk

L'Ariégeoise
France
Road

A Pyrenean sportive that enjoys UCI Golden Bike status

Atlantic Ocean

EUROPE

The Pyrenees are your playground and, more specifically, the beautiful Ariège region of France opens up before you at this well-known, well-organised event. In fact it's so well organised that cycling's governing body, the UCI, has given its stamp of approval and included the sportive as part of its Golden Bike series, which is as good as a gold star and a guarantee that

this is a top-end sportive well worthy of your attention.

A handful of hardy types even opt to remain in the Pyrenees to compete in L'Ariégeoise following their ride in the Quebrantahuesos the weekend before in order to bag a double-whammy of two of the very toughest events on the sportive calendar.

Statistics

Location
Ariège
Distance
161/117/69 km
100/72.7/42.9 miles
(2012)
Highest point
1,785 m (2012)
Terrain
Tarmac
Field size
Over 4,000
First event
1995
Website
www.cyclosport-ariegeoise.com
Contact
ariegeoise.cycloclub@
wanadoo.fr

The ride finishes at Plateau de Beille, the course's highest point

Tour de France
France
Pro stage race

The world's biggest and best bike race

Since its first edition in 1903, the Tour de France has been an indelible part of the French summer, and indeed the bike race by which all others are judged. There simply was no bedding-in period; right from the beginning, after Géo Lefèvre suggested to his editor, Henri Desgrange, that a bike race around France would be a great way to publicise their newspaper, L'Auto, the race's popularity has been huge, truly capturing the imagination of the French public and, later, the rest of the world's, too.

The race's second edition, in 1904, however, almost signalled the end of the road for the Tour as riders jumped onto trains to avoid riding the horribly long stages, while others were beaten up by rivals' fervent fans. However, by 1905 it was back, and soon more popular than ever.

The iconic leader's yellow jersey only made its first appearance in 1919, worn by Frenchman Eugène Christophe, although it was a Belgian, Firmin Lambot, who finished the race in Paris in yellow that year.

The green points jersey was first awarded in 1953, while 1975 saw the introduction of both the polka-dot 'King of the Mountains' jersey and the white jersey to signify the race's best young rider.

Statistics

Location
Liège, Belgium to
Paris, France (2012)
Distance
3,479 km/2,162 miles
over 21 stages (2012)
Highest point
2,115 m (2012)
Terrain
Tarmac
Record wins
Lance Armstrong
(USA) (seven wins)
Field size
198
First event
1903
Website
www.letour.fr
Contact
cyclisme@aso.fr

Samuel Sanchez won the King of the Mountains competition in 2011

The first major climb to be included was the Ballon d'Alsace, in the Vosges, in 1905, while the Pyrenees followed in 1910 and the Alps in 1911. Since then, both mountain ranges have defined the race, and iconic climbs such as the Col du Tourmalet and Alpe d'Huez have often provided the springboard for overall victory.

When France's Jacques Anquetil recorded his fifth win in 1964, it became the measure of the race's greatest champions, and four more riders were to reach five wins in later years: Belgian Eddy Merckx (1974), Frenchman Bernard Hinault (1985), Spain's Miguel Indurain (1995) and the USA's Lance Armstrong (2003).

The Galibier is one ▲ of the highest cols that the tour climbs

Armstrong, though, went one – and then two – better, winning his seventh Tour in 2005, making him statistically the race's best ever rider.

In 1998 – the year before Armstrong's first Tour triumph – there were shades of the drama and cheating of the 1904 Tour when a drugs scandal – the 'Festina affair' – broke, and threatened the race's very existence. Willy Voet, a Belgian member of staff at the French Festina team, was caught with a carload of doping products at the Belgium-France border while on his way to Dublin, Ireland, for the start of the Tour. He later admitted to French police that there was a programme of organised doping on the team.

Festina – which contained French stars Richard Virenque and Laurent Brochard – were kicked off the race, which nevertheless rumbled on – just – amid continued police raids, recriminations and rider unrest. However, the Tour proved itself to be bigger than any team or rider and it rallied to continue – some would say greater and stronger than ever as the scandal forced change upon the sport by way of increasingly effective drug-testing methods. While the Tour has continued to unearth participants cheating by way of drugs, the general consensus is that there has been a real sea change, and the Tour is more secure, both financially and in the minds of the public, than ever.

In 2011, the Tour demonstrated its truly international reach when it had its first Australian winner in Cadel Evans. Rumours abound of a possible non-European start – Qatar and Japan have shown interest – but for now it remains on European shores, a French institution, albeit one with non-French winners of late. The nation has been impatiently waiting since Hinault's 1985 victory, although it doesn't look like a home win is on the cards any time soon.

Cadel Evans passes the Arc de Triomphe on his way to victory during the final stage of the Tour in 2011 ▶

Cadel Evans scooped cycling's top prize in 2011, becoming the first Australian in history to do so

Tour of Austria
Austria

Pro stage race

A mountainous stage race that goes up against the Tour de France on the calendar

Like the Tour of Poland, the Tour of Austria has become an alternative to racing the Tour de France thanks to its July calendar slot. Former pro mountain biker Fredrik Kessiakoff of Astana convincingly won the 2011 edition, but the Swede has yet to prove himself in a grand tour, and was forced to pull out of the 2012 Giro d'Italia a week before the start citing a lack of fitness. If the Tour de France didn't beckon instead, then he may have got the chance to return to Austria to defend his title.

In fact, 2011 Tour de France champion Cadel Evans is a two-time Austria winner – in 2001 and 2004 – but that was when riders would use the race to hone Tour form, and its calendar slot change to July since 2005 has meant it hasn't attracted as many high-profile names as it once did.

Statistics

Location
Northern Austria

Distance
1,142 km/709 miles
over 8 stages (2012)

Terrain
Tarmac

Record wins
Wolfgang Steinmayr
(Aut) (four wins)

Field size
144

First event
1949

Website
www.oesterreich-rundfahrt.at

Contact
martin.roseneder@
sportpress.at

The peloton races through Hafenberg

There is no shortage of climbing in mountainous Austria ▶

Maratona dles Dolomites
Italy
Road

Classic climbing in the Dolomites in this always oversubscribed event

The Maratona dles Dolomites – the 'dles' means 'of the' in the local dialect – has established itself as one of the world's must-ride sportives, in part thanks to its heritage (2012 will be the twenty-sixth edition of the event), but also thanks to the stunning surroundings in which it takes place. As the organisers say of their event, "The Maratona belongs to the Dolomites; the Maratona is the Dolomites."

The event starts and finishes in the Alta Badia ski area, with three distances to choose from – 138 km, 106 km or 55 km. The profile of the full Maratona route is a true clichéd shark's teeth one: it takes in seven major climbs, which include the Passo Pordoi and the 2,236 m high Passo Giau, with its almost 10 per cent gradient over 10 km.

A place among the 9,000-rider field is as hard to come by as a spot in the London Marathon, and similarly a lottery system has to pick out the lucky 9,000, leaving more than 20,000 people disappointed in 2012. The week preceding the Maratona is Riders' Week, with training rides, drinks receptions and exhibitions, and there's even a mountain time trial up the Pordoi the day after the sportive – for those that still have the legs, that is.

Statistics
Location
La Villa to Corvara
Distance
138/106/55 km
85.7/65.9/34.2 miles
(2012)
Highest point
2,236 m (2012)
Terrain
Tarmac
Field size
9,000
First event
1987
Website
www.maratona.it/en
Contact
info@maratona.it

Italy's Dolomites dominate the skyline

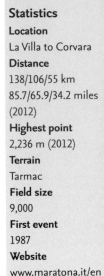

Thousands of riders head for the impenetrable-looking crags ▶

Beaumont Trophy
United Kingdom

Pro one-day race

British Premier Calendar event where Bradley Wiggins has twice been a winner

The Beaumont Trophy celebrated its 60th anniversary in 2012 and today it's part of a four-day cycling festival that also includes sportives, criterium racing and family rides.

A memorable race in its own right, the Beaumont can nevertheless boast having Bradley Wiggins as a two-time winner, and perhaps can go as far as to say it helped him towards his fourth place overall at the 2009 Tour de France, Wiggins having won the race just a

couple of weeks before he headed to France.

'Wiggo' was back at his old tricks again at the 2011 Beaumont, which incorporated the road race national championships, winning his red, white and blue jersey with another solo move.

However, there was no chance of him showing up to the 2012 edition, as the Tour de France was already under way, having been moved back a week due to the Olympics.

Statistics

Location
Tyneside

Distance
173.8 km/108 miles (2012)

Terrain
Tarmac

Record wins
Ray Wetherell (Gbr) (five wins)

First event
1952

Website
www.virginmoney cyclone.co.uk

Contact
info@virginmoney cyclone.co.uk

Bradley Wiggins has won the event on two occasions

Morocco Bike
Morocco
Mountain bike

The Atlas Mountains await you in this long-weekend adventure

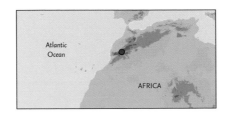

Starting in Marrakech, Morocco Bike takes riders into the Atlas Mountains, and through deserts and forests during an action-packed three days of riding before coming full circle to finish back in Marrakech. Such diverse and stunning terrain on UK riders' doorstep, just a few hours' flight away, makes this a huge adventure that can be enjoyed over not much more than a long weekend. Distances are tough enough over the rough stuff, but doable at 34 km on the first day, 56 km on the second and 26 km on the third day. Riders pledge to raise £1,800 for Action Medical Research, the medical research charity for children.

Statistics
Location
Atlas Mountains
Distance
116 km/72 miles
over 3 days (2012)
Terrain
Dirt roads, rocky and sandy trails
Website
www.action.org.uk
Contact
Via website

Morocco's rugged Atlas Mountains are the rider's playground

La Marmotte
France
Road
Making cyclists suffer since 1982...

It's already long at 174 km, but throw in climbs of the calibre – and difficulty – of the Col du Glandon, the Col du Galibier and the finish on the mythical Alpe d'Huez, and you've got one of the toughest sportives on the circuit. It's also one of the oldest sportives still running today, having started in 1982 and run ever since, which also gives it some extra cachet against the new kids on the block. In fact, so well known is it these days that La Marmotte boasted no fewer than forty-one different nations setting off from Bourg d'Oisans at the foot of Alpe d'Huez in the 2011 edition.

Statistics
Location
Bourg d'Oisans to Alpe d'Huez
Distance
174 km/108.1 miles (2012)
Highest point
2,645 m (2012)
Terrain
Tarmac
Field size
Over 4,000
First event
1982
Website
www.sport communication.com
Contact
Via website

Thousands of riders from a multitude of nations take part each year

The course is steeped in tough climbs as well as history ▶

Sjaelland Rundt
Denmark
Road

One of Denmark's best-loved sportives around
the stunning roads of Zealand

Sjaelland – or Zealand, as it's known in
English – is Denmark's biggest island,
with the country's capital, Copenhagen,
situated on its east coast. Roskilde – site
of arguably Europe's second-best-known
music festival after Glastonbury – is in the
centre of the island, although it's missed
out by the massive 293 km route of the
Sjaelland Rundt, which sticks more to
the southern half of the island. Køge,

40 km southwest of Copenhagen, is the
start and finish town, with riders setting
off from 6 am with a long day ahead of
them. The route takes participants on quiet,
picture-postcard roads, through forests
and past farms, and the feed stations
tend to be at village halls where you
receive a warm welcome and even
hotter sustenance.

Statistics

Location
Around the island
of Sjaelland
Distance
293 km/182.1 miles
(2012)
Terrain
Tarmac
First event
1980
Website
www.kcrv.dk/sjaelland-
rundt-paa-cykel
Contact
info@kcrv.dk

Køge, Sjaelland

Gran Fondo Highwood Pass Canada

Road

Take on the Canadian Rockies in this gran fondo, but watch out for bears...

The Highwood Pass is Canada's highest paved road at 2,207 m, and it's pretty much uphill all the way from the start to get there. You start in Longview – southwest of Calgary, Alberta – and the top of Highwood comes after around 80 km into this 147 km gran fondo in the Canadian Rockies. However, once you make it up there, relief: you've then got pretty much 70 km of descending to the finish at the Stoney Nakoda resort, where a celebration party awaits.

The organisers warn seriously about keeping your eyes peeled for any hungry bears while you've stopped for lunch, but you can also expect moose, deer and sheep – slightly less scary, unless you're descending and they're on the road.

Statistics

Location
Longview to Morley, Alberta

Distance
147 km/91.3 miles (2012)

Highest point
2,207 m (2012)

Terrain
Tarmac

Field size
600

Website
www.granfondo
highwoodpass.com

Contact
info@granfondo
highwoodpass.com

Beware of the animals as well as the ascents

Etape du Tour
France
Road

As close to riding the Tour de France as mere mortals are ever going to get

Despite not being the oldest sportive event by a long shot, the Etape du Tour has become the event that every amateur rider worth their salt would like to say that they've done at least once. Why? Because the 'Tour' part of its title refers to the Tour – the Tour de France – with participants riding a stage of the race on exactly the same roads as the pros.

While competition for a place on the Etape is fierce, it's no less competitive out on the road. French pros who might not have been selected to ride the Tour de France often choose to ride the Etape, taking on, and usually beating, the amateur front runners – perhaps showing their pro team managers what they've missed at the same time.

In 2012 separate timing for the major climbs was introduced, allowing for bragging rights with your friends as to who was 'King of the Mountains', while your overall finish time is still recorded, too, of course.

Statistics

Location
Act 1: Albertville to La Toussuire (2012)
Act 2: Pau to Bagnères-de-Luchon (2012)

Distance
Act 1: 152 km/ 94.4 miles (2012)
Act 2: 201 km/ 124.9 miles (2012)

Highest point
Act 1: 2,000 m (2012)
Act 2: 2,115 m (2012)

Terrain
Tarmac

Field size
10,000

First event
1993

Website
www.letapedutour.com

Contact
letapedutour@aso.fr

The Etape is a bona fide Tour de France experience

Because this really is as close to riding the Tour as most riders are ever going to get, demand for places has always been understandably high since the first edition of the Etape in 1993. As a result, a second Etape was introduced as of 2011 to help cater for the number of people wanting to ride, and the two separate events are now called 'Act 1' and 'Act 2'.

The toughest Tour ▲ stages are selected for the Etape

In 2011, while riders struggled with 37 °C heat during Act 1 between Modane Valfréjus and Alpe d'Huez, Act 2 between Issoire and Saint Flour through the Massif Central just a week later was a struggle for completely different reasons, with very few riders finishing due to unexpected extreme weather that included sleet and heavy rain. Five busloads of riders had called it a day by the first feed station, while many of those who pressed on but later gave up were left stranded for hours as the race organiser's resources were pushed to the limit to come and rescue them, with reports of riders shivering in phone boxes, desperate to warm up.

Such extreme weather is rare in France in July, even in the mountains, and the event remains as popular as ever. Failure to secure an individual place is not the end of the world, however, as a number of 'preferred partners' around the world – the major cycling holiday companies – are allocated places, too, and so are worth a look as a way in.

Just be ready for a tough day in the saddle, and be prepared for the worst that the weather in the Alps, Pyrenees or Massif Central can throw at you.

Sweltering conditions hinder riders during Act 1 in 2011 ▶

Determined cyclists battle against the wind and rain during Act 2 in 2011

La Fausto Coppi
Italy
Road

'Il Campionissimo' remembered in this extremely tough gran fondo

Fausto Coppi was arguably Italy's greatest ever climber – Coppi or Gino Bartali anyway; it divided the nation. Either way, it's no great surprise that a sportive using Coppi's name is positively dripping with climbs. Big ones, too.

The Colle Sampeyre is a nasty climb, especially as it comes after a long drag from the first feed zone after you've left your base in Cuneo. With an average grade of 8.5 per cent and 16 km long, if you weren't warmed up at the start, you will be after the Sampeyre. Then it's the descent, but immediately you're on to another Alpine monster: the Colle Fauniera – aka the Colle dei Morta, or 'the Hill of the Dead', which rises to 2,485 m, although another feed zone at the top is well placed. After a long descent, the Madonna del Colletto should seem like a baby at 'only' 1,310 m, but with around 180 km of the 198 km gran fondo under your belt, you'll be looking forward to the post-race pasta party – a prerequisite, this being an Italian event – and wishing you'd plumped for the 111 km medio fondo instead. Still, when competitors are all obliged to wear the same event jersey that comes with your entry fee, the pain quickly fades as you realise just how great you all look. How very Italian.

Statistics

Location
Cuneo

Distance
198/111 km
123/69 miles (2012)

Highest point
2,485 m (2012)

Terrain
Tarmac

Website
www.faustocoppi.net

Contact
info@faustocoppi.net

Riders all wear the mandatory event jersey

'Coppi' cats emulate Italy's greatest ever cyclist

Tour de Donut
USA
Road

A 'hole' new way to run a bike race

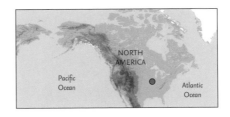

Statistics

Location
Staunton, Illinois
Distance
51.2 km/32 miles
(2012)
Terrain
Tarmac
First event
1989
Website
www.bebikeclub.com/
tourdedonut
Contact
nonfctr@yahoo.com

As odd bike-event concepts go, the Tour de Donut is certainly right up there with the Naked Bike Ride – although rather different in execution. The Tour de Donut is a 32-mile bike race that takes place each year in Staunton, Illinois, with two checkpoints – aka donut stops – at which riders eat as many donuts as they can, with each one consumed getting them a five-minute bonus off their finishing bike time.

In 2011, Randy Santel ate a quite phenomenal forty donuts, but the 2011 Tour de Donut champion – despite scoffing only a paltry thirty-eight donuts along the way – was KC Merckel, by virtue of a very rapid ride. Not easily done following the checkpoints, either, no doubt.

Professional eater Randy Santel scoffed a whopping forty donuts in 2011

GranFondo Los Angeles
USA

Road

Sportive riding in the Santa Monica Mountains around Malibu, California

Thanks to rider feedback from the 2011 Gran Fondo Los Angeles, which started and finished in the heart of Beverly Hills, a new venue slightly further out of town was chosen for the 2012 edition. The arguably even more stunning setting for the start and finish is among the vineyards of Saddlerock Ranch, home of Malibu Family Wines. Riders can choose between a 75-mile or 40-mile route through the Santa Monica Mountains around Malibu, just west along the coast from Los Angeles.

Just as he did at the previous Gran Fondo Miami, 1997 Tour de France winner Jan Ullrich was all set to ride the 2012 version of the Gran Fondo Los Angeles, too, and, even though he's been retired for a while, he might well have given some riders a run for their money in the mountains.

Statistics

Location
Malibu, California
Distance
120.7/64.4 km
75/40 miles (2012)
Terrain
Tarmac
Website
www.granfondo-world.com
Contact
info@granfondo
usa.com

Malibu, California

Jurassic Classic
United Kingdom

Road

Enjoy East Devon by bike at this sportive, which offers a choice of 100 km or 100 miles

The Jurassic Classic sportive offers the choice between the 100-mile Epic route or the 100-km Challenge, and both '100s' help to raise money for The Prostate Cancer Charity.

Both distances start in Exmouth, with the Challenge's most challenging climb coming at Gittisham Hill, after the route turns inland after the feed station at Sidmouth, while the Epic continues along the Jurassic coastline and up and over Salcombe Hill, all the way along to Lyme Regis before heading north. The routes come together again at Honiton and complete the circle back to Exmouth where the events village will have kept friends and family fed, watered and entertained, and then will do the same for you.

Statistics

Location
Exmouth, Devon
Distance
160.1/100 km
100/62.1 miles (2012)
Terrain
Tarmac
Website
www.jurassic-classic.
org.uk
Contact
cycling@prostate-
cancer.org.uk

Breathtaking Jurassic coastline at Lyme Regis, Devon

Tour of Qinghai Lake
China

Pro stage race

Chinese stage race with a knack of producing stars of the future

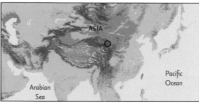

The Tour of Qinghai Lake is a true climbers' event, and a list of past winners of this Chinese stage race reads like a who's who of today's big stars, with most of them on their way up when they won here. Tom Danielson won the very first event in 2002, and although he's showed flashes of brilliance since then, he truly came alive at the 2011 Tour de France, where he finished ninth at his first attempt. Qinghai Lake champion in 2003, Italian Damiano Cunego, blossomed quickly and won the Giro d'Italia the following year, while 2006 winner Maarten Tjallingii won the Tour of Belgium the same year as his victory in China, and has since developed into a very useful Classics rider, coming third at the 2011 Paris–Roubaix.

Statistics

Location
Qinghai Province, Gansu Province and Ningxia Hui, northwest China

Distance
2,680 km/1,665.3 miles over 13 stages (2012)

Terrain
Tarmac

Field size
154

First event
2002

Website
www.tdql.cn

Contact
tdql2010@hotmail.com

Tom Danielson won the inaugural event in 2002

Tour of Poland
Poland

Pro stage race

Top-notch stage race that sets up stars of
the future

This UCI WorldTour event runs concurrently
with the Tour de France, but has never had
any trouble attracting the big-name riders
who aren't in the hunt for the yellow jersey
in Paris. The Tour of Poland began life as
an amateur race in 1928, and only opened
its doors to professional riders in 1993.
Despite that, that year local rider Dariusz
Baranowski took his third straight Tour of
Poland title, and the then 21 year old clearly
impressed somebody, as he was riding for
US Postal a couple of years later. He went
on to ride for Banesto, and won the King of
the Mountains title at the 2002 Dauphiné
Libéré, before going on to finish twenty-
fourth overall at that year's Tour de France.

The race has acted as a stepping stone
for younger riders in more recent years, too,
with Garmin's Dan Martin winning the 2010
edition, and then being pipped for the win
the following year by Liquigas's Peter Sagan.
The race was looking for a new champion
to succeed the Slovakian, however, as both
Martin and Sagan were stepping up to ride
their first Tour de France in 2012.

Statistics

Location
Karpacz to Krakow
(2012)
Distance
1,234.7 km/767.2 miles
over 7 stages (2012)
Terrain
Tarmac
Record wins
Dariusz Baranowski
(Pol),
Marian Wieckowski
(Pol)
(both three wins)
Field size
200
First event
1928
Website
http://tourdepologne.pl
Contact
kontakt@langteam.
com.pl

Future stars cut their teeth in Poland

**Locals turn out
in force to cheer
the top pro teams** ▶

Craft Bike TransAlp
Germany, Austria and Italy
Mountain bike
The ultimate MTB Alpine challenge

The TransAlp is a mountain bike stage race for teams of two which takes them through the German, Austrian and Italian Alps, across eight stages, covering around 600 km with a vertical gain of almost 20,000 m. It's not for the faint of heart, and is very much a stage race rather than a sightseeing pootle – concerned as the organisers genuinely are, however, to ensure the race takes in a spectacular route through the Alps.

The race starts in Oberammergau in Bavaria, in the south of Germany, and takes the riders across a variety of terrain from gravel roads to single track, and over Austria's mighty 2,753-m-high Idjoch climb on stage three, all the way to Riva del Garda in northern Italy.

Participants can choose to either camp or stay at hotels along the route, while a pasta party is provided each evening for hungry riders to refuel for the next day.

Statistics
Location
Oberammergau,
Bavaria to Riva
del Garda
Distance
600 km/372.8 miles
over 8 stages (2012)
Terrain
Gravel, tarmac and
dirt roads
Field size
1,100
(550 teams
of two)
Website
www.bike-magazin.de/
event/bike-transalp
Contact
o.ruesche@delius-
klasing.de

Riva del Garda, Italy

Trails and tracks over
the Bavarian Alps are
for starters ▶

Tour of the California Alps Death Ride USA

Road

Choose the number of climbs you want to tackle yourself, but make sure you're back in time for dinner

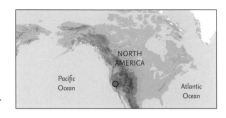

The Death Ride may not sound that appealing, but one look at the terrain this sportive covers in the California Alps, just south of Lake Tahoe, will have you dying to ride it... The full five-pass route takes you on a 129-mile ride with more than 15,000 ft of climbing on the menu: both sides of Monitor Pass, both sides of Ebbetts Pass with the climb of Carson Pass to finish. However, there is also the option to do any number of the climbs, and no matter if you do one or all five, you'll be well looked after with a proper lunch served en route, as well as massage and dinner in the evening.

Statistics

Location
Alpine County, California

Distance
207.6 km/129 miles (2012)

Highest point
2,660 m (2012)

Terrain
Tarmac

Field size
3,500

Website
www.deathride.com

Contact
info@deathride.com

Carson Pass is the stunning finale

La Pina Cycling Marathon
Italy
Road

Pinarello welcomes riders to a classic gran fondo
in Treviso

Statistics
Location
Treviso
Distance
168.5/118.5 km
104.7/73.6 miles (2012)
Terrain
Tarmac
Website
www.lapinarello.com
Contact
info@lapinarello.com

Like all the best Italian fondos, both a gran
fondo and a medio fondo are offered when
it comes to La Pina – over 168.5 km or
118.5 km respectively. Both start and finish
in Treviso on the Piazza del Grano – a place
dearly loved by the company's marketing
manager, and son of founder Giovanni,
Andrea Pinarello, who passed away in
August 2011 aged just 40, and who the gran
fondo will remember in 2012.

The gran fondo followed a new route in
2012, including for the first time a climb
called the Praderadego – 7 km long with
gradients of up to 16 per cent.

La Pina is also one of just six events that
make up the UCI's Golden Bike series,
chosen as being on top of their game and
as working hard to continue to promote
cycling positively.

Treviso

Urban Hill Climb
United Kingdom

Road
A tough hill climb in leafy North London

After a successful first event in 2010, Urban Hill Climb organisers Rollapaluza – best known for their roller racing evenings – decided to ramp up the evening's excitement even more in 2011 by introducing a race format that included two semi-finals, a third-place ride-off, and a final.

The qualifying round was otherwise the same as the previous year: 120 cyclists of all abilities, shapes and sizes – entry on a first-come, first-served basis – duking it out one-by-one against the clock up the 800-m-long Swain's Lane climb in Highbury, north London. Screamed on their way by hundreds of enthusiastic friends, family members, club-mates and general cycling fans, most make it up in between two and three minutes. The very fast guys, however, pile-drive their way up in less than a minute-and-a-half, often trading climb records before the evening's out. With the top four qualifiers going into the semi-finals, where they had to use tactics as well as brute strength to make it to the top first, in 2011 Michael Smith (Corley Cycles) and 16-year-old rising star Germain Burton (De Ver Cycles) made it through to the final, and in what was their third ascent of the evening, Smith managed to overpower Burton to take the title.

This appears to be a much-loved event that's here to stay, with Rollapaluza managing to get Swain's Lane closed to other traffic for the duration of the event. Those who want to give it a try themselves have to be quick, though – entries sell out in a matter of minutes.

Defeated 2011 finalist Germain Burton

Statistics
Location
London
Distance
800 m/0.5 miles (2012)
Terrain
Tarmac
Field size
120
First event
2010
Website
www.urbanhillclimb.com
Contact
Via website

Pain on Swain's Lane only lasts a couple of minutes, but it's intense ▶

Tour de Wallonie
Belgium
Pro stage race
Stage race in French-speaking Belgium

Britain's Russell Downing, then with Team Sky, won the final stage in a bunch sprint and with it did enough to take the overall classification of the 2010 edition of this five-day stage race in French-speaking Belgium. In 2011, it was a home win for Belgium as Greg Van Avermaet showed his rivals a clean pair of heels in the sprints, but it's the type of race where you need to be a good all-rounder – like both Van Avermaet and Downing – always staying in the front group and being able to fight for the bonus seconds on offer at the finish, too, which often decide the race.

Statistics
Location
Wallonia
Distance
885.8 km/550.4 miles
over 5 stages (2011)
Terrain
Tarmac
Record wins
Mario Kummer (Ger)
(two wins)
First event
1974
Website
www.trworg.be
Contact
info@trworg.be

Tournai, Wallonia

Greg Van Avermaet, 2011 winner ▶

BHF South Downs Way Off-Road Bike Ride
United Kingdom
Mountain bike

Winchester to Eastbourne via the South Downs Way

The South Downs Way is a 100-mile-long bridleway stretching from Winchester all the way to Eastbourne via Devil's Dyke in the hills just north of Brighton. The 65-mile option of this British Heart Foundation charity ride along the muddy, chalky tracks, ends at the Dyke, offering stunning views and a pub at which to recover, and is plenty

for a very tough day's mountain biking. Although, for those who are really after a challenge, the extra 35 miles to Eastbourne will certainly provide it. The British weather is normally kind in July, but come prepared with warm and waterproof clothing, as not every edition can be guaranteed sunshine.

Statistics
Location
Winchester, Hampshire to Eastbourne, East Sussex
Distance
160.1/104.6/56.3 km
100/65/35 miles (2012)
Terrain
Chalk bridleways and muddy single track
Website
www.bhf.org.uk
Contact
Via website

Thirsty riders can recuperate at the Devil's Dyke pub

Tour Ride
United Kingdom
Road
The Tour of Britain's Etapes du Tour

The Tour Ride routes are inspired by the Tour of Britain pro stage race route, and in 2012 started with the Tour Ride East Anglia on 22 July. While they're essentially the Tour of Britain version of the Tour de France's Etape du Tour, they're aimed at being a little more inclusive of riders of all abilities, while offering five venues around the country to allow people to find an event close to home.

The Tour Ride Wales took place on 12 August, while the Tour Ride Scotland was on 26 August and took riders on sections of stage three between Jedburgh and Dumfries covered by the pros on 11 September, with the Tour Ride road show then heading to Stoke-on-Trent for a round there on 23 September. The final Tour Ride was to take place on the final day of the Cycle Show at the NEC in Birmingham on 30 September.

Statistics

Location
Multiple rides, nationwide

Distance
Various

Terrain
Tarmac

First event
2009

Website
www.tourride.co.uk

Contact
cycling@prostate-cancer.org.uk

The Scottish edition passes the Borders town of Jedburgh

Mount Evans Hill Climb
USA

Road

A 27-mile hill climb that sorts the men from the boys

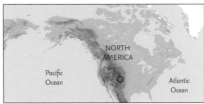

The Mount Evans Hill Climb in Colorado is a mass-start race that has run each year since 1962, and although things are a little chaotic at the start, everyone soon finds their rhythm. They have plenty of time to, too: at 27.4 miles long, it puts most European climbs in the shade, and at 4,348 m high, it's the highest paved road in North America.

The race's official title is the Bob Cook Memorial Mount Evans Hill Climb, named in memory of five-time winner Cook, who died from cancer aged just 23.

Colorado-based pro riders in particular have always done battle not only to try to win the event but also to set a new record for the climb, which currently stands at 1:41:20, set in 2004 by three-time winner Tom Danielson. Other past winners include Garmin manager Jonathan Vaughters (three wins) and Durango-based mountain bike legend Ned Overend (two wins).

Statistics

Location
Mount Evans, Colorado
Distance
44.1 km/27.4 miles (2012)
Highest point
4,348 m (2012)
Terrain
Tarmac
Record wins
Scott Moninger (USA) (six wins)
Field size
600 to 1,000
First event
1962
Website
www.bicyclerace.com
Contact
Via website

'The road into the sky' attracts the local pros

Mount Evans boasts the highest paved road in North America ▶

MOUNT EVANS
ROAD
ELEV. 14,130 FT.

Sachsen Tour
Germany
Pro one-day race

After two years away, the Sachsen Tour returns as a one-day race

The Sachsen Tour – the Tour of Saxony – was a five-day stage race around the state in eastern Germany, which was once part of the former East Germany. It ran from 1985 to 1995 as an amateur event, although a young Jens Voigt – also a product of East Germany – managed to keep the pros at bay and win the race in his final year as an amateur in 1996.

In 2010, a loss of sponsorship meant that the race was cancelled, and that was the case again in 2011. However, with a concerted effort from the organisers and with the support of cycling fans, as well as a bit of help from 2011 time trial world champion Tony Martin, who was born in East Germany, the Sachsen Tour International was all set to make its return as a one-day race for 2012 as part of the UCI Europe Tour. "Comeback 12", the organisers were calling it, and why not? In cycling, it's extremely rare to see a race make a return once it's been cancelled due to financial difficulties, so it's an event that is, luckily, bucking the trend.

Statistics

Location
Dresden, Saxony
Terrain
Tarmac
Record wins
Uwe Ampler (Ger),
Jörn Reuss (Ger),
Thomas Liese (Ger)
(all two wins)
First event
1985
Website
www.sachsentour.org
Contact
info@sachsen-tour-international.de

Two-time winner Uwe Ampler

The former East German race has a new lease of life

Dresden Race
Germany
Road

A Saxony sportive on the same day as the pro Sachsen Tour

The historic city of Dresden, in Saxony, Germany, hosts both the start and finish of the Dresden Race for 'Jedermann' (everyone). With the sportive taking place on the same day as the pro Sachsen Tour – the former stage race that became a one-day race in 2012 after having been cancelled for the previous two years – it gives all participants that warm glow of pride that they, too, have been there and done it as the pros later scream across the same finish line. Riders have a choice between a 106 km or 75 km route, and just to make sure everyone's kept happy, there's also a ride for 6 to 13 year olds.

Statistics

Location
Dresden, Saxony
Distance
106/75 km
65.9/46.6 miles (2012)
Terrain
Tarmac
Website
www.sachsentour.org
Contact
info@raceday-dresden.de

Dresden's famous Semperoper

TransRockies Challenge
Canada

Mountain bike
British Columbia to Alberta via the
Canadian Rockies

Since 2002, the TransRockies Challenge
has been offering exactly that to mountain
bikers keen to find out what real adventure
tastes like. Across 400 km of tough
Canadian Rockies terrain from Fernie,
British Columbia to Canmore, Alberta, riders
have experienced what MTBs were made for
– albeit fully supported by the TransRockies
guys to ensure everything runs smoothly.

For those who don't fancy the whole
hog cold, there are also options for those
riders who want to ease them into such
a challenge a little more slowly by simply
riding an individual stage or a few stages.
With race starts no earlier than 9 am, and
dinner and presentations at a reasonable
hour in the evening to give you plenty of
time to relax, the organisers describe their
event as "tough but doable", and you can't
say fairer than that.

Statistics
Location
Fernie, British
Columbia to
Canmore, Alberta
Distance
360 km/223.7 miles
over 7 stages (2012)
Terrain
Off-road
First event
2002
Website
www.transrockies.com
Contact
info@transrockies.com

Canmore, Alberta

Graeme Obree Classic
United Kingdom
Road

Join 'The Flying Scotsman' on the roads
of Ayrshire

Graeme thoroughly enjoyed being out on
the road and chatting with everyone at the
inaugural Graeme Obree Classic sportive in
2011, and so was there for more of the same
in 2012.

With this event being the third and
final round of the Scottish Sportive Series,
Graeme Obree was also on hand to
present certificates to those who have
done the treble.

The sportive, around Ayrshire, has
two distance options: a 48.5-mile
'intermediate' ride or the 68.5-mile
'endurance' ride. There's plenty of climbing
in both, but the longer option includes
the brutal climb of Nick o' the Balloch, so
choose wisely.

This is a sportive likely to go from
strength to strength – especially when
participants get to meet and ride with one
of their heroes, which certainly can't be said
of too many sportives.

Statistics
Location
Auchincruive, Scotland
Distance
110.2/78 km
68.5/48.5 miles (2012)
Terrain
Tarmac
First event
2011
Website
www.obree.com/
sportive2012.php
Contact
charlie@
maximisesport.com

Auchincruive, Ayrshire

Dunwich Dynamo
United Kingdom
Night

Night-riding between London and the Suffolk coast

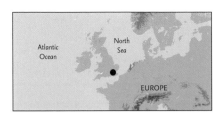

The Dunwich Dynamo is a night ride between London Fields in Hackney and the coastal town of Dunwich, in Suffolk, and is an event that the organisers are keen to keep relatively low-key, despite the hundreds who turn up year in, year out. It started as an informal ride by a few mates, and that's what it essentially still is. It's a fun ride, and not a race, and riders are encouraged to keep noise to a minimum as they purr through villages along the way, and of course to keep all their litter with them. Reaching Dunwich beach, riders reward themselves with breakfast or a dip in the sea, plus a little sleep for those who need it, before heading to the return coaches that have been made available in recent years for riders and their bikes to get back to London.

Statistics

Location
London Fields, Hackney to Dunwich, Suffolk

Distance
200 km/124.3 miles (2012)

Terrain
Tarmac

First event
1992

Website
www.londonschool
ofcycling.co.uk

Contact
patrick@londonschool
ofcycling.co.uk

Riders prepare to set off from London Fields

Tour of Burgos
Spain
Pro stage race

Five-day stage race that allows the Spanish
climbers to shine

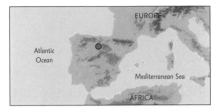

The Tour of Burgos is a Spanish stage race
held in the northern province of Burgos.
The area is extremely hilly, which makes
it very much one for the climbers, with
Spanish mountains specialists like Joaquim
Rodriguez and 2008 Olympic road race
champion Samuel Sanchez dominating the
race in recent years.

The race was first held in 1946, but only
reappeared in the Eighties after just a
couple of editions. Then, as now, star
Spanish climbers such as 1988 Tour de
France champion Pedro Delgado,
Marino Lejaretta – a four-time winner –
and Abraham Olano made the race theirs,
although British climbing legend Robert
Millar, in the twilight years of his career,
won the mountains jersey at Burgos
in 1994.

Statistics

Location
Burgos
Distance
646.6 km/401.8 miles
over 5 stages (2012)
Terrain
Tarmac
Record wins
Marino Lejaretta (Spa)
(four wins)
Field size
120
First event
1946
Website
www.vuelta
burgos.com
Contact
vueltaburgos@
diputaciondeburgos.es

Burgos attracts the top Spanish pros

The 2011 event had a
mountain-top finish
on stage one ▶

Brighton Big Dog
United Kingdom
Mountain bike

A 6-hour MTB race for individuals or teams on a tough south-coast course

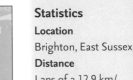

The Brighton Big Dog is one of those mountain bike events that has quickly established itself as one essential to tick off the list – and then to keep going back to as it was so enjoyable. The first edition was held in 2009, and the race has kept the same Stanmer Park location just north of Brighton, with a very challenging 8-mile course that riders try to cover as many times as possible in 6 hours, either as an individual or as part of a two- or three-man relay team. There's also a retro-bike category and separate youth races.

This being the UK in the summer, weather conditions can vary greatly from year to year, and even hour to hour on race day, so riders need to be prepared. The 2010 event, for example, could have been a complete washout were it not for the enthusiasm of the competitors and general positivity of the organisation, and some riders came away having enjoyed themselves in the mud more than if it had been dry.

The other aspect of the Big Dog that keeps people coming back year after year is the social side: both during the event, which has a very friendly vibe, but also afterwards down on Brighton seafront at the Fortune of War pub, where competitors receive a free drink to get them warmed up for a fun evening out with new friends.

Statistics

Location
Brighton, East Sussex
Distance
Laps of a 12.9 km/
8 mile course (2012)
Terrain
Off-road
First event
2009
Website
www.brighton
bigdog.com
Contact
Via website

Stanmer Park, East Sussex

Broad trails as well as wiggly singletrack make up the course ▶

Tour of Elk Grove
USA

Pro stage race

An Illinois cycling festival for everyone, from pros to the whole family

The Tour of Elk Grove is a three-day festival of cycling held just outside Chicago which includes a three-day pro women's race, various category races, fun rides, time trials and kids' races.

The men's race became a UCI event in 2011, and for 2012 it was bumped up from a 2.2 category to a 2.1, which meant that the Elk Grove organisers were hoping for an even better, even more international field than normal for the three-day, three-stage men's race, having already had fifteen nationalities represented in 2011.

The main event consists of a short opening time trial, a longer road race and a criterium – all held in and around the community of Elk Grove Village, and offering a tidy prize purse to the overall winner.

Statistics

Location
Elk Grove Village, Illinois
Distance
277 km/172.1 miles over 3 stages (2012)
Terrain
Tarmac
Field size
200
First event
2006
Website
www.tourof elkgrove.com
Contact
fnewton@ chicagoevents.com

International teams compete in Elk Grove

Eneco Tour
Netherlands and Belgium
Pro stage race

A sprinter and time triallists' stage race straddling Holland and Belgium

This Belgo-Dutch stage race was chosen to be Alberto Contador's comeback race in 2012, the day after his doping suspension ended.

Along with the E3 Harelbeke, the Eneco Tour shares the distinction of featuring the infamous, but much loved, cobbled climb of the Muur van Geraardsbergen, which was dropped from the Tour of Flanders route for 2012.

Eneco is a race that has often been won by time triallists; most stages end in a bunch sprint, and so the TT stage has usually been the deciding factor. For 2012, with

the Olympic time trial just ten days before the Eneco TT, recent Eneco winners Edvald Boasson Hagen and Tony Martin were able to hone their time trialling form perfectly.

That TT aspect was exaggerated further in 2012, although to the tune of needing to be as strong as your whole team against the clock with the introduction of a team time trial. It provided riders with a dress rehearsal for the team time trial world championships in Limburg in September, which, unlike the road race and the time trial, features trade teams rather than national squads.

Statistics
Location
Waalwijk, Netherlands to Geraardsbergen, Belgium
Distance
1,200 km/745.6 miles over 7 stages (2012)
Terrain
Tarmac
Record wins
José Ivan Gutierrez (Spa), Edvald Boasson Hagen (Nor) (both two wins)
Field size
176
First event
2005
Website
www.enecotour.com
Contact
chris.vannoppen@golazo.com

José Ivan Gutierrez wins the prologue in 2008

Edvald Boasson Hagen dominated the 2011 race, winning all the overall jerseys ▶

Tour of Utah
USA

Pro stage race

A stage race in 'the beehive state' which attracts a top field of American and international riders

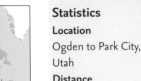

"America's toughest stage race", claim the organisers, and who are we to argue having seen the kinds of climbs Utah has to offer, including the 8.3-mile climb of Little Cottonwood Canyon, with an average grade of 9.2 per cent, but with ramps of up to 12 per cent? The 2012 event was the fifth consecutive time the climb up to the Snowbird ski resort had been used, or six if you count its introduction in 2006; the 2007 Tour of Utah was cancelled due to a lack of sponsor interest.

It's that man Levi Leipheimer yet again who holds the record for most wins at Utah, having won in both 2010 and 2011, adding to three Tour of California titles, two Tour of the Gila wins and the 2011 US Pro Cycling Challenge title. Despite him being Europe-based, are there any US races the Californian hasn't won?

Statistics

Location
Ogden to Park City, Utah
Distance
881.4 km/547.7 miles over 6 stages (2012)
Terrain
Tarmac
Record wins
Levi Leipheimer (USA) (two wins)
Field size
128
First event
2002
Website
www.tourofutah.com
Contact
info@toutofutah.com

Utah is packed with steep climbs

The peloton races towards Park City in 2011 ▶

Tour de l'Ain
Pro stage race
France

Stage race that captures the imagination of the French public still drunk on the Tour de France

Coming just two weeks after the finish of the Tour de France, the Tour de l'Ain tends to attract the bigger French names who have shown themselves to the French public on TV over the course of three weeks, and so draws some decent-sized crowds.

The six-stage race around the Ain département in central-eastern France mixes either an individual or team time trial with flat and hilly stages, creating a mini-Tour de France for Ain residents' enjoyment.

In 2011, 21-year-old Frenchman Thibaut Pinot of FDJ, a second-year pro, put in an impressive performance to win two stages of the race, but it was another Frenchman, David Moncoutié, who took the top honours, although Pinot did carry that form over to take the overall win at the Settimana Lombarda just a couple of weeks later.

Statistics
Location
Montmerle-sur-Saône to Lélex
Distance
679.8 km/422.4 miles over 6 stages (2012)
Highest point
1,130 m (2012)
Terrain
Tarmac
Field size
96
First event
1989
Website
www.tourdelain.com
Contact
contact@tour delain.com

The Grand Colombier in the Jura mountains is a key climb

David Moncoutié won the 2011 event in front of a home crowd ▶

Tour de l'Ain Cyclosportif
France
Road

Get the true pro experience with this multi-stage sportive event

This basically is the pro Tour de l'Ain – just without the pros, or the time trials. Enter as many of the five stages as you wish as though they were individual sportives, but if you want the chance to compete for the leader's jersey, the 'King of the Mountains' jersey or the team prize with your team-mates – there's no points jersey for wannabe Cavs, unfortunately – then you'll need to sign up for all five stages. This being the Continent, the Tour de l'Ain Cyclosportif is extremely good value for money at 32 euros per single stage – for those who just want the 'normal' sportive experience' – or 150 euros for all five stages. There is also the 'pro pack' option, however, at considerably more expense – 1,650 euros – but then you do get a daily massage, all transport, meals and a room at the same hotel as the pro teams. It really is the real deal.

Statistics

Location
Montmerle-sur-Saône to Lélex

Distance
653 km/405.8 miles over 5 stages (2012)

Highest point
1,130 m

Terrain
Tarmac

Website
www.tourdelain.com

Contact
contact@tourdelain.com

Take on the Grand Colombier just like the pros do

Tour of Utah Ultimate Challenge USA

Road

Take on the 'Ultimate Challenge' on Utah's toughest stage

The Tour of Utah's sportive – the Ultimate Challenge – takes on the route of the 'queen stage' – 100 miles between Newpark Town Center in Park City and the Snowbird Ski and Summer Resort via the 8.3-mile climb of Little Cottonwood Canyon. It's an early start to ensure everyone's off the course ahead of the pros coming through, but as well as the 100-mile option, there's a 74-miler to Alpine and a 35-mile option finishing in Midway. Both towns host intermediate sprints, so sportive riders will be on hand to watch the pros duke it out, and then watch the rest of the stage on TV screens.

Statistics

Location
Park City to Snowbird Ski and Summer Resort

Distance
160.1/119/56.3 km
100/74/35 miles (2012)

Terrain
Tarmac

Field size
600

Website
www.tourofutah.com

Contact
info@toutofutah.com

The route swerves up Little Cottonwood Canyon

Leadville Trail 100
USA

Mountain bike

Prestigious Colorado Rockies MTB race – as ridden by Lance Armstrong

The Leadville 100 is an out-and-back 100-mile mountain bike race through the Colorado Rockies, starting and finishing in Leadville, and reaching a breathtaking elevation of 12,424 ft.

It's an event that has become so popular that entry these days is by lottery, London Marathon style, although similarly to the marathon there are also charity places available.

It's unlikely that the 2010 winner Levi Leipheimer or his former team-mate

Lance Armstrong had to enter the lottery to get in, though. Armstrong, who had been pipped to the title in 2008 by Colorado local and six-time winner David Wiens, came back in 2009 to beat Wiens by almost half an hour – a puncture with 17 miles to go and all – although as Wiens rightly pointed out, Armstrong was racing Leadville off the back of his comeback Tour de France that year. "Last year he was just coming off the couch," laughed Wiens.

Statistics
Location
Leadville, Colorado
Distance
160.1 km/100 miles (2012)
Highest point
3,787 m (2012)
Terrain
Forest trails and mountain roads
Record wins
David Wiens (USA) (six wins)
First event
1994
Website
www.leadville raceseries.com
Contact
Via website

American legends Levi Leipheimer (left) and Lance Armstrong have both won the event

Riders are faced with a tough off-road course through the Colorado Rockies ▶

Highlander Radmarathon
Austria
Road

Austria's Vorarlberg region invites you to come and sample its mountains...

Austria's mountainous Vorarlberg region, in the westernmost tip of the country, bordering Liechtenstein, Switzerland and Germany, plays host to the Highlander Radmarathon. Austria may not at first seem like an obvious choice of sportive destination, but when you consider the challenging, but stunning, terrain it has to offer, and then look a little closer and see the plethora of sportive events it holds during the summer months, it becomes a total no-brainer.

The town of Hohenems is your host for the 'Highlander Weekend' with a party and evening criterium race on the Saturday night, and then the 187 km Radmarathon and the slightly shorter Rund um Vorarlberg, over 160 km, with fewer climbs, both taking place on the Sunday.

Statistics

Location
Hohenems
Distance
187 km/116.2 miles (2012)
Terrain
Tarmac
Field size
1,000
First event
1975
Website
www.highlander-radmarathon.at
Contact
office@highlander-radmarathon.at

For spectacular bike riding, Austria has it all

The Devil in the Downs
United Kingdom
Road

A devilish new sportive around the High Weald and the South Downs

Founded in 1887, Worthing Excelsior Cycling Club is one of the oldest in the UK, and it celebrated its 125th anniversary in 2012 with this new sportive challenge on its doorstep in the stunning South Downs.

Dial Post Village Hall, near Horsham, West Sussex, is the starting point from where riders then choose the full 125 km route, chock-full of devilishly tough climbing through the High Weald and the South Downs, or the only slightly flatter profile of the 85 km 'Little Devil'. Or

there's 'The Imp' – a shorter, 50 km option for those just getting into sportive riding.

Devil's Dyke, above Brighton, is one of the area's most iconic climbs, and having dragged themselves up there to the finish, riders can look back over High Weald stretching away towards the North Downs from whence they came – before enjoying a pint in the pub at the top to toast a job well done. Money raised will benefit the Chestnut Tree House – a Sussex-based children's hospice.

Statistics

Location
Dial Post, West Sussex
Distance
125/85/50 km
77.7/52.8/31.1 miles
(2012)
Terrain
Tarmac
First event
2012
Website
www.worthing
excelsior.co.uk/
devil-in-the-downs
Contact
Via website

The event takes its name from Devil's Dyke

The rolling hillsides of the South Downs are devilishly difficult by bike ▶

GranFondo Garneau–Cascades Canada

Road

Quebec-based sportive for all abilities from the organisers of the Tour de Beauce

The GranFondo Garneau-Cascades runs the 110 km from Trois-Rivières to Quebec City, and is very firmly aimed at riders of all abilities. The frontrunners will be aiming to be the first ones home, while slower riders will be happy to just enjoy the ride in this stunning part of the world, knowing that profits from the event go to the Friends of the Elderly Organization, which provides help and company to senior citizens who find themselves alone in the world.

The only climb of note is the finish one up to sponsor Louis Garneau's factory. Garneau is one of Canada's best-known cycling and triathlon clothing manufacturers, and provides kit, helmets and shoes across the pond to France's favourite pro rider, Thomas Voeckler, and his Europcar team. The entry fee includes your own Garneau-Cascades jersey, while there's also a shuttle service available from Quebec City back to Trois-Rivières.

Statistics

Location
Trois-Rivières to Quebec
Distance
110 km/64.4 miles (2012)
Highest point
82 m (2012)
Terrain
Tarmac
Field size
2,000
First event
2009
Website
www.quebec granfondo.com
Contact
granfondo@ louisgarneau.com

The journey begins at Trois-Rivières

Château Frontenac, Quebec's landmark hotel ▶

San Sebastian Classic
Spain

Pro one-day race

Spanish one-day race that favours climbers straight out of the Tour de France

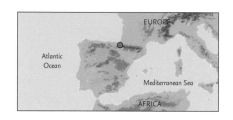

The Clásica de San Sebastián is the first major race after the Tour de France and, as a result of being a climber's race, it should suit whoever won the Tour down to the ground. Although Tour de France champions Miguel Indurain and Lance Armstrong have won in San Sebastian, both did so ahead of their first French win, and there has never been a 'double' winner in the same year.

The main climb on the route is the famed Alto de Jaizkibel, with its gradients of up to 8.5 per cent, and it's climbed twice in the final 80 km of the race, followed each time by the shorter and slightly less steep climb of the Arkale, from the top of which, the second time, the finish line is just 15 km away.

Despite being the biggest one-day race in Spain, and despite the big-name riders who frequent it, the race, which has been run since 1981, has recently faced an uncertain future, along with a number of other Spanish races suffering in today's economic climate. However, local Basque banking group Sabadell Guipuzcoano's injection of cash for San Sebastian, as well as for the Tour of the Basque Country stage race, has ensured its survival for the length of the two-year sponsorship deal at least.

Statistics

Location
San Sebastian

Distance
227 km/141.1 miles (2012)

Terrain
Tarmac

Record wins
Marino Lejaretta (Spa) (three wins)

Field size
168

First event
1981

Website
http://clasica-san-sebastian.diariovasco.com

Contact
contactanos@diariovasco.com

The winner is given a traditional Basque *txapela* hat

Joaquim Rodriguez leads an escape ▶

Tour du Limousin
France
Pro stage race

A French stage race held in perfect cycling country

This four-day stage race takes place around the French region of Limousin, in the Massif Central, which is perfect cycling country being France's least populated mainland region, beaten only by Corsica. It's a race that, since its first edition in 1968, has attracted all the big-name French riders, and past winners include such leading lights as Bernard Hinault, Marc Madiot, Eric Boyer and Charly Mottet. The French teams tend to dominate proceedings, as was the case in 2011 with two stage wins for FDJ sprinter Matthieu Ladagnous and a stage for Cofidis's Tony Gallopin, but it was stage one winner, the Belgian Björn Leukemans, riding for the Dutch Vacansoleil team, who upset the French apple cart and took the leader's jersey all the way to the finish in Limoges.

Statistics

Location
Limousin
Distance
611.7 km/380 miles
over 4 stages (2012)
Terrain
Tarmac
Record wins
Francis Duteil (Fra),
Charly Mottet (Fra),
Patrice Halgand (Fra),
Bernard Hinault (Fra),
Pierrick Fédrigo (Fra)
(all two wins)
Field size
120
First event
1968
Website
www.tourdu
limousin.com
Contact
communication@
tourdulimousin.com

Björn Leukemans, 2011 winner

Open de Suède Vårgårda
Sweden
Pro one-day race

Two rounds of the UCI women's World Cup for the price of one in southwest Sweden

Vårgårda, a pretty town in an active, outdoorsy area of southwest Sweden, hosts not one but two rounds of the nine-leg UCI women's World Cup, with the world's best female riders descending on the town to ride both events in the space of three days.

The team time trial takes place on an out-and-back 42.5 km route, with teams of six having to do battle with strong winds on what is a mainly flat parcours.

Two days later, the same teams line up in Vårgårda for the road race – twelve laps of an 11 km circuit around the town for 132 km in total, with a major climb out on the circuit, and a short, sharp rise out of the town itself to keep everyone on their toes.

Statistics
Location
Vårgårda
Distance
132 km/82 miles
(road race)
42.5 km/26.4 miles
(TTT) (2012)
Terrain
Tarmac
First event
2006 (TTT 2008)
Website
www.
worldcupvargarda.se
Contact
info@
worldcupvargarda.se

Marianne Vos won the race in 2011

Vuelta a España
Spain

Pro stage race

Spain's national tour, and the world's third
biggest stage race

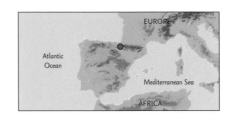

The Tour of Spain – or the Vuelta a España
– is cycling's third biggest stage race after
the Tour de France and the Giro d'Italia, with
the triumvirate of three-week races making
up the sport's 'grand tours'.

Yet, the Vuelta sits very much in the shade
of its two older cousins – a certain lack of
confidence or sense of place somehow
missing from this event.

The three-week race used to take place
in April, but was moved to its current
August/September slot in 1995 as it was
considered to be too close on the calendar
to May's Giro. However, it now comes so
late in the season that there are relatively
few riders who target it as their number-one
goal as a result. Many riders are tired, but
those whose other objectives have fallen
by the wayside due to illness or injury,
plus riders who are targeting the world
championships at the end of September

or early October, will look to the Vuelta.
Few races like to be considered either a
consolation prize or a warm-up act for
another race, though.

For riders, spectators and journalists who
are fans of a late start – and who isn't? – and
a late finish, corresponding with Spain's
fondness for a late evening meal, the race
is perfect. In fact, there are more than a few
journalists who rate it as their favourite race
of the year thanks to the opportunity to
unwind in the evening and the later start the
next day.

Unlike a number of smaller Spanish races
that have fallen by the wayside in recent
years, the Vuelta's future seems assured. In a
bid to help it on its way, the race organisers,
Unipublic, are now supported by Tour de
France organisers ASO, who have helped to
beam the TV coverage to more countries
than ever.

Statistics

Location
Pamplona to Madrid
(2012)
Distance
3,300 km/2,049 miles
over 21 stages (2012)
Highest point
2,252 m (2012)
Terrain
Tarmac
Record wins
Tony Rominger (Swi),
Roberto Heras (Spa)
(both three wins)
Field size
198
First event
1935
Website
www.lavuelta.com
Contact
info@unipublic.es

Riders needing a big win often target the Vuelta

**The Vuelta is as hotly
contested as the Giro
and the Tour** ▶

Mount Washington Hill Climb USA

Road

A 7.6-mile hill climb up the famous New Hampshire mountain, with a sting in the tail

Just like July's Mount Evans Hill Climb in Colorado, the Mount Washington Hill Climb is a mass-start event, with the first rider to the top the winner. However, where Colorado's Mount Evans has the edge on height and is the much longer climb at 27.4 miles, Mount Washington is 7.6 miles long but offers gradients of up to 22 per cent, with an average of 12 per cent.

Three-time Mount Evans winner Tom Danielson has also won twice on Mount Washington, and holds the record time for both ascents, setting a time of 49 minutes 24 seconds on Mount Washington in 2002.

The road that winds its way up the mountain is called the Auto Road, and also hosts both a running race and a car race. Apart from the difficulty of the 'must do' cycling event, the fact that the Auto Road is a private road, and only open a few times a year, adds to the appeal.

The extreme weather sometimes experienced at the summit has required the race to be cancelled three times since it began in 1973, for the last time in 2007 when gale-force winds and freezing temperatures turned the August race into a wintry no-go zone. As a result, the race is always planned for a Saturday so that if weather conditions do conspire against the event, the Sunday can be used as a back up day to prevent disappointment.

In 2006, Newton's Revenge was created

– a July race following the same format as the original Mount Washington Hill Climb to help cater for the overspill of disappointed riders not getting a place in the 600-rider-limit August race.

Tom Danielson, record holder

Statistics

Location
Mount Washington, New Hampshire

Distance
12.2 km/7.6 miles (2012)

Highest point
1,917 m (2012)

Terrain
Tarmac

Record wins
Tyler Hamilton (USA) (four wins)

Field size
600

First event
1973

Website
www.mtwashington bicyclehillclimb.org

Contact
Via website

Mount Washington, New Hampshire ▶

Velofondo Vårgårda
Sweden
Road

A sportive held on the day between the two women's World Cup events in Vårgårda, Sweden

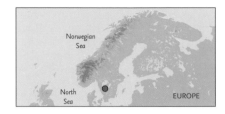

The two women's UCI World Cup events in Vårgårda might be girls only, but Velofondo Vårgårda, which takes place on the day in between, is a sportive that everyone can take part in, and the organisers really do want to attract every type of rider – experienced or otherwise – to take part in the 60 km version around Vårgårda, that features a couple of little climbs to keep things interesting.

The 140 km route is for the slightly more discerning, and those really wanting to go for it can compete with the elite riders up at the front end, but most of the competitors are there just for the challenge and to experience the stunning scenery of southwest Sweden. Then there's the party afterwards – and again, everyone's invited.

Statistics

Location
Vårgårda

Distance
140/60 km
87/37.3 miles (2012)

Terrain
Tarmac

Website
www.velofondo.se

Contact
vargardack@scf.se

Vårgårda

Fyen Rundt
Denmark
Road

Denmark's 'middle island' is your host for this relaxed and enjoyable sportive

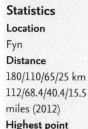

Fyn – or Funen in English; Fyen is the old Danish way to spell it – is Denmark's middle island, and this friendly but competitive sportive, first run in 1894, goes some way to proving that the little Scandinavian country is far from flat. The idyllic, quiet country roads on a warm summer's day are hard to beat, and apart from the extremely challenging full 180 km route, there are also 110 km, 65 km and 25 km options, so something for everyone, starting and finishing just west of the island's main city, Odense – birthplace of Hans Christian Andersen – where the post-race barbecue also takes place.

Statistics

Location
Fyn
Distance
180/110/65/25 km
112/68.4/40.4/15.5
miles (2012)
Highest point
118 m (2012)
Terrain
Tarmac
First event
1894
Website
http://fyenrundt.dk
Contact
fyen-rundt@
sporteventfyn.dk

Local team Capinordic compete in the 2009 event

Tre Valli Varesine
Italy

Pro one-day race

Head to Lombardy for the Trittico Lombardo 'summer Classics'

The Tre Valli Varesine is a one-day Italian semi-Classic based around Varese, in Lombardy, and is the first event in the Trittico Lombardo – the 'Lombardy Triptych', if you will – followed by the Coppa Ugo Agostoni the next day, and the Coppa Bernocchi on the third day.

"It's a little like the Tour of Mallorca," says journalist and Italian cycling expert Daniel Friebe. "Riders drop in or out for whichever races suit them – most do two, not all three – although there is an overall classification for the most consistent rider who rides all of them."

Along with races such as the now defunct Giro del Lazio, the Tre Valli Varesine, Agostoni and Bernocchi made up the once prestigious 'summer Classics', Friebe explains. "Riders would use them to hone their form for the world championships when they were held in August."

However, since the world championships moved from August to a later September/ October slot in the calendar, the summer Classics have lost a little of their importance. From a spectator's point of view, three consecutive days of top-notch Italian pro cycling in Lombardy – sunshine almost guaranteed – is an economical way to get your fix of race-watching, helped by the wealth of airports surrounding Milan, which is a quick and easy hop from the UK.

Statistics

Location
Varese
Distance
195 km/121 miles (2012)
Highest point
484 m (2012)
Terrain
Tarmac
Record wins
Gianni Motta (Ita), Giuseppe Saronni (Ita) (both four wins)
Field size
152
First event
1919
Website
www.trevalli varesine.com
Contact
Via website

Historic Varese hosts this once-prestigious race

Davide Rebellin won Varesine in 2011 ▶

Vattenfall Cyclassics
Germany

Pro one-day race

Germany's most prestigious one-day race, held
in Hamburg

The Vattenfall Cyclassics began life as
the HEW Cyclassics in 1996, and quickly
established itself on the cycling calendar
thanks to the popularity of the sport in
Germany following Jan Ullrich's Tour de
France victory in 1997. Ullrich also won
the Cyclassics that year, crowd-pleaser that
he was, although since then the race has
been very much the domain of the sprinters:
Erik Zabel, Johan Museeuw, Oscar Freire
and Robbie McEwen have all won here,
while it is US sprinter Tyler Farrar of the
Garmin team who holds the honour of the
record number of wins in Hamburg – which
stands at just two, demonstrating that the
crowd has seen a varied list of winners over
the years.

The race, which became the Vattenfall
Cyclassics in 2006, takes place on a circuit
based around Hamburg, and achieved UCI
World Cup status in 1998 following Ullrich's
victory, and subsequently became a ProTour
event when the season-long, elite-level
competition took over from the World Cup
in 2005. Today, it remains a round of what is
now called the WorldTour.

In the sportive version of the event,
22,000 members of the public get to take
part in a mass ride held on the morning
before the pro race.

Statistics
Location
Hamburg
Distance
246.7 km/153.3 miles
(2012)
Terrain
Tarmac
Record wins
Tyler Farrar (USA)
(two wins)
Field size
168
First event
1996
Website
www.vattenfall-
cyclassics.de
Contact
Via website

Edvald Boasson Hagen celebrates his victory in 2011

The Vattenfall
invariably ends
with a super-fast
sprint finish ▶

Vattenfall Cyclassics
(sportive) Germany
Road

Ride the professional course before the pros do,
then sit back and watch them do it faster!

This is how all sportives should be: a
huge festival of cycling – 22,000 riders in
all – taking to the roads, around Hamburg
in this case, for an enjoyable, safe, well
run event before being able to relax with
something to eat and drink and watch
the pros do their thing on the same course.
There are three distance options – 55 km,
100 km or 155 km – with all of them
covering the pro route, rather than just
the longer option, which can often be the
case with other sportives. Here, the shorter
distance covers the western loop of the pro
course, the middle distance the southern
loop of the course, while the longer distance
combines both.

Statistics

Location
Hamburg
Distance
155/100/55 km
96.3/62.1/34.2 miles
(2012)
Terrain
Tarmac
Field size
22,000
First event
1996
Website
www.vattenfall-
cyclassics.de
Contact
Via website

The Vattenfall is run with legendary German efficiency

Thousands of cyclists
ride the roads of the
pro event ▶

Haute Route
Switzerland and France

Long distance

It's mountains all the way from Geneva to Nice via the Alps' toughest climbs

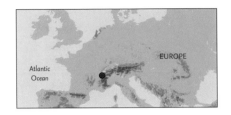

The Haute Route is the name given to a nineteenth-century mountaineering route in the Alps between Chamonix and Zermatt. Although both walkers and skiers still take on the classic route, the name has now also been adopted by the organisers of the self-styled 'hardest sportive in the world', which isn't far off the mark in its description.

Riders cover 780 km in seven days, and face nineteen climbs over the seven stages. All the classic climbs are there, from the Colombière to the Madeleine, the Glandon to the Izoard, and Alpe d'Huez – twice.

The first edition saw 300 riders from twenty-seven different countries take on the Haute Route in 2011, and that increased to 500 for the second edition in 2012. Everyone is timed on each of the stages, but it's up to the riders how hard they want to push themselves – not that it's possible to have an easy time due to the terrain.

In 2012, after starting in Geneva on day one, and plunging headlong into the mountains, the third stage took riders from Courchevel over the Madeleine and the Glandon before the tackling the twenty-one hairpin bends up to the finish on the mythical Alpe d'Huez. The next day was an individual time trial up Alpe d'Huez before finally leaving the famous climb behind on stage five – destination Col d'Izoard. Stage seven, on the final day, took in the Col de la Couillole, and then from the top of the Col de Vence it was a straight downhill run into Nice, where a beachside cold beer was the reward for everyone completing such a challenging event.

Statistics

Location
Geneva to Nice

Distance
780 km/484.7 miles over 7 stages (2012)

Highest point
2,802 m

Terrain
Tarmac

Field size
500

First event
2011

Website
www.hauteroute.org

Contact
julie@hauteroute.org

Alpe d'Huez is one of many classic climbs along the way

Col de la Couillole ▶

USA Pro Cycling Challenge
USA

Pro stage race

Colorado's premier stage race gives the Tour of California a run for its money as US top dog

Essentially a Tour of Colorado in all but name – it's a trademark issue – the USA Pro Cycling Challenge challenges a pro peloton with the biggest, baddest and best climbs in the state, with Durango, Crested Butte, Aspen, Boulder and state capital Denver all present and correct on the route of the 2012 edition.

The inaugural event in 2011 was won by the USA's Levi Leipheimer of the RadioShack team, by just 11 seconds from compatriot Christian Vande Velde (Garmin), and in fact the first five places were filled by American riders, all keen to perform on home ground in front of their adoring fans. Leipheimer – a three-time winner of the

Tour of California – described the crowds at the finish in Denver as the biggest he'd ever seen at a US cycling event.

"I don't know if I've ever raced in a place where the crowds have been so appreciative," added 2011 Tour de France champion Cadel Evans, who finished seventh overall in Denver. The Australian was no doubt tired after his efforts in July, but clearly there was boundless enthusiasm from the spectators – as well there might be at a race that not only welcomed Evans and the biggest American stars, but which also attracted Ivan Basso, the Schleck brothers, Robert Gesink and perennial crowd favourite Jens Voigt.

Statistics

Location
Durango to
Denver, Colorado
Distance
1,100 km/683 miles
over 7 stages (2012)
Terrain
Tarmac
Field size
136
First event
2011
Website
www.usaprocycling
challenge.com
Contact
info@usapro
cyclingchallenge.com

The peloton negotiates a tight turn in Denver

Frank Pipp rides
the prologue of
the 2011 event in
Colorado Springs ▶

Paris–Brest–Paris
France
Long distance

Such a long ride that it's only held once every four years

Paris–Brest–Paris is one of the world's oldest cycling events, having been run for the first time across the 600 km between Paris and the Breton city of Brest, and then back again, in 1891.

It began as an event for both professional and amateur riders, organised by Pierre Giffard to promote his newspaper, Le Petit Journal. It would be well over a decade later that journalist Géo Lefèvre would hit upon the idea of a race around the whole of France – a Tour de France – to promote Henri Desgrange's paper, L'Auto.

However, Giffard soon found that the first Paris–Brest–Paris was extremely difficult, and immediately decided that it should only be organised every ten years as a result.

By the 1931 event, the balance had swung very much in the 'tourist' riders' favour as 155 amateurs and only twenty-eight pro riders lined up – riding such a long event didn't do the pros much good when the majority of races had begun to be raced over distances more like we know them today.

These days, 'PBP' is a brevet, or randonnée – a style of event that existed way before the cyclosportive, and which is about being a good, strong, able cyclist, capable of going the distance, but not racing, working together with fellow cyclists and simply enjoying the ride for what it is.

It's a ride for riders looking for one of cycling's toughest challenges, and since 1975 the event has been held every four years, with participants' goal being to attempt to dip under the magic ninety hours completion time. Stories abound of exhaustion and toil, with some riders managing to get their heads down for a little kip in an inviting bus stop, or even catching forty winks simply at the side of the road.

Like all 'Paris to...' bike races these days, PBP has to start a little outside the French capital – in Saint-Quentin-en-Yvelines, 20 km southwest of Paris, but that changes very little: completing Paris–Brest–Paris still puts you in a very exclusive club indeed.

Statistics
Location
Paris to Brest and back
Distance
1,200 km/745.6 miles (2012)
Terrain
Tarmac
First event
1891
Website
www.paris-brest-paris.org
Contact
julien.bon@audax-club-parisien.com

Brest

The inaugural event ▶ was organised to promote a newspaper

Le Petit Journal

SUPPLÉMENT ILLUSTRÉ

TOUS LES VENDREDIS
Le Supplément Illustré
5 Centimes

Huit pages : CINQ centimes

TOUS LES JOURS
Le Petit Journal
5 Centimes

Deuxième Année   **SAMEDI 20 SEPTEMBRE 1891**   Numéro 44

M. CHARLES TERRONT

Vainqueur de la course nationale de Paris à Brest
organisée par le « Petit Journal »

Cyclo Morbihan
France
Road

Plouay's cyclosportive rides attract riders from far and wide to this cycling-mad Breton town

In Brittany, the popularity of cycling is right up there with the national obsession for football. Bernard Hinault, of course – arguably France's best-ever cyclist – was a Breton, and the search for his successor continues. A good place to start is August's Four Days of Plouay – a long weekend of cycling, both riding and racing, which includes the GP Ouest-France pro race. The Cyclo Morbihan is a series of rides on the Friday that includes mountain-bike routes and sportive distances of 117 or 161 km, plus more leisurely 'tourist' rides over the same distances, plus two shorter options over 60 and 91 km. There's something for everyone, then, and little excuse for British riders not to join in with their French cousins, who number more than 3,000 for the rides, thanks to Plouay's accessibility from the UK.

Statistics

Location
Plouay
Distance
161/117 km
100/72.7 miles (2012)
Terrain
Tarmac
Field size
3,500
First event
1986
Website
www.grandprix-plouay.com
Contact
comiteplouay@orange.fr

The department of Morbihan is rural and pretty

Kongeetapen
Denmark
Road

The Tour of Denmark's hardest stage makes for a great sportive event – and it's far from flat

The Kongeetape, meaning 'king stage' – although more often than not a race's toughest stage is known as the 'queen stage' in English – is the Tour of Denmark's hardest, which in the 2012 edition took the pro peloton over the short but very sharp climb of Kiddesvej in Vejle, Jutland, on stage three from Silkeborg.

The term is borrowed as the name of the Tour of Denmark's sportive event, which covers the route of stage three just ahead of the pros. Kiddesvej might only be 350 m long, but with maximum gradients of 21 per cent, coming after 170 km of undulating roads, it's the kind of climb where riders have to truly dig deep to avoid the ignominy of having to put their foot down and walk. The same goes for the pros, too.

Statistics
Location
Silkeborg to Vejle
Distance
170 km/105.6 miles (2012)
Terrain
Tarmac
Field size
1,000
First event
2009
Website
www.kongeetapen.dk
Contact
skov_haderslev@ tdcadsl.dk

Silkeborg

Le Mans 24 Heures Vélo
France
Long distance

A long day in the saddle... unless you've got team-mates!

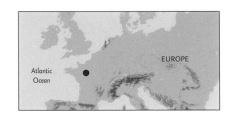

It's a race against time at this 24-hour event ridden on the famous Le Mans circuit. There's even a Le Mans-style start, with hundreds of riders in slippery cleats running to their bikes. From there, it's a case of changeovers in the pit lane for teams and pairs, and a relentless plodding on for the brave souls riding as individuals. It's up to you, of course, how often you stop or swap with your team-mates, but there's a campsite for setting up your tent and getting a bit of sleep between rides, while those doing the night shift are well lit up thanks to the floodlit track. Other than the main goal of trying to record as many laps of the circuit as possible, there's also a 'best lap' prize for those who are feeling particularly fast having just come back from a sleep.

Statistics

Location
Le Mans motor circuit

Distance
Laps of a 4.2 km/
2.6 mile circuit

Highest point
81 m

Terrain
Tarmac

Field size
2,000
(400 teams of five)

First event
2009

Website
www.24heures
velo.fr/en

Contact
Via website

World-famous Le Mans circuit

Glenurquhart Highland Games cycling events
United Kingdom
Track

Track racing – Highland Games style!

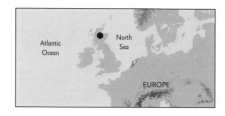

Glenurquhart is a glen, or small valley, running from Loch Ness to the village of Drumnadrochit, where the Games take place. On the western edge of Loch Ness, the village attracts the tourists looking for a sight of the monster, but in late August it's the Glenurquhart Highland Games that people come for, and Nessie has to take a back seat. All sorts of throwing and running events are included, while the cycling takes place on a flat grass track where there are short, fast races over 800, 1,500 and 3,000 m. Then there's arguably everyone's favourite track cycling event, the Devil Take the Hindmost – or, as it is in Scotland, the De'il Tak the Hindmost – where the last rider in the line each lap is eliminated from the race until just two riders remain to duke it out for victory.

Statistics

Location
Drumnadrochit, Loch Ness, Scottish Highlands
Distance
Different distances up to 3,000 m (2012)
Terrain
Grass track
First event
1945
Website
www.glenurquhart-highland-games.co.uk
Contact
info@glenurquhart-highland-gathering.co.uk

The peaceful village of Drumnadrochit sees annual cycling craziness

Gruyère Cycling Tour
Switzerland
Road

Cheesy grins all round for this Swiss sportive

La Gruyère is a picture-postcard town in the west of Switzerland – and yes, it is the place famous for its cheese: a hard Swiss cheese, which works perfectly in a fondue…

The sportive began life in 1996 to celebrate the seventy-fifth anniversary of neighbouring town Bulle's cycling club, La Pédale Bulloise, which was a great success, welcoming 500 riders. However, having called it the Classic du 75ème Anniversaire, the organisers wanted a 'name' to give to the event, both to attract even more riders and to avoid adding a year to the event title each time.

So in came Swiss pro and 1996 Olympic road race champion Pascal Richard, and the Classic Pascal Richard was born. He stayed involved until 2007, when the event became the Gruyère Cycling Tour.

In 2011, the sportive had 1,800 riders lining up in Bulle, and for 2012 the running of the event – at which riders can choose between a 125 km or 85 km route – was taken over by Chassot Concept, organisers of the Tour of Romandy pro stage race.

Statistics

Location
Bulle

Distance
125/85 km
77.7/52.8 miles (2012)

Terrain
Tarmac

Field size
1,800

First event
1996

Website
www.gruyere-cycling-tour.ch

Contact
info@sports-evenements.ch

Gruyère

GP Ouest-France
France
Pro one-day race

Top-class racing on a spectator-friendly circuit around Plouay

Atlantic
Ocean

EUROPE

Bretons love their cycling, and there's no exception when it comes to their enjoyment of the GP Ouest-France in the small town of Plouay. People come from far and wide, often in their camper vans, which litter the race route, to enjoy the annual festival of cycling there each August over a long weekend. A sportive event, the Cyclo Morbihan, takes place on the Friday before the racing starts with the amateur race, the GP de Plouay, on the Saturday morning, and continues with the women's World Cup race that afternoon, with the pro men's race on the Sunday.

"There's a real festival atmosphere, and the crowds just keep building throughout the weekend," says Dan Kogan, an elite amateur rider with the British Twenty3c-Orbea team, who spent the 2011 season living and racing near Plouay, and rode the amateur event. "Even the amateur race is a big deal – an event everyone wants to win in front of such big crowds – and the race blows apart. The area looks flat, but the course is deceptively hilly."

All the racing takes place on a road circuit around the area, and it's an enjoyable weekend of racing that's easily accessible for British cycling fans.

In recent years, Kogan explains, local spectators would walk the circuit during the pro race, catching sight of local heroes such as Thomas Voeckler multiple times in different places, but for 2012, the men's pro race and the women's race used a new, longer 27 km circuit, putting paid to all but the most ardent walking fan's efforts, while the amateur race used a 14 km circuit.

Statistics

Location
Plouay

Distance
195 km/121.2 miles (2012)

Terrain
Tarmac

Record wins
Philippe Bobo (Fra),
Armand Audaire (Fra),
Emile Guérinel (Fra),
Fernand Picot (Fra),
Jean Jourden (Fra),
Jacques Bossis (Fra),
Gilbert Duclos-Lassalle
(Fra) (all two wins)

Field size
192

First event
1931

Website
www.grandprix-plouay.com

Contact
comiteplouay@orange.fr

World champion Thor Hushovd rode the 2011 event

Thomas Voeckler is a favourite with the home crowd ▶

Tour de l'Avenir

France

Pro stage race

A race where future Tour de France stars are moulded

The Tour de l'Avenir – the 'Tour of the Future' – first saw the light of day in 1961, and was the brainchild of the L'Equipe newspaper's editor Jacques Marchand. His idea was to have a race similar to the Tour de France where nations that didn't have any professional trade teams could bring their riders, and at first it was open only to amateur riders on national squads. During the Eighties it changed to allow pro teams, although still with a strong focus on youth, which then became its raison d'être, allowing only riders under the age of 25. Later, the age limit dropped to under 23, and it reverted to national squads once more.

Star names such as Greg LeMond, Laurent Fignon and Miguel Indurain all won while on their way up, and more recent winners include Lars Bak and Bauke Mollema, proving themselves on diverse routes based mainly around the French Alps that distil a Tour de France's worth of sprinting, climbing and time trialling into one week, with the same yellow, green and polka-dot jerseys giving wide-eyed young riders a chance to experience what might be to come in their future careers – if they play their cards right.

Bauke Mollema

Statistics

Location
Dole to Le Grand Bornand
Distance
835.7 km/519.3 miles over 7 stages (2012)
Highest point
1,993 m (2012)
Terrain
Tarmac
Record wins
Serguei Soukhoroutchenkov (Rus) (two wins)
Field size
108
First event
1961
Website
www.letour.fr
Contact
cyclisme@aso.fr

Denmark's Lars Bak ▶

La Granfondo Les Deux Alpes France

Road

Mythical Tour climbs to conquer at this late-summer Alpine sportive

As the organisers put it, this is a sportive to celebrate the end of summer, although hopefully that's not quite the end of it already in late August. The famous ski resort of Les Deux Alpes – France's second oldest after Chamonix – is the start and finish point for both the 164 km 'Master' distance, which also crosses the Col de Parquetout and the Alpe du Grand Serre, and the 65 km 'Senior' distance which takes an easier route via Bourg d'Oisans before looping back to tackle the finish up to Les Deux Alpes.

The climb up to the ski resort will always be remembered as the climb on the rain-soaked fifteenth stage of the 1998 Tour de France where Italy's Marco Pantani won the race, first attacking Jan Ullrich on the Col du Galibier, and then extending his lead on the climb up to the finish at Les Deux Alpes, beating the German by nine minutes on the line. From there, Pantani never let go of yellow again.

Statistics

Location
Les Deux Alpes

Distance
164/65 km
101.9/40.4 miles (2012)

Highest point
1,650 m (2012)

Terrain
Tarmac

Website
www.sport
communication.info

Contact
Via website

The climbs around Les Deux Alpes await the Granfondo participants

Sean Kelly Tour of Waterford Ireland

Road

Ride with 'King Kelly' at this sportive based around the Irish hero's home town

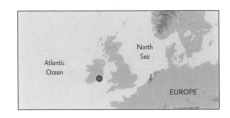

Arguably Ireland's greatest-ever cyclist, Sean Kelly – and it would be Stephen Roche who would quite rightly be arguing – lends his name to the Tour of Waterford sportive. Kelly was born in Waterford in 1956, and would go on to become one of the greatest cyclists of all time, never mind Ireland, winning Paris–Roubaix twice, the green jersey at the Tour de France four times, and the overall Tour of Spain title in 1988.

The Tour of Waterford offers sportive distances over 50 or 160 km, while the Kelly Heritage 100 km ride was added for 2012, exploring west Waterford, on many of the same roads Kelly himself trained on as a youngster.

There's also a 10 km family ride the day before the sportives, open to all aged seven and above.

Statistics

Location
County Waterford
Distance
160/100/50 km
99.4/62.1/31.1 miles
(2012)
Terrain
Tarmac
Field size
4,500
First event
2007
Website
www.itsafeeling.com
Contact
kphelan@waterford
sportspartnership.ie

In the wheeltracks of the great Sean Kelly

'Kelly country' attracts thousands of cyclists every year ▶

Ötztaler Radmarathon
Austria
Road

A mountainous Austrian adventure through the North Tyrol and Italy's South Tyrol

The four climbs faced on the 238 km route of the Ötztaler Radmarathon certainly aren't for shrinking violets; this is one tough route, and considered by some to be one of the hardest sportives in the world.

From the start in Sölden you can enjoy a descent until the start of the day's first climb, the Kühtai – 18.5 km with a horribly high maximum gradient of 18 per cent. Heading south, and having entered Italy's South Tyrol region via the long but gradual Brennerpass, riders loop southwest and over the Jaufenpass. The route back into the North Tyrol and Austria is via the Timmelsjoch – and the organisers have saved the best till last. The climb gets considerably steeper as it goes on, 29 km long and maxing out at 14 per cent, which is quite enough by this stage of the ride. From there, though, bar one little blip, it's a downhill run all the way back to Sölden.

Statistics

Location
Sölden
Distance
238 km/147.9 miles (2012)
Terrain
Tarmac
Field size
5,000
First event
1982
Website
www.oetztaler-radmarathon.com
Contact
radmarathon@oetztal.com

Dare to to take on the giddying Timmelsjoch?

Settimana Ciclistica Lombarda Italy

Pro stage race

A hilly, week-long Italian stage race around Bergamo

Lombardy is a hotbed of cycling, and there are a number of races in the region as a result. However, when they all seem to use 'Lombardy' in their title, it's easy to get confused as to which is which.

The Settimana Ciclistica Lombarda is a week-long stage race in the hills and valleys around Bergamo, but is not to be confused with either 'Lombardy Week' – the unofficial build-up to the Tour of Lombardy – or the Trittico Lombardo series of one-day semi-Classics.

Before jumping on the 'Lombarda' bandwagon, it used to be known as the Settimana Bergamasca, and was the scene of Lance Armstrong's first European stage-race win in 1991 while riding for the small Subaru-Montgomery squad.

Statistics

Location
Bergamo, Lombardy
Distance
685.8 km/426.1 miles over 4 stages (2011)
Terrain
Tarmac
Record wins
Pavel Tonkov (Rus) (three wins)
First event
1970
Website
www.settimana ciclisticalombarda.it
Contact
grupposportivo domus@libero.it

Bergamo's hillsides host the race

Twinings Pro-Am Tour Saturday Sportives
United Kingdom
Road

Test yourself on the hills around Salisbury

Twinings – yes, the tea people – sponsor this new weekend of cycling, with a Premier Calendar pro race on the Sunday, and a series of rides on the Saturday. Saturday's main event is the sportive, and there's a choice of 60 or a 100 miles. The 60-mile route takes in the Avon Valley and Salisbury Plain, and goes as far as Andover – home of Twinings, where there's a tea stop to recharge before the 30 miles home. The 100-mile sportive follows the same outward 30-mile route, but then heads north as far as Hungerford and Marlborough before the southern stretch back to Salisbury.

There's also the Twinings Pro-Am Tour Corporate Challenge, in which four colleagues ride the 100-mile sportive on Saturday, and then on Sunday morning ride a team time trial with their work-mates in Salisbury city centre – and the winning team gets to ride in a VIP car during the afternoon's pro race.

Tea-time in Salisbury

Statistics

Location
Salisbury

Distance
160.1/96.6 km
100/60 miles (2012)

Terrain
Tarmac

Field size
100

First event
2011

Website
www.twiningstour.com

Contact
info@twinings
tour.com

Twinings Pro-Am Tour
Pro Race United Kingdom

Pro one-day race

See the top British teams in action in the newest Premier Calendar race

The Twinings Pro-Am Tour cycling weekend was a new-for-2011 event consisting of a Saturday dedicated to family rides and sportives, and a Sunday for the pro race, which is part of the British Premier Calendar series. Wilton, near Salisbury, is the race base, and used for both the start and finish. The race takes the riders out on two loops of the Wiltshire countryside – first four laps of a hilly 17-mile circuit, out towards Fovant and the famous Fovant Badges – the huge regimental badges cut into the chalk at Fovant Down – and then six shorter, flatter loops of a circuit around Wilton town centre. All the major UK teams take part, including Endura Racing and Rapha Condor Sharp, and the race has quickly established itself as one of the Premier Calendar's showcase events.

Statistics

Location
Salisbury
Distance
162.5 km/101 miles
(2012)
Terrain
Tarmac
First event
2011
Website
www.twiningstour.com
Contact
info@twinings
tour.com

Fovant Badges, Wiltshire

Tour of Denmark
Denmark
Pro stage race

Scandinavia's premier stage race that attracts top stars directly from the Tour de France

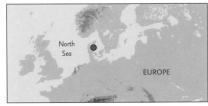

The Tour of Denmark attracts the country's biggest stars, as well as a number of big names in flying form straight from the Tour de France, although the 2012 edition started in late August to ensure as strong a field as ever as many riders were heading to the Olympic Games during the Tour of Denmark's usual early August slot.

New-for-2012 Australian team GreenEdge's Simon Gerrans was one of those who came to the race in 2011 from the Tour de France and used his fitness to win the race for his then team, Sky.

"I just hit some really good form, and went well on what are shorter climbs in Denmark, and did well in the short time trial," says Gerrans. "It's just a great race, and there's a lot of enthusiasm for it, as there aren't that many big pro events in Scandinavia."

The six-stage race normally starts in Jutland, in the west of Denmark, that borders Germany, with Randers the start town in 2012. It then makes its way across the middle island, Fyn, with the traditional mid-race time trial often taking place there, before heading to the eastern island of Sjaelland and Copenhagen. The final stage in the centre of the capital, in particular, brings out huge crowds thanks to its spectator-friendly finishing circuit.

Statistics

Location
Randers to Frederiksberg, Copenhagen (2012)

Distance
864.5 km/537.2 miles over 6 stages (2012)

Terrain
Tarmac

Record wins
Jakob Fuglsang (Den) (three wins)

Field size
120

First event
1985

Website
www.postdanmark rundt.dk

Contact
cyclingworld@ cyclingworld.dk

Simon Gerrans celebrates his overall win in 2011

The peloton races ▶ through Copenhagen

World Ports Classic
Netherlands and Belgium

Pro stage race

The Netherlands and Belgium united by sport in this brand new pro cycling event

New for 2012, but destined to become a classic race in its own right, the World Ports Classic brings together two of the world's greatest sea ports – Rotterdam and Antwerp – and at the same time unites two of cycling's greatest nations in the Netherlands and Belgium.

Rotterdam's Tour de France Grand Départ in 2010 was a great success, and it was during its planning that the idea for the new event was conceived. Likewise, Tour owners ASO are the organisers behind the new two-day race.

The World Ports Classic brings back top-level racing to the Rotterdam area, while Antwerp is no stranger to cycling, or sport in general, having hosted the 1920 Olympic Games, while Tom Boonen hails from nearby Mol.

Strong men like Boonen will feel at home, too, as equally strong sea breezes are likely to characterise the new race, passing from Holland to Belgium on day one, and then back again on the second day, with the most consistent rider crowned king of the two ports.

North Sea

EUROPE

Statistics

Location
Rotterdam to Antwerp and back
Distance
362.5 km/225.2 miles over 2 stages (2012)
Terrain
Tarmac
First event
2012
Website
www.letour.fr
Contact
cyclisme@aso.fr

Antwerp, Belgium

Port of Rotterdam, Netherlands ▶

Verbier–La Romandie Classic Switzerland

Road

Get the pro experience at this sportive organised by the team behind the Tour of Romandy

With 5 km left to go, Alberto Contador's attack on the climb up to Verbier set the 2009 Tour de France alight, dropping the likes of Andy Schleck, Bradley Wiggins and, perhaps most importantly, dropping his Astana team-mate Lance Armstrong. It left little doubt as to who the squad's main man was, and the Spaniard held the yellow jersey all the way to Paris to take his second Tour title.

Contador's career took something of a nosedive later when, following the 2010 Tour, which he also won, he tested positive and had that year's victory annulled. However, the organisers of the Tour of Romandy stage race, who also organise this sportive, are clearly very proud of the action on the road to Verbier that day in 2009, and offer participants the chance to recreate it themselves, with times on the final climb recorded so that riders can measure themselves against the pros.

For those wanting to enjoy the riding in this scenic and pretty part of Switzerland without the stress and strain of the final climb, it's possible to end your ride after 70 km – instead of 78 km – at Le Châble and take the cable car up to the top, and still join in the pasta party put on at the finish. The rides start in Aigle at cycling governing body UCI's headquarters.

Statistics

Location
Verbier

Distance
78 km/48.5 miles (2012)

Highest point
1,490 m (2012)

Terrain
Tarmac

Website
www.tourde
romandie.ch/classic

Contact
info@tourde
romandie.ch

The ride begins at Aigle

Participants finish on a high at Verbier, 1,500 m ▶

La Cyclo'Manche
France
Road

A scenice route through French countryside that's easy to reach from the UK

La Cyclo'Manche starts and finishes in the Normandy town of Sainte-Mère-Eglise, site of some of the fiercest D-Day fighting in the Second World War and featuring in The Longest Day, starring Richard Burton. Both the area's history and proximity to the UK, just across la Manche – the Channel – means that this is a no-brainer for British riders wanting to easily access the experience of a full-on French sportive, with Cherbourg barely a 40-km drive away. Distance options are 184 km, 133 km or 50 km, and although the area's not flat, there's nothing too brutal to distract from an enjoyable day on the bike in a beautiful area of France that is truly a hidden gem.

Statistics

Location
Normandy
Distance
184/133/50 km
114.3/82.6/31.1 miles
(2012)
Highest point
159 m (2012)
Terrain
Tarmac
Website
www.sport
communication.com
Contact
Via website

The memorial to paratrooper John Steele hangs from the church tower in Sainte-Mère-Eglise

La Ronde Picarde
France
Road

Pretty Picardy by bike in a French sportive that's
popular with Brits

La Ronde Picarde is another French sportive
that is easily accessible for riders from the
UK, with the start town of Abbeville a 60-km
drive east from Dieppe, or 100 km down
from Calais. Abbeville, in Picardy – a town
virtually flattened by German bombs during
the Second World War – sets riders out on
a choice of an undulating 185 km 'Master'

route, the 131 km 'Senior' or the 53 km
'Maritime', which, despite its name, actually
takes riders inland, unlike the other two
rides, which head for the coast. The circular
routes all come back to Eaucourt, only just
outside Abbeville, where a pasta party awaits,
which will fuel you for the kilometre or so
back to your car and your easy trip home.

Statistics
Location
Abbeville, Picardy
Distance
185/131/53 km
115/81.4/32.9 miles
(2012)
Highest point
156 m (2012)
Terrain
Tarmac
Website
www.sport
communication.com
Contact
Via website

All routes start from Abbeville

Giro di San Francisco
USA

Road

Top-notch criterium racing in the very heart of
San Francisco

The City by the Bay, San Francisco, plays
host to North America's top pro teams and
amateur racers of all abilities in a series of
different criterium races, from category-five
men to kids' races, to elite women to the
main event, which pits the pros against first-
and second-category racers on the 0.75-mile
circuit. The race was first run in 1975, and
the 1978 edition even included a descent of
San Fran's famously wiggly Lombard Street.
Today's circuit is just a stone's throw away
from the eastern end of Lombard Street,
based around Levi Strauss Plaza and the
eastern end of Union Street.

Riders charge through the Golden Gate city

Statistics

Location
San Francisco

Distance
Laps of a 1.2 km/
0.75mile circuit

Terrain
Tarmac

Record wins
Men: Greg LeMond
(USA) (two wins);
Women: Melody Wong
(USA) (three wins)

First event
1975

Website
www.metromint
cycling.com

Contact
Via website

**San Francisco has
some of the world's
steepest streets** ▶

Alpine Challenge
France
Long distance

Closed roads, tough climbs and an overall classification makes you feel like a pro in this sportive around Annecy

HotChillee is the company behind the 'London to Paris' ride, which was first run in 2003. Over the years, it's grown to become the must-ride event it is today, turning swathes of people away once its 450 spots have been filled. The first Alpine Challenge, in 2010, grew out of that demand, as well as from feedback from 'L2P' riders ready for an even tougher challenge. Numbers are still kept down – there were 230 places in 2012 – but that allows for the riders and the organisers to all fit into a couple of hotels in central Annecy, France, eating together and getting to know one another, and creating that authentic pro atmosphere that the event tries to foster, with massage available each evening, and general classification print-outs handed out at the dinner table.

Out on the road, the timed first stage sorts riders into ability groups, and from there it's game on, with timed climbing sections on the next three stages, while riders enjoy each other's company in between trying to beat each other. The top group is fast, while even the slow group requires a high level of fitness due to the tough climbs around the Annecy area.

The rolling road closures, thanks to the skilled motorbike outriders, who are a constant presence, allow riders to concentrate solely on their cycling, while another pro touch is the mechanics who will take care of post-ride problems, while you relax on the massage table, or at the bar with a beer.

Despite being so well looked after, it's a tough few days on the bike, but the bonus is the breathtaking scenery. Lake Annecy provides a stunning backdrop to every stage, while also offering the chance of an early-morning swim or, even better, a post-ride dip each day to help soothe aching muscles.

Statistics

Location
Annecy
Distance
323.5 km over 4 stages (2011)
Terrain
Tarmac
Field size
230
First event
2010
Website
www.thealpine challenge.com
Contact
Via website

Participants relax at beautiful Lake Annecy

Riders make their way around Annecy, including Stephen Roche (right) ▶

Grand Prix Cycliste de Québec Canada

Pro one-day race

The first of two Canadian grands prix, which form part of the UCI's WorldTour circuit

The Grand Prix Cycliste de Québec and its cousin in Montreal, two days later, are two new races that were introduced in 2010, coming in at cycling body the UCI's highest level of race ranking, WorldTour, to help the continued growth of bike racing internationally – or 'mondialisation' as it tends to be called. The races' high-quality organisation, enthusiastic crowds and top-notch hotels help keep the sport's best riders happy and motivated as they head towards the end of the season.

The Quebec City race is held in the heart of the old town, on a hilly 12.6 km circuit beside the city's famous St Lawrence River. Riders cover the circuit 16 times, for a total distance of just over 200 km, making it almost unbeatable for spectators.

Both races are particularly well loved by the pro riders, not only for the opportunity to spend a little time in the stunning cities they're held in, but also for the high-quality accommodation the organisers tend to provide. In Quebec, it's the amazing Fairmont Le Château Frontenac, which is as grand in reality as its name suggests. When you're an international jet-setting sports star, such things begin to matter...

Statistics

Location
Quebec

Distance
201.6 km/125.3 miles (2012)

Terrain
Tarmac

Field size
176

First event
2010

Website
http://gpcqm.ca

Contact
info@gpcqm.ca

Tight turns on the Québec circuit

Deloitte Ride Across Britain United Kingdom

Long distance

Land's End to John o' Groats with like-minded people and full support

Double Olympic gold-medal-winning rower turned adventurer James Cracknell and two friends are the brains behind the Deloitte Ride Across Britain. Riding from Land's End to John o' Groats was nothing new – they knew that – but they wanted their Ride Across Britain to be a mass ride during which participants could enjoy one another's company and the scenery, and not have to worry about carrying all their equipment with them, as most 'end-to-end-ers' are wont to do. The 960 miles, and 20,000 metres of climbing, are broken down into nine stages of relatively equal length, but if that sounds tough – and it is – the emphasis is nonetheless on enjoyment, and the most picturesque back roads have been chosen for the route rather then the most direct, busier roads.

Statistics

Location
Land's End to
John o' Groats

Distance
1,545 km/960 miles
(2012)

Terrain
Tarmac

Field size
700

First event
2010

Website
www.rideacross
britain.com

Contact
info@rideacross
britain.com

Olympic gold medallist James Cracknell is the man behind the ride

Still smiling after
960 miles ▶

Paris–Brussels
France and Belgium
Pro one-day race

Spanning two countries, this one-day race is one for the sprinters

Similarly to the Paris-Tours WorldTour race that comes the following month, Paris–Brussels is very much a race for the sprinters, despite the lumpy, cobbled climbs that are stacked up towards the end of the race.

The race starts some 80 km northeast of Paris, in Soissons, and finishes on the outskirts of Brussels. Having first been held in 1893, it's one of the oldest races in France. Australian sprinter Robbie McEwen, who

retired following the 2012 Tour of California, holds the record for the most number of wins, with five.

Rising Russian sprint star Denis Galimzyanov won the 2011 edition, but second placed Yauheni Hutarovich, of Belarus, might well make a claim for the race being his after Galimzyanov was caught, and admitted to, having taken EPO to improve his performances in an out-of-competition test in March 2012.

Statistics

Location
Soissons to Brussels
Distance
219.5 km/136.4 miles (2012)
Terrain
Tarmac
Record wins
Robbie McEwen (Aus) (five wins)
Field size
200
First event
1893
Website
www.paris-bruxelles.be
Contact
wim.vanherreweghe@flandersclassics.be

Denis Galimzyanov

Robbie McEwen holds the record for most victories, winning the event five times ▶

Stilettos on Wheels
United Kingdom

Mountain bike

Women-only mountain bike races, with a September race in Brighton and a May one in Derbyshire

'Stilettos on Wheels' may not sound that comfortable, but it's in fact the name of the UK's first women-only mountain-bike races – a series of two – based on circuits that riders must complete as many laps of as possible in a choice of either a two- or four-hour event. You can enter as either a solo rider – simply riding as many laps as possible in the allotted time – or in pairs, which means one rider out on the course at a time, sharing the load with a relay changeover in the pit area each lap or so. The Brighton course uses much of the route of the now-famous Brighton Big Dog MTB race, in Stanmer Park, while Birchall, in Derbyshire, is the venue for the other race.

Statistics

Location
Brighton

Distance
As many laps as possible in two or four hours on a 4.2 km/2.6 mile circuit (2012)

Terrain
Off-road

First event
2012

Website
http://stilettoson wheels.com

Contact
info@stilettoson wheels.com

The rolling hills of Stanmer Park host the event

La Lucien Aimar
France
Road

A sportive in the south of France held in honour of the 1966 Tour de France winner

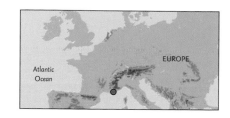

This sportive honours 1966 Tour de France champion and now Tour of the Mediterranean organiser Lucien Aimar. The start and finish town is Aimar's birthplace, Hyères, just east of the port of Toulon, where Aimar takes his Tour of the Med up the Mont Faron each year.

There are three distance choices – 61 km, 93 km or 145 km – all 'out and back' inland into the jaw dropping Massif des Maures, a huge expanse of virtually unspoiled rolling hills and forest that stretches to Fré, 100 km east along the coast past the rather more populated Saint Tropez. The longer version takes riders over the Col de Notre Dame des Anges – a tough climb that Aimar often also includes on the route of the Tour of the Med pro race.

Statistics

Location
Hyères
Distance
145/93/61 km
90/57.8/37.9 miles
(2012)
Highest point
710 m (2012)
Terrain
Tarmac
Website
http://letourmed.fr
Contact
occostebelle@
wanadoo.fr

Hyères

Tour of Britain
United Kingdom

Pro stage race

The 'British Tour de France' welcomes the world's
top pro teams to UK shores

In its current guise, the Tour of Britain
has been running since 2004, when it
was resurrected with a model of using
local authorities and a number of smaller
sponsors to support the race, rather than
relying on a headline sponsor who would
shoulder most of the responsibility, but
who could potentially pull out and leave
the event high and dry, as had happened
in the past.

Its precursor, the PruTour, survived for
just two editions, between 1998 and 1999,
while until 1994 the much-loved Kellogg's
Tour of Britain ran concurrently with the
arguably even better-loved Milk Race from
1987. The Milk Race was an amateur Tour

of Britain that had run since 1958 (and was
once ridden by Jimmy Savile), becoming
'pro-am' in 1985 before disappearing in 1993.
The Kellogg's Tour waved what was to be
only a temporary farewell to an enthusiastic
public the following year.

The 2004 Tour of Britain was held over
five days, but by 2012 had grown to become
an eight-day race. The 2012 route starts in
Ipswich and finishes in Guildford 1,350 km
later after visits to Nottingham, Dumfries,
Caerphilly and Dartmouth, avoiding a
finish in London, which will no doubt be
recovering from the Olympic Games, and
a major sporting event passing through
would be the last thing on its mind.

Statistics

Location
Ipswich to Guildford
(2012)
Distance
1,350 km/838.3 miles
over 8 stages (2012)
Terrain
Tarmac
Field size
96
First event
2004
Website
www.tourofbritain.com
Contact
peterh@thetour.co.uk

The British Tour showcases the UK's rolling landscape

A stage in central
London has been the
traditional finale ▶

Etape Cymru
Wales

Road

A fully closed-road sportive that takes on the climbs of North Wales

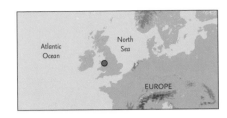

There might have been teething problems during the inaugural Etape Cymru in 2011, but even the Tour de France struggled in the beginning. Problems such as roads that were too narrow for so many riders, feed stations running out of water and traffic getting onto the closed-road event were all set to be addressed for the 2012 edition.

The route has been tweaked as a result, but wherever you look, there's stunning scenery. Horseshoe Pass is the North Wales route's main obstacle – more than 6 km in length, with sections at up to 20 per cent – with the start and finish of this 147 km sportive at Bangor-on-Dee racecourse, just outside Wrexham.

Statistics

Location
Wrexham, Wales (2012)

Distance
147 km/91.3 miles (2012)

Terrain
Tarmac

Field size
1,700

First event
2011

Website
www.etape-cymru.co.uk

Contact
info@participatesport.com

Horseshoe Pass

Riders negotiate narrow roads in 2011 ▶

Grand Prix Cycliste de Montréal Canada

Pro one-day race

The second of Canada's WorldTour Classics, held on a tough circuit in downtown Montreal

The Grand Prix Cycliste de Montréal is Canada's second grand prix after the first race in Quebec City two days earlier, and which are part of the UCI's WorldTour calendar. Like the Quebec race, the Montreal event is held on a very spectator-friendly circuit based on the University of Montreal on Mount Royal. The Côte Camilien-Houde – 1.8 km long with an average gradient of 8 per cent – is the main difficulty on the 12 km circuit, and although that's nothing compared to some of the mountains the pro riders face in Europe, it's on a course that never really flattens out, and has to be covered seventeen times for a distance total of 205 km, so repeated ascents quickly take their toll. It's an uphill drag to the finish, too, and it was here that Movistar's Rui Costa, of Portugal, outwitted Frenchman Pierrick Fédrigo to win the 2011 event, with Belgian Classics specialist Philippe Gilbert the best of the rest in third. The Netherlands' Robert Gesink, a specialist climber, had won the inaugural event in 2010, indicating just how tough a circuit it is.

Statistics

Location
Montreal

Distance
205.7 km/127.8 miles (2012)

Highest point
211 m (2012)

Terrain
Tarmac

Field size
176

First event
2010

Website
http://gpcqm.ca

Contact
info@gpcqm.ca

The peloton heads towards Old Port of Montreal

Rui Costa won in 2011, beating Philippe Gilbert (right) and Pierrick Fédrigo ▶

GP de Fourmies
France
Pro one-day race

Traditional French one-day race that tends to be one for the sprinters

The Grand Prix de Fourmies is a one-day race that has run every year since 1928, bar a few editions during the Second World War, and even then it did run in 1941 and 1943. Situated in the northern French town of Fourmies, right on the border with Belgium, it's no great surprise that French and Belgian riders dominate the list of past winners. However, it's also been a happy hunting ground for British riders on a couple of occasions, too, with Barry Hoban taking victory there in 1971, and Max Sciandri winning twice, in 1993 and 1995. However, only 1995 can really be claimed as a British win, as Sciandri was Italian in 1993 before becoming a British national – thanks to his mother – in early 1995.

Statistics
Location
Fourmies
Distance
200 km/124.3 miles
(2012)
Terrain
Tarmac
Record wins
Albert Barthelemy
(Fra),
Jean-Luc
Vandenbroucke (Bel)
(both three wins)
Field size
168
First event
1928
Website
www.grandprix
defourmies.com
Contact
gpf@mairie-
fourmies.fr

Jean-Luc Vandenbroucke has won the race a record three times

Southern Sportive
United Kingdom
Road

The South Downs are your stomping ground, with the introduction of a 'super' distance for 2012

The organisers of the Southern Sportive have added events such as the Wight Riviera Sportive, The Joker and the Great Western Sportive to their stable in recent years, but their original and best event remains the Southern Sportive, started in 2006. Although they promised they wouldn't ever mess with the 155 km classic route – and they haven't – for those looking for an even bigger challenge, 2012 heralded the introduction of the Wilier Gauntlet, a 192 km option that tacks on an extra 37 km loop and 2,500 feet of climbing to a route that already had 6,500 feet of climbing through the best hills the South Downs have to offer. In addition to the 'full' and 'super' routes, there's also the 112 km 'mid' route and the 71 km 'short' route, which still isn't that short, and far from flat.

Event headquarters for all distances is at Churcher's College in Petersfield, Hampshire.

Statistics

Location
Petersfield, Hampshire

Distance
192/155/112/71 km
119.2/96.3/69.6/44 miles
(2012)

Highest point
235 m

Terrain
Tarmac

First event
2006

Website
www.southernsportive.
com

Contact
info@southernsportive.
com

Petersfield, Hampshire

GP de Wallonie
Belgium
Pro one-day race

It's like spring Classics racing again as one-day riders refocus on the world champs

The Belgian spring Classics feel like a lifetime ago as the Grand Prix de Wallonie gets under way. This is Wallonia – French-speaking Belgium – this time, although the racing is very much the same as in nearby Flanders. The GP is often a key race for riders targeting the world championships road race, with a tough finishing climb up to the citadel in Namur. In 2011, Belgian champion Philippe Gilbert left the chasing pack in his wake as he demonstrated just how good he is at these Ardennes-style finishes. Despite many then naming him as one of the favourites for the upcoming world championships in Copenhagen, the Belgian's efforts were completely neutralised in Denmark by a British squad hell-bent on delivering Mark Cavendish to a world champ's title in a bunch sprint.

Statistics

Location
Chaudfontaine to Namur

Distance
203 km/126.1 miles (2011)

Terrain
Tarmac

Record wins
Adolf Braeckeveldt (Bel),
Nick Nuyens (Bel) (both three wins)

Field size
176

First event
1935

Website
www.trworg.be

Contact
info@trworg.be

Namur, the finish

Belgian Nick Nuyens is joint holder of the record for most wins ▶

Giant's Causeway Coast Sportive United Kingdom

Road

Northern Ireland's northern coast roads provide both the challenge and the scenery at this sportive

The northern coast of Northern Ireland provides the stunning backdrop for the Giant's Causeway Coast Sportive. There are three distance options: the 35-mile Causeway Coaster, on a relatively flat route, the 78-mile Glens and Coast Route or the 115-mile Giant Killers, with the principal difficulty in the two longer rides being the brutal Torr Head, although the medium option does offer a 'shortcut' option – an alternative section of the route that misses the climb out altogether. There's plenty of climbing, even on the shorter route, and some very steep descents, too, so care is needed, particularly in wet weather, which is a real possibility on the edge of the Irish Sea.

Ballycastle, in County Antrim, is the start and finish town for all distances, where competitors can enjoy swapping stories over a beer once it's all over.

Statistics

Location
Ballycastle, County Antrim, Northern Ireland

Distance
185.1/125.5/56.3 km
115/78/35 miles (2012)

Highest point
350 m (2012)

Terrain
Tarmac

Field size
1,000

First event
2011

Website
www.giantscauseway
coastsportive.com

Contact
info@cycleni.com

The route takes riders along Northern Ireland's rugged coastline

En route to Ballycastle for a well-deserved 'recovery' beer ▶

UCI/NRC Grand Prix
USA

Pro one-day race

The race formerly known as the Univest Grand Prix

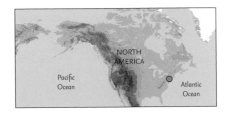

Known as the Univest Grand Prix since its beginnings in 1998, Univest, a banking and insurance group, has been a long-time supporter of the race and its sportive event, but has decided to concentrate its efforts on helping non-profit organisations struggling in the current economic climate for 2012. The race, however, will continue under the moniker the UCI/NRC Grand Prix, opening an action-packed weekend of cycling based around the town of Souderton, Pennsylvania. The 100-mile race, which sees the top North American teams take part, takes place on laps of two spectator-friendly circuits, and there's also a pro criterium in Doylestown the next day, which is only open to those who finish Saturday's Grand Prix.

Statistics

Location
Souderton and
Doylestown,
Pennsylvania
Distance
161 km/100 miles
(2012)
Terrain
Tarmac
Field size
132
First event
1998
Website
www.univest
grandprix.com
Contact
jde@spartacycling.com

The top US teams fight it out over 100 miles

UCI/NRC Grand Prix Cyclosportif USA

Road

Take on Pennsylvania's tough terrain ahead of the pros, with a choice of two distances

As part of what is a packed weekend of cycling, this sportive event – with a choice of a 100 km or 50 km route – kicks things off at 8 am on the Saturday, giving riders plenty of time to complete the circuit that takes on parts of the pro UCI/NRC Grand Prix race route before the pros get under way themselves. Downtown Souderton, Pennsylvania, is where it all starts and finishes, and your entry fee includes well-stocked feed zones out on the course, an event t-shirt and, perhaps most importantly of all, lunch provided at the end while you watch the pros gather for the main event.

Statistics

Location
Souderton, Pennsylvania

Distance
100/50 km
62.1/31.1 miles (2012)

Highest point
264 m (2012)

Terrain
Tarmac

Field size
1,500

Website
www.univest
grandprix.com

Contact
brian@sparta
cycling.com

Sauderton

Pisgah Stage Race
USA

Mountain bike

Off-road stage racing at its best over five days in North Carolina

The Pisgah National Forest in North Carolina is the stunning venue for this five-day mountain-bike stage race. Daily distances range between 25 and 43 miles, and these are ridden at full race pace; the organisers are at pains to stress that this is a race and not a sightseeing tour, but neither is it a survival trip, and there are food stops and mechanical assistance available on each stage. That's not to say that you can't enjoy the area, however, and no matter how fast you ride, you're going to appreciate the tough terrain and technical single-track. Take on the pros as an individual rider – although there are also age and ability categories – or buddy up as a duo team, with the clock stopping on the second man each stage, or compete as a relay team of two to five riders, taking it in turn to ride the stages.

Statistics

Location
Pisgah National Forest, North Carolina

Distance
313.8 km/195 miles over 5 stages (2012)

Terrain
Off-road

First event
2009

Website
www.blueridge adventures.net

Contact
info@blueridge adventures.net

The Pisgah National Forest boasts miles of single-track

Milan–Turin
Italy

Pro one-day race

Back on the calendar: Italy's oldest bike race

Italy's oldest bike race, first held in 1876, Milan–Turin returned in 2012 after five years away, having last been held in 2007 when Danilo Di Luca took top honours. The race has been pushed and pulled around the calendar, from being held in spring, prior to Milan–San Remo, to a late autumn slot and back again a few times. Now, it rests in the week between the world championships and the Tour of Lombardy. The race is also infamous for the 1995 incident when a vehicle got onto the course and crashed head-on into Marco Pantani, breaking his leg in multiple places, and forcing a long period of rehabilitation, with 'The Pirate' only returning to his best at the 1997 Tour de France.

Statistics

Location
Milan to Turin

Distance
199 km/123.7 miles (2012)

Terrain
Tarmac

Record wins
Costante Girardengo (Ita) (five wins)

First event
1876

Website
www.gazzetta.it/ Speciali/Minisiti_ Ciclismo/milano-torino

Contact
marketing.sport@rcs.it

Danilo Di Luca won the race in 2007

Rothaus RiderMan
Germany
Road

A three-stage sportive through Germany's Black Forest

The Black Forest in the deep south of Germany is the picturesque setting for this sportive, which in 2012 added a stage to become a three-day event and part of the German Cycling Cup series.

Day one consists of an individual time trial over 16 km of undulating terrain – taken very seriously indeed by the local fastmen, most of whom will roll down the start ramp on low-profile TT bikes.

Day two is a mass-start road ride that heads out from the event centre at Bad Dürrheim, a spa town and health resort, for an 81.5 km hilly circuit.

Day three's 86 km finale serves up more of the same, with over 1,000 metres of climbing.

At the end, find your place in the general classification – there are age group categories too – and celebrate (or commiserate) with a few bottles of the sponsor's excellent beer and a big plate of Bratwurst and sauerkraut.

Statistics

Location
Bad Dürrheim,
Black Forest

Distance
183.5 km/114 miles
over 3 stages (2012)

Highest point
896 m (2012)

Terrain
Tarmac

Climate
15 to 25°C

First event
2000

Website
www.riderman.de

Contact
Via website

The tough terrain of the Black Forest is no piece of cake

Giro del Piemonte
Italy

Pro one-day race

Piemonte is a last test for many riders ahead of the Tour of Lombardy

It's officially called the Gran Piemonte these days – yet another RCS-organised Italian race with a name change, like 'Il Lombardia' for the Tour of Lombardy – but the Giro del Piemonte does what it says on the tin: it's a tour of Piedmont, albeit one in a straight line. The start is in Piasco, and the finish comes 199 km later in Novi Ligure directly east. In 2012, it will take place the day after the revamped Milan–Turin and will be used to hone form for Il Lombardia just a few days later. In 2011, it was Katusha's Daniel Moreno who outsmarted Greg Van Avermaet (BMC) to win the sprint from a 14-man group.

Statistics

Location
Piedmont
Distance
199 km/123.7 miles
(2012)
Terrain
Tarmac
Record wins
Costante Girardengo
(Ita),
Aldo Bini (Ita),
Gino Bartali (Ita),
Fiorenzo Magni (Ita)
(all three wins)
Field size
144
First event
1906
Website
www.gazzetta.it/
Speciali/Giro
Piemonte/it
Contact
marketing.sport@rcs.it

Fiorenzo Magni and Costante Girardengo have won the race three times

Picturesque Piedmont plays host to the race▶

Il Lombardia
Italy

Pro one-day race

A race which heralds the winding-down of the pro season, that no one is slowing down for

The Giro di Lombardia – the Tour of Lombardy – might have officially been renamed Il Lombardia by organisers RCS, but old habits die hard when it comes to this, one of the oldest, toughest and most important one-day events on the Italian cycling calendar.

Traditionally, the race has signified the end of the European racing season, although for 2012 the race was moved a little forward in the calendar, and is now held in September, rather than October, to take advantage of riders' good form coming out of the world championships, which will have taken place just the week before.

The race remains based around Lake Como, while the main climb is the Ghisallo, these days the penultimate climb on the route. The course has changed frequently since the first edition back in 1905, with Como or Bergamo the usual finish towns, while the start has usually been in Milan. From 2011, Lecco, on the edge of Lake Como, became the new finish town, with Milan continuing as the start city. The sole British winner remains Tom Simpson, in 1965, while Irishman Sean Kelly is the only other English-speaking rider to have triumphed there, albeit three times, in 1983, 1985 and 1991. Otherwise, it's remained mainly the domain of the Italians, who have won on home soil sixty-seven times against Belgium's twelve.

Fausto Coppi holds the record for most wins, triumphing on five occasions

Statistics

Location
Milan to Lecco

Distance
241 km/149.8 miles (2012)

Highest point
1,340 m (2012)

Terrain
Tarmac

Record wins
Fausto Coppi (Ita) (five wins)

Field size
200

First event
1905

Website
www.gazzetta. it/Speciali/ GiroLombardia/en

Contact
marketing.sport@rcs.it

The route takes riders around the stunning Lake Como ▶

Duo Normand
France
Pro one-day race

'Two-up' time trialling in Normandy against the sport's top pro riders

The Duo Normand is a 'two-up' time trial where your two-man team shares the effort, with the clock stopping on the second rider. Where other events give you as close to the pro experience as possible, the Duo Normand doesn't even have to try: you really are racing against the pros. Okay, so there are separate categories – mixed pairs and corporate teams, for example – but everyone sets a time on the 54.3 km circuit, starting and finishing in Marigny, which is easily accessible from the Cherbourg ferry port.

You can even have a friend or family member drive behind you with a support car containing spare wheels or even a spare bike, but the best part of it is that you get a name plate for the front of the car with both riders' names on it. It doesn't get much more pro than that...

The race has had some big-name winners since its first edition in 1982, including Bradley Wiggins, Jonathan Vaughters and Filippo Pozzato, with a tidy prize purse, currently standing at €5,000, for any duo capable of beating the 1999-winning time set by Jens Voigt and Chris Boardman of 1 hour, 4 minutes and 47 seconds. Chris Boardman also won the 1993 edition, with Frenchman Laurent Bezault, and in 1996 took the win with fellow Brit Paul Manning.

Statistics

Location
Marigny, Normandy

Distance
54.3 km/33.7 miles
(2012)

Terrain
Tarmac

Record wins
Chris Boardman (Gbr)
(three wins)

First event
1982

Website
www.duonormand.
com

Contact
Via website

Paris–Roubaix hero Johan Vansummeren won in 2011 with Dutchman Thomas Dekker

Jens Voigt has set the fastest time along with Chris Boardman ▶

Giro del Lazio
Italy
Pro one-day race

Historic one-day race makes its return for 2012

The Giro del Lazio makes a welcome return to international cycling for 2012, having been cancelled in 2009 due to its proximity to the Memorial Cimmuri on the calendar, which was attracting the big teams and riders despite Lazio's long history as a fixture on the Italian circuit since 1933.

The more modern Memorial Cimmuri was subsequently cancelled in 2010, having only run since 2005 and, in 2012, the Giro del Lazio finally makes its return, albeit in a new September spot.

Past winners include Gino Bartali, Felice Gimondi and Roger De Vlaeminck while the last Lazio winner, Italian climber Francesco Masciarelli, today rides for the Kazakh Astana squad, and would have been hoping to return and defend the title he's held for the past four years.

Statistics

Location
Rieti to Nettuno (2012)
Distance
196 km/121.7 miles (2012)
Terrain
Tarmac
Record wins
Francesco Moser (Ita), Andrea Tafi (Ita) (both three wins)
First event
1933
Website
www.gazzetta.it/Speciali/Minisiti_Ciclismo/giro_lazio
Contact
marketing.sport@rcs.it

Andrea Tafi has triumphed a record three times

Hilly Lazio is perfect for cycle racing ▶

Levi's GranFondo
USA

Road

Ride with Levi Leipheimer in this spectacular Californian sportive

Having a gran fondo event named after you must mean that you've made it in the world of cycling, and there are few more deserving of such an accolade than American rider Levi Leipheimer. He virtually owns US cycling – arguably even more so than that other American rider – having won the Tour of California, the Tour of Utah, the USA Pro Cycling Challenge and the Tour of the Gila, and all that despite spending most of his time based in Europe.

Levi's GranFondo is in fact also known as the King Ridge Gran Fondo, taking in the heights of the brutal King's Ridge Road as it does – a favourite climb of Leipheimer's. The race starts and finishes in his home town of Santa Rosa, and follows a route out to

the Pacific, through the spectacular coastal mountains and back to Santa Rosa. Being on his doorstep, Levi himself takes part, and as a proud Californian he enjoys showing off his state to the thousands of keen amateurs who join him. If the full 103-mile distance sounds a little daunting, there's also a 65-mile 'medio' distance, which still takes you as far as the coast, but misses out King's Ridge, and a 'piccolo' route over 32 miles which stays closer to Santa Rosa, although still in spectacular countryside, making it an ideal introduction for beginners. Good luck getting in, though: the ride attracts thousands of riders each year, and spaces fill up very quickly, which isn't bad for an event that was only first held in 2009.

Statistics

Location
Santa Rosa, California
Distance
165.8/104.6/51.5 km
103/65/32 miles (2012)
Highest point
527.9 m (2012)
Terrain
Tarmac
Field size
7,500
First event
2009
Website
www.levisgranfondo.com
Contact
fish@bikemonkey.net

Thousands of riders prepare to start in Santa Rosa

Chase the shadow of Levi Leipheimer over California's best climbs ▶

Three Peaks Cyclo-Cross
United Kingdom
Cyclo-cross

The Yorkshire Dales host arguably the world's toughest cyclo-cross race

The three peaks of Ingleborough, Whernside and Pen-y-ghent are the principle challenges in the annual Three Peaks Cyclo-Cross that takes place in the Yorkshire Dales.

The race distance has increased over the years to the 61 km it is today, well up from the 40 km of the first event in 1961. There have been various rule changes, too, such as the required exclusive use of cyclo-cross bikes today, whereas in years past riders would switch to road bikes for the on-road sections of the course. Competitors can still change bikes and receive spares and assistance, but the race wishes to remain very much a cyclo-cross event.

Statistics

Location
Helwith Bridge, Yorkshire Dales

Distance
61 km/37.9 miles (2012)

Highest point
736 m (2012)

Terrain
Road, tracks, paths, steep mountain climbs and descents

Record wins
Rob Jebb (Gbr) (eight wins)

Field size
600

First event
1961

Website
www.3peakscyclocross.org.uk

Contact
john3peaks@hotmail.com

Ingleborough is too steep to ride

Britain's Rob Jebb holds the record number of wins with eight, with his winning streak between 2000 and 2008, broken only when the race was cancelled in both 2001 and 2007 due to outbreaks of foot and mouth. Jebb took his eighth title in 2010, but in recent years has been challenged by Nineties mountain bike star Nick Craig, who first won the Three Peaks back in 1991, but has held back the hands of time by winning again in 2009 and 2011. Louise Robinson holds the women's record with five wins.

"Rob Jebb and Nick Craig both have very different approaches to the race," says Simon Scarsbrook of the Mosquito RT squad, and a veteran of 14 Three Peaks races. "Rob has people all over the course with spare bikes and wheels, whereas Nick just has one bike and is very self-sufficient."

Rob Jebb's name is ▲ on the winner's list a record eight times

Scarsbrook used his cross-country running fitness to good effect at his first Three Peaks in 1986, he says. "But as I've got older, I've trained for the race a bit more specifically."

Despite it being a bike race, the walking/running side of the race is not to be underestimated. Scarsbrook's cyclo-cross training includes step-ups on his wall in the garden, with his bike on his back. Then, he and a colleague realised that the 20 floors of the building they worked at provided the perfect opportunity to put in some lunchtime training, albeit without a bike.

"Instead, we'd use shoulder bags filled with books," Scarsbrook smiles. "Then we'd do the stairs up to the twentieth floor, go back down in the lift and do it three more times before the end of our lunch break. It worked well," he adds.

It takes skill and concentration to negotiate the course's rocky descents ▶

The course passes the Ribblehead Viaduct

Giro dell'Emilia
Italy

Pro one-day race

Tradition-rich Italian one-day race that attracts the big names for an end-of-season showdown

This Italian one-day race, first held in 1909, may fall late in the season, but one look at the list of past winners reveals just how illustrious a race it is: Eddy Merckx, Roger De Vlaeminck, Tony Rominger and Frank Schleck have all taken victory here. Held in the northern Italian region of Emilia-Romagna, riders set off from Bologna for a 200 km loop that finishes with four 10 km laps over the Colle della Guardia climb, finishing at the magnificent Sanctuary of the Madonna of San Luca church at the top, just outside Bologna. The 2011 winner, Acqua e Sapone's Colombian climber Carlos Alberto Betancur, used the final 2 km climb to put 24 seconds into his pursuers, led home by Rabobank's Bauke Mollema.

Statistics
Location
Bologna,
Emilia-Romagna
Distance
200 km/124.3 miles
(2012)
Highest point
760 m (2012)
Terrain
Tarmac
Record wins
Costante Girardengo
(Ita) (five wins)
Field size
160
First event
1909
Website
www.gsemilia.it
Contact
gsemiliaciclismo@
tin.it

Riders finish at the Sanctuary of the Madonna of San Luca church

Nationale Sluitingsprijs Putte–Kapellen Belgium

Pro one-day race

One of the last races of the European season gives riders one more chance to save their year

Belgium's 'end race' around the the village of Putte, in the Belgian municipality of Kapellen, as the race name loosely translates, is one of the last chances for the sprinters to chalk up a win if their season hasn't gone as successfully as they'd hoped. In 2010, British rider Adam Blythe, who has made Belgium his home, outsprinted the late Wouter Weylandt for the win.

Weylandt died during the 2011 Giro d'Italia after crashing on a descent.

The 2011 Sluitingsprijs went to the Belarus sprinter Yauheni Hutarovich, taking his fourth win of the season in a bunch sprint after eleven spectator-friendly laps of a 16.7 km circuit around the village, which sits right on the border with the Netherlands.

Statistics

Location
Putte, Kapellen

Distance
183.5 km/114 miles (2012)

Terrain
Tarmac

Record wins
Frans Van Looy (Bel), Adri Van Der Poel (Ned) (both three wins)

Field size
168

First event
1929

Website
www.sluitingsprijs.be

Contact
mail@sluitingsprijs.be

Yauheni Hutarovich, 2011 winner

L'Eroica
Italy
Road

Tuscany's 'white roads' provide a Paris–Roubaix-esque challenge in this throwback sportive

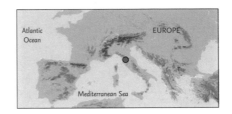

Tuscany's 'white roads', the strade bianche – essentially unmade, gravel roads – define this fantastic sportive in northern Italy. First held in 1997, the organisers have always encouraged vintage clothing and bicycles but for the first time in 2012 they made pre-1987 bicycles obligatory for all participants. The appeal, of course, is that this was the kind of road surface that road racers past used to have to contend with. While in most of Europe dirt tracks gave way first to cobbles, and later tarmac, a number of Tuscany's chalky roads remain, used by farm vehicles – and hardy cyclists.

The Eroica also paved – or, rather, gravelled – the way for the Strade Bianche pro event over the same roads, which, having first been held in October 2007, now enjoys a more Roubaix-esque March calendar slot, and indeed in years to come could even come to challenge Paris–Roubaix itself as the 'off-road road event' of choice.

Unlike Roubaix, however, there are some tough climbs, with gradients reaching 20 per cent, which those taking part in the sportive version really don't want to be walking up in their retro leather cycling shoes, so be sure to come armed with low gear ratios.

The pro event is one to watch, both as a spectator and in terms of its development, while the sportive version is very much one to ride, being one of the most different, difficult and enjoyable sportives out there.

Statistics

Location
Gaiole in Chianti
Distance
205/135/75/38 km
127.4/83.9/46.6/23.6 miles (2012)
Terrain
Tarmac and gravel roads
Field size
Over 4,000
First event
1997
Website
www.eroica-ciclismo.it
Contact
info@eroica.it

Gaiole in Chianti is wine country

Ride on the famous strade bianche in homage to the riders of yesteryear ▶

Paris–Tours
France
Pro one-day race

One of France's oldest races, 'the sprinters' Classic' often comes down to a frenetic bunch gallop in Tours

'The sprinters' Classic' is another 'Paris to...' race that struggles to start too close to the French capital, and even from the early days the race start has been held well outside Paris. In 2012, the town of Châteauneuf-en-Thymerais, around 80 km southwest of the city, plays host to the start of the race, which then runs along a 230 km route further southwest to Tours, where it does finish in the city centre, on the Avenue de Grammont. However, the long, straight finish was greatly reduced in length in 2011 due to the installation of new tram tracks, and was perhaps not to the sprinters' liking as BMC's Greg Van Avermaet shed the remainder of a breakaway group to win by a gap of two seconds from Vacansoleil's Marco Marcato.

The bunch was led home almost a minute and a half down by the now-retired Australian sprinter Robbie McEwen, with Mark Cavendish, in his new world champion's rainbow jersey, never really in contention, though it is a race he's surely destined to win one day.

Paris–Tours was first held in 1896, but a second edition wasn't held until 1901, and then a third in 1906. Since then, however, it's been an annual event, put on by the same organisers as the Tour de France, and is rare in that only the two world wars have interrupted it being staged each year.

It's also famous for being one of the few big races that Eddy Merckx failed to win. The Belgian rider Noël Vantyghem once joked that between him and Merckx, they had won all of cycling's Classic races – Vantyghem the 1972 edition of Paris-Tours, and Merckx all the rest.

Statistics
Location
Châteauneuf-en-Thymerais to Tours
Distance
230 km/142.9 miles (2012)
Highest point
155 m (2012)
Terrain
Tarmac
Record wins
Gustave Daneels (Bel),
Guido Reybroeck (Bel),
Paul Maye (Fra),
Erik Zabel (Ger)
(all three wins)
Field size
200
First event
1896
Website
www.letour.fr
Contact
cyclisme@aso.fr

Greg Van Avermaet pips Marco Marcato to victory in 2011

Flamboyant Gothic Tours Cathedral ▶

L'Etape Argentina
Argentina
Road

Argentina's Etape du Tour – organised by the
team behind the real thing too

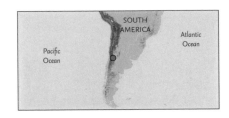

L'Etape Argentina – or La Etapa Argentina
– is organised by ASO, organisers of both
the Tour de France and L'Etape du Tour. It's
quite a coup for enthusiastic Argentinian
amateur riders to have an event organised
by the team behind the most famous race
in the world and the most famous sportive
in the world on their doorstep. While these
days the Etape in France has become so
popular that two separate 'acts' are now
included, the Argentinian version has been
organised as a two-stage sportive from the
off in 2011, when it took on the roads of the
country's cycling heartlands in Mendoza
and San Juan, and was so successful that it
seems likely to become a permanent fixture
on the sportive calendar.

Statistics

Location
Mendoza and
San Juan

Distance
250 km/155.3 miles
over 2 stages (2011)

Terrain
Tarmac

First event
2011

Website
www.laetapa
argentina.com

Contact
info@laetapa
argentina.com

Mendoza and San Juan provinces offer spectacular cycling

Catford CC Hill Climb
United Kingdom
Road
Probably the oldest bike race in the world...

The Catford CC Hill Climb claims to be the oldest still-continuing bike race in the world, having first been held in 1886. Some 125 years later, these uphill time trials haven't exactly become mainstream cycling events, but the huge crowds that turn out on York's Hill near Sevenoaks each October for this 707-yard uphill struggle are happy to keep it their little secret. Some hardy souls even ride the Bec CC Hill Climb in Titsey, Surrey, later in the afternoon – the two are

always held on the same Sunday – while the day before Brighton Mitre promotes their 'double' hill climb: a morning hill climb up the fearsome Steyning Bostal in Sussex, followed by a hill climb up Mill Hill in nearby Shoreham-by-Sea in the afternoon, with the combined times deciding the winner. Together with the Catford and Bec hill climbs, these make up the 'Four Hills' competition, with a prize for the best rider overall.

Statistics
Location
York's Hill, Sevenoaks, Kent
Distance
0.65 km/0.4 miles (2012)
Terrain
Tarmac
Record wins
Max Pendleton (Gbr) (eight wins)
First event
1886
Website
www.catfordcc.co.uk
Contact
hongensec@catfordcc.co.uk

York's Hill has gradients of up to 25 per cent

Bec CC Hill Climb
United Kingdom

Road

Racing uphill against the clock, riders have to contend with the '1 in 4' gradients of White Lane

White Lane, in Titsey, near Limpsfield, Surrey, is the venue for this 700-yard-long afternoon hill climb promoted by the Bec Cycling Club, and organiser Garry Beckett – a former T-Mobile and Saturn team soigneur, and one of Bradley Wiggins's helpers during his track days.

The climb starts off at a 1 in 8 gradient, but soon ramps up to 1 in 6. Approaching the top, it maxes out at 25 per cent, and so is a cruel hill, steepening as it goes.

Pair it with the Catford CC Hill Climb that morning – which arguably has the slight edge as the older event and an extra 7 yards to climb – and you can make a real day of it. Both claim to have the biggest, loudest and most enthusiastic crowd, although it's often simply the same bunch of riders and spectators attending both fantastic events.

Statistics
Location
White Lane, Titsey, Surrey
Distance
0.64 km/0.4 miles (2012)
Terrain
Tarmac
First event
1956
Website
www.beccycling club.co.uk
Contact
Via website

It's no pain, no gain at White Lane

Tour of Beijing
China

Pro stage race

One of top-level pro racing's newest events takes riders back to the site of the 2008 Olympics

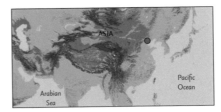

A perfect example of cycling's 'mondialisation', the Tour of Beijing is the newest addition to the UCI's WorldTour circuit, and now becomes the final race in the series, taking over from the Tour of Lombardy, which has shifted forward to the end of September from its traditional early-October slot.

A number of riders expressed doubts about heading so far afield at the end of a long season ahead of the first edition of the Tour of Beijing in 2011, but it was deemed a great success, both by the organisers and the riders

The five-day race kicks off with a time trial and, in 2011, Germany's Tony Martin showed a clean pair of heels to a quartet of British TT specialists – David Millar, Alex Dowsett,

Chris Froome and Steve Cummings – to win the first stage, set in the Olympic Park between the 'Bird's Nest' stadium and the Water Cube, and he didn't relinquish the jersey all the way to the finish back at the Olympic Park, via the Summer Palace, the Great Wall and Tiananmen Square. That was despite Irish pair Philip Deignan and Nicolas Roche – son of 1987 Tour de France champion Stephen Roche – having tried, along with Froome, to blow the race apart on the Great Wall 'queen stage'. Martin, though, stood as strong as the Great Wall itself and, despite having set out his stall on the first stage, fought hard to maintain his lead and become the new event's first ever winner.

Statistics

Location
Beijing

Distance
617.8 km/383.9 miles over 5 stages (2011)

Highest point
892 m (2011)

Terrain
Tarmac

Field size
152

First event
2011

Website
www.tourofbeijing.net

Contact
tourofbeijing@ jumpmedia.com.au

Alpine-style climbs make the peloton feel at home

The Great Wall of China is a surreal sight in a bike race ▶

Roc d'Azur
France
Mountain bike

There's something for everyone at the world's biggest mountain bike event on France's Côte d'Azur

This is one of those events that really is a must-do for mountain bikers everywhere. Since 1997, the Roc d'Azur has grown to become the huge five-day festival of cycling based around Fréjus on France's Côte d'Azur that it is today.

The programme of events is mind-boggling, and on offer are kids' races, leisure rides and evening criterium races around Fréjus's old town and nearby Roquebrune-sur-Argens the following night. For the first time in 2012, the programme includes Tri Roc – an off-road triathlon made up of a Mediterranean swim leg, a MTB cycle leg and a trail run to finish things off.

There's also a show running across the final four days attracting 250 of the sport's biggest manufacturers as exhibitors, as well as displays of trials riding and BMXing. In addition to the 20,000 competitors across all the events, the Roc d'Azur attracts 170,000 spectators and visitors, making it by far the biggest mountain biking event in the world.

The jewel in the crown, however, is the main event on the final day: the Roc d'Azur. Over a 56 km course, riders are faced with extremely challenging terrain – plenty of climbing, but plenty of technical descending, too – and, best of all, the weather is, or at least should be, extremely pleasant as southern Europe enjoys the last of the warm temperatures before autumn sets in.

Statistics

Location
Fréjus, Roquebrune-sur-Argens and Sainte Maxime

Distance
56 km/34.8 miles (main event, 2012)

Terrain
Off-road

Field size
20,000 (all events)

First event
1984

Website
www.rocazur.com

Contact
klazarew@aso.fr

Moritz Milatz wins Roc d'Azur 2011 ahead of Christoph Sauser

Roquebrune-sur-Argens, southeast France ▶

Herald Sun Tour
Australia
Pro stage race

The 'original Tour Down Under' has had some big-name winners over the years

The Jayco Herald Sun Tour is Australia's oldest pro stage race, having started in 1952. Held across five days in Victoria, the race is sponsored by the state's newspaper, the Herald Sun, based in Melbourne, where the race finishes with a criterium. In recent years it's added caravan and mobile-home manufacturer Jayco – a big supporter of Australian cycling – as a main sponsor.

Most of the current crop of Aussie pros have won here, and past winners include Baden Cooke, Matt Wilson, Simon Gerrans and Stuart O'Grady. In 2009, Bradley Wiggins became the third Briton to win the title, following Malcolm Elliott and Dave Mann, off the back of fourth place at that year's Tour de France. Wiggins's late father, Gary, was Australian, and Wiggins gave the Herald Sun the perfect sound bite: "If I was going to pick a tour to win other than the Tour de France, the Jayco Herald Sun Tour is the one." He added that racing in front of such huge Melbourne crowds gave him goose bumps, and that he felt very much at home.

It was his first-ever overall stage-race victory, but since then he's added the 2011 Critérium du Dauphiné and the 2012 Paris-Nice and Tour of Romandy, and headed into the 2012 Tour de France as joint favourite with Australian Cadel Evans.

Statistics

Location
Victoria

Distance
672 km/417.6 miles over 5 stages (2011)

Terrain
Tarmac

Record wins
Barry Waddell (Aus) (five wins)

Field size
108

First event
1952

Website
www.heraldsun tour.com.au

Contact
jaycoheraldsuntour@ jumpmedia.com.au

Stuart O'Grady is one of a host of Australian winners

Top international teams turn out for Australia's oldest stage race ▶

Tour de Vendée
France
Pro one-day race

The cycling-mad Vendée region hosts this well-loved French one-day race

Despite its name, this is a one-day race in the Vendée region, in western France, departing from Le-Poire-sur-Vie and finishing 205 km later, after three 5 km finishing circuits, in the town of La-Roche-sur-Yon. Appropriately enough, local lad Jean-René Bernaudeau was the first pro winner of the Tour de Vendée in 1980 – the first year it was organised as a pro event, having been for amateurs between 1972 and 1979. Bernaudeau was riding then for the Renault-Gitane team, led by Bernard Hinault. The team would become even more famous in the early 1980s when it added Laurent Fignon and Greg LeMond to its ranks. Today, Bernaudeau is the boss of the Vendée-based Europcar team, which gets the biggest cheers of all at this race, as well as at the Tour de France when it passes through the region, frequently as it does, with team leader Tommy Voeckler a real crowd favourite.

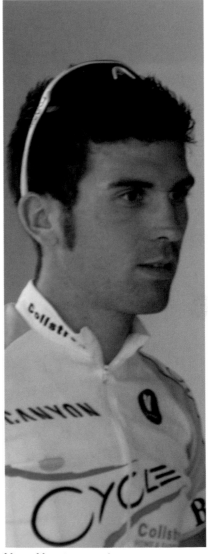

Marco Marcato, 2011 winner

Statistics

Location
Vendée
Distance
205 km/127.4 miles (2012)
Terrain
Tarmac
Record wins
Jaan Kirsipuu (Est) (four wins)
Field size
128
First event
1972
Website
www.tourdevendee.fr
Contact
Via website

The Swazi Frontier
Swaziland
Mountain bike

A three day mountain-bike race through the tiny but spectacular southern African nation of Swaziland

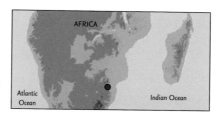

'Spectacular' perhaps doesn't do justice to the route this three-day mountain-bike race takes through the small, southern African nation of Swaziland, across plains, along forest tracks, down 25 km descents, across streams, and through villages of enthusiastic spectators.

Unlike some multi-day mountain-bike events where tents are the order of the day, the Swazi Frontier houses participants in top-notch resort hotels, which isn't a bad way to recover from your efforts. One of the goals of the event is to promote tourism in Swaziland, thus showcasing quality accommodation, but it exists also to promote mountain biking and to bring a top sports event to the people in the towns and communities it passes through.

Anyone is welcome to enter and requests can be made via email. Once entries open, usually around March, slots are filled on a first come, first served basis.

Statistics

Location
Hawane Resort to Maguga Lodge
Distance
180.9 km/112.4 miles over 3 stages (2012)
Highest point
1,800 m (2012)
Terrain
Off-road
Field size
180 (90 teams of two)
First event
2006
Website
www.theswazifrontier.sz
Contact
info@theswazifrontier.sz

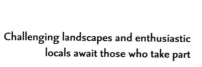
Challenging landscapes and enthusiastic locals await those who take part

Jayco Teams Classic Charity Ride Australia

Road

An Australian Etape du Tour giving riders a chance to experience a stage of the Herald Sun Tour

This sportive runs alongside the Jayco Herald Sun Tour in Victoria, Australia, and is based on the idea of the Etape du Tour whereby amateurs get the opportunity to ride a stage of the race in support of the event's charity partners, which in 2011 included MS Australia, diabetes charity HypoActive and the KIDS Foundation, helping children deal with life-changing injuries.

The 2011 ride was based on stage four between Sorrento and the famous climb of Arthurs Seat – which features regularly in the Sun Tour – and which was timed so that participants could compare their efforts against the pros up the hill. A 100 km or 45 km route was on offer, with both finishing well ahead of the pro race to allow time to get a prime position to watch the pros come home.

Statistics

Location
Victoria

Distance
100/45 km
62.1/30 miles (2011)

Terrain
Tarmac

Website
www.heraldsuntour.
com.au

Contact
jaycoheraldsuntour@
jumpmedia.com.au

A climb up Arthurs Seat frequently features on the route

Red Hook Crit Milano
Italy
Night

*Brakeless, 'fixie' crit racing all the way from
Brooklyn – Italian style*

Since it began in 2008, Brooklyn's Red Hook
Crit has become the New York bike race
every cool cat worth their salt wants to win.
So why not transplant it to Milan, Italy?
The Red Hook neighbourhood may be
specific to Brooklyn, but the name's
travelled with the concept, too. The first
Milan edition took place in October 2010,
with a dozen North American racers making
the trip over to Italy to showboat in front of
a curious, 1,000-strong crowd, who weren't
left disappointed. In 2011, the race brought
in sponsorship from Nike, and a 5k running
race was added to the programme. On the
bike, this time it was Neil Bezdek – winner
of the 2009 Brooklyn event – who beat
Basque rider Jonander Ortunodo, who had
beaten him in Milan the year before.

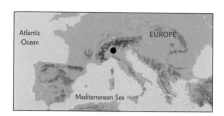

Statistics

Location
Milan
Distance
18 laps of a 1.8 km/
1.1 mile course (2012)
Terrain
Tarmac
First event
2010
Website
http://redhookcrit.com
Contact
Via website

Pro rider Neil Bezdek won in 2011

Crocodile Trophy
Australia
Mountain bike

Mountain-bike stage racing through some of the Australian Outback's toughest terrain

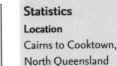

The Crocodile Trophy is dubbed one of the longest and hardest mountain-bike races in the world, and indeed this nine-day event through the Outback of North Queensland, Australia, shares more than a few things in common with the Tour de France. Riders compete for a leader's jersey over nine stages but, like the Tour, there's a race within the race for the points jersey, rewarding consistent finishing, while teams also compete for a prize.

Unlike the Tour, however, while there are mechanics available at the start and finish of each stage, during the stage itself you're on your own when it comes to fixing your bike. There were some changes and additions to

the 2012 event: the introduction of two-man teams to join the existing classifications for the three-man teams or individual riders.

Also new, outside the racing, is a guided ride along the route of the Crocodile Trophy, without the pressure of competition and time limits. Led by former pro mountain biker and Crocodile Trophy silver medallist Valentin Zeller, the tour runs concurrently with the race, and offers riders an opportunity to genuinely enjoy the amazing scenery rather than seeing it flash by under race conditions. Participants are even allowed to use electric bikes, whose purring motors should at least help keep the crocodiles away...

Statistics
Location
Cairns to Cooktown, North Queensland
Distance
933 km/579.7 miles over 9 stages (2012)
Terrain
Off-road
Record wins
Jaap Viergever (Ned) (four wins)
First event
1995
Website
www.crocodile-trophy. com
Contact
schoenbacher@croc.at

Double trouble: tandem riders run the gauntlet with the crocs

Earth, air, water . . . and the fire rages in the bellies of Croc Trophy racers ▶

Mad Anthony Cyclocross USA

Cyclo-cross

A spectacular Michigan cyclo-cross race through the grounds of Detroit's Fort Wayne

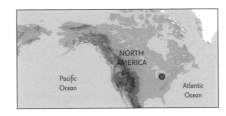

The Mad Anthony Cyclo-Cross race has taken place in the grounds of Fort Wayne, in Detroit, Michigan, since 2009, and has quickly made a name for itself thanks to its truly spectacular backdrop.

And Mad Anthony? General Anthony Wayne got his nickname thanks to his feisty mood and his exploits during the American Revolutionary War (1775-1783). He went into politics afterwards and died from gout in 1796, aged fifty-one.

It is from Wayne that the fort took its name upon completion in 1851, but by then peace had broken out between the USA and Great Britain, and it stood empty until 1861, after which it became an induction centre for US troops, and continued in that capacity until the Vietnam War.

Today, Fort Wayne is maintained as one of the USA's historic sites, but the Mad Anthony cyclo-cross race takes advantage of its rolling grounds, passing by disused tanks and through dark munitions tunnels, creating a stunning circuit for riders and spectators alike.

Statistics

Location
Detroit, Michigan

Terrain
Off-road

Field size
209 (all categories, 2011)

First event
2009

Website
http://madanthonycx.blogspot.co.uk/

Contact
madanthonycx@gmail.com

Riders do battle with tough terrain in Fort Wayne

Chrono des Nations
France

Pro one-day race

One-day time trial in which the best protagonists against the clock battle it out for supremacy

This single-day time trial, which takes place in the town of Les Herbiers, in the Vendée region of France, is essentially the Chrono des Herbiers by another name. The now defunct Grand Prix des Nations was a similar time trial held between 1932 and 2004, latterly around Dieppe. From 2006, the Chrono des Herbiers took on part of the race's name to become the Chrono des Nations, helping to keep the older race's legacy alive.

The first Chrono des Herbiers in 1982 was won by British rider Gary Dowdell, and there was a second British win the following year thanks to David Akam. Since then, an eclectic mix of nationalities have added their name to the trophy, but Chris Boardman brought it home to Britain again in both 1993 and 1996, while David Millar smashed the course record in 2010 to record the fifth British win in the race's history. However, that record of 58 minutes 53 seconds – the first time anyone had ever dipped under the 59-minute mark for the 48.5 km circuit – was short-lived, as in 2011 Germany's Tony Martin delivered a new best time of 56 minutes 20 seconds – equivalent to a huge 51.7 kph average speed.

German time trial specialists had also dominated the GP des Nations in the event's latter years, with Jens Voigt, Uwe Peschel and Michael Rich, twice, winning the final four editions of the race before it merged with the Chrono des Herbiers. With British Sky rider Alex Dowsett finishing third in 2011, having stepped up from the under-23 ranks, the 2012 Chrono des Nations was gearing up to be a real battle between German and British riders.

Serhiy Honchar has won three times

Statistics

Location
Les Herbiers, Vendée
Distance
48.5 km/30.1 miles
(2012)
Terrain
Tarmac
Record wins
Serhiy Honchar (Ukr)
(three wins)
First event
1982
Website
www.chronodes
nations.com
Contact
chronodesnations@
wanadoo.fr

British time trial champion Alex Dowsett (top) will hope to challenge Germany's Tony Martin's (right) record time ▶

Muddy Hell
United Kingdom

Cyclo-cross

Halloween fun at London's Herne Hill at this spooky cyclo-cross race

Muddy Hell organisers Rollapaluza are the same bunch that bring you the roller-racing, but since 2009, they've been bringing something really quite different to the table: a cyclo-cross race in Halloween costumes around the grounds of London's legendary Herne Hill velodrome.

For many, this is the highlight of the season: a silly, fun race, with the chance to dress up at the end of the season when many are still in great form, to really entertain the crowd. Those who can pull some radical moves over some of the jumps get the biggest cheers of the night – save, perhaps, for the "oohs" for those who fail to make it over the barriers in the beer tent, as the route runs straight through the middle.

The racing, taking place at the weekend closest to Halloween, gets under way as night approaches, and it's pitch black once the seniors start, adding to the spooky atmosphere. But worry not – you'll know when the ghosties, ghoulies – and even Mr Blobby – are approaching, as front lights are obligatory, which only helps add to the atmosphere.

It's a great way to finish the season, but be quick: all categories – senior men, women, vets, novices, juniors, youths – fill up quickly.

Halloween at Herne Hill

Statistics
Location
Herne Hill, London
Distance
60 mins on a 2 km/ 1.2 mile course (seniors, 2012)
Terrain
Off-road
Field size
330
First event
2009
Website
www.muddyhell.cx
Contact
Via website

Grafton to Inverell Cycle Classic Australia

Pro one-day race

A long and hilly one-day pro race through New South Wales

The Grafton to Inverell Cycle Classic was established by Harold Strahley in 1961 – planned, in theory, years before, but only a possibility following the construction of a road through the Gibraltar Range between Grafton on the east coast of New South Wales and Inverell almost 230 km along the road inland. Detractors said the race would be too long and too hard, but the riders showed up, although few could ever deny that it's not a tough race. They certainly know about it when they first hit the Gibraltar Range 70 km into the 228 km race, climbing for 18 km until things flatten out a little, and then it's pretty much a downhill run for the 50 km to Inverell.

The elite A grade race sets off first, and is part of Cycling Australia's National Road Series. It is followed 15 minutes later by a B grade and separate C grade race over the same route, with riders allowed nine hours to complete the course.

Statistics

Location
Grafton to Inverell
Distance
228 km/141.7 miles (2012)
Highest point
1,190 m (2012)
Terrain
Tarmac
Record wins
Jamie Drew (Aus) (two wins)
First event
1961
Website
www.graftontoinverel
cycleclassic.com.au
Contact
Via website

The race begins in Grafton

Japan Cup Cycle Road Race
Japan

Pro one-day race

A hilly race in Japan that gives local teams the chance to take on some of the world's best riders

ASIA

Pacific Ocean

Held in the city of Utsunomiya, in Tochigi prefecture, 100 km north of Tokyo, the Japan Cup one-day race is part of the UCI Asia Tour, and uses a hilly 153 km course that suits the sport's real climbers, with recent winners including Denmark's Chris Anker Sørensen (2009) and Ireland's Dan Martin (2010). In 2011 Australia's Nathan Haas added the Japan Cup title to the 2011 Jayco Herald Sun Tour title the Genesys Wealth Advisers rider won just a week earlier, which helped secure him a spot with Jonathan Vaughters's Garmin-Barracuda ProTeam for the 2012 season.

First held in 1992, that first edition was won by former Omega Pharma-Lotto team directeur sportif Hendrik Redant. Italian climber Claudio Chiappucci won the following three editions, and holds the record of most wins with compatriot Sergio Barbero.

Large, knowledgeable crowds turn out to give it a real flavour of European pro racing, with many of the top UCI ProTeams making the trip over for what is often riders' last race of the season, including Liquigas, Saxo Bank, Astana and Lampre.

Statistics

Location
Utsunomiya, Tochigi
Distance
153 km/95 miles (2012)
Terrain
Tarmac
Record wins
Sergio Barbero (Ita),
Claudio Chiappucci
(Ita) (both 3 wins)
Field size
105
First event
1992
Website
www.japancup.gr.jp
Contact
japancup@brandex.
co.jp

KING OF MOUNTAIN

The world's best hit the hills around Utsunomiya

Rapha Super Cross
United Kingdom
Cyclo-cross

The perfect combination of top-notch cyclo-cross racing and fun in three events over nine days

Statistics

Location
West Yorkshire, Leicestershire and London

Distance
60 mins (senior, 2012)

Terrain
Off-road

First event
2011

Website
www.rapha.cc/super-cross

Contact
ian@rouleur.cc

The success of the inaugural Rapha Super Cross series in 2011 paved the way for a second year of the cyclo-cross events, with two new venues and the return of a third for 2012. Beautiful Broughton House in Skipton, Yorkshire – the Tempest family's home since 1597 – hosts the opening round in its grounds, and a week later it's on to Misterton Hall, near Lutterworth in Leicestershire, for round two at a venue a little more used to hosting cyclo-cross races. The next day sees the finale return to London's iconic Alexandra Palace.

While also competing for individual glory in each round, the elite riders' main prize is the teams classification at the end of all three rounds, which was won by the Hope Technology squad in 2011.

All those halls and palaces make it sound rather high class, but the onus is on fun and making the racing as entertaining for the crowd to watch as it is for the riders to race, and to that end the 'tequila short-cut' makes a very welcome return to the novice race. It is what it sounds like: a quicker route, chopping off part of the course, in exchange for the rider downing a shot of tequila. For those watching, perhaps a more delicious combo than hard liquor and lung-busting racing is the availability of Belgian-style chips, pies and beers, all enjoyed to a soundtrack of jangling, supporter-rattled cowbells.

Series organiser Ian Cleverly describes proceedings as "a mix of American and continental cyclo-cross – the best of everything". Whether you go along just for a look, or take the plunge and take part, it's not to be missed.

Sludging through mud or downing tequila, either way it's messy

Exmoor Beast
United Kingdom
Road

*A tough event to close the British sportive season,
which takes riders around a wind-blasted Exmoor*

Not to be confused with the Beast of
Exmoor – the sheep-worrying, big-cat
creature that supposedly resides nearby,
this nevertheless beastly sportive, starting
and finishing in Minehead, will push riders
hard thanks to a number of tough climbs
over a choice of a 100 km or 100 mile route
around Exmoor. While the pros are ending
their seasons in European races such as
the Tour of Lombardy and Paris–Tours, the

Exmoor Beast heralds the winding-down of
the British sportive season as the weather
takes a turn for the worse. The event, which
has run since 2007, often bears the brunt
of it, too, and apart from rain, the wind has
a major impact on how tough a ride it is.
Riders who thrive on that 'Belgian hardman'
image, keen to tick it off their 'must ride' list,
will love it, but as the organisers warn, it's
not called the beast for nothing.

Statistics

Location
Exmoor
Distance
160.1/100 km
100/62.1 miles (2012)
Highest point
486 m (2012)
Terrain
Tarmac
Field size
1,500
First event
2007
Website
www.exmoorbeast.org
Contact
Via website

Get blown away by gruelling climbs around Exmoor

Melbourne to Warrnambool Cycling Classic Australia

Road

Race against top Aussie pros at one of the world's oldest bike races

Warrnambool is a coastal city on one of the southern-most points of the state of Victoria, Australia, and has often featured on the route of the Herald Sun Tour pro stage race. Melbourne, 250 km east along the coast as the crow flies, regularly hosts the finish of the Herald Sun Tour, too, but the Melbourne to Warrnambool Cycling Classic is a separate, one-day race that has been held over virtually the same route since 1895, albeit back to front, from Warrnambool to Melbourne on thirty-two occasions. The very first race was held in that direction, in fact, but today Werribee racecourse, on the western outskirts of Melbourne, is the start point for this 262 km race, which pitches amateur riders who fancy their chances over such a long, tough route, against the best Australian pro teams.

Statistics

Location
Melbourne to Warrnambool

Distance
262 km/162.8 miles (2012)

Terrain
Tarmac

Record wins
Peter Besanko (Aus) (three wins)

First event
1895

Website
www.melbourneto
warrnambool.com

Contact
info@caribou.net.au

Melbourne

La Ruta Costa Rica
Costa Rica
Mountain bike

Extreme mountain-bike racing across the unforgiving climbs and jungles of Costa Rica

Costa Rica's Ruta de los Conquistadores celebrates its twentieth edition in 2012, and remains one of the toughest endurance events in the world, cycling or otherwise. At three days long, it's nowhere near as long as the three-week Tour de France, but packing in 240 miles of extreme, mountainous terrain pushes riders to their absolute limits. The route honours that which the Spanish conquerors of South America took on horseback between the Atlantic and the Pacific in 1560.

La Ruta Costa Rica isn't one of those events you'll be able to 'wing'; around 40 per cent of riders each year don't finish due to the difficulty of the course. Exposed beaches, dense jungle, humidity, altitude, rain, and the resultant waist-deep mud all combine to conspire against the athletes, yet the highest point of the race, the still-active Irazú at 11,259 feet, makes you feel like you're standing on top of the world.

Only the toughest competitors withstand the relentless obstacles encountered throughout Costa Rica's jungles

Statistics
Location
Jaco to Limón
Distance
386.2 km/240 miles
over 3 days (2012)
Highest point
3,432 m (2012)
Terrain
Gravel, jeep roads,
tarmac and
single-track
First event
1993
Website
www.larutadeloscon
quistadores.com
Contact
info@adventure
race.com

Gran Fondo Colnago
Miami USA

Road

Gran fondo riding in Florida with a choice of distances starting and finishing in central Miami

Unfortunately, the final round of the Gran Fondo USA series in the normally sun-soaked Floridian city of Miami experienced some rain showers for its inaugural running of the Gran Fondo Colnago Miami in 2011, but it couldn't dampen the spirits of more than 1,400 riders who rode their choice of a 100-, 55- or 25-mile route. They were joined by 1997 Tour de France champion

Jan Ullrich, who was riding his bike again after a bit of a break, as well as two-time Giro d'Italia champion Gilberto Simoni. The longer route takes riders out of the city and into the surrounding tropical countryside of South Florida before heading back to the Miami City Hall where, in the best tradition of gran fondos, all participants tuck into an energy-restoring pasta party.

Statistics

Location
Miami, Florida
Distance
161/88.5/40.2 km
100/55/25 miles (2012)
Terrain
Tarmac
First event
2011
Website
www.granfondo-world.com
Contact
info@granfondo
usa.com

Downtown Miami

Ghent Six
Belgium
Track

If you're only ever going to go to one six-day track race, Ghent is the one to go to

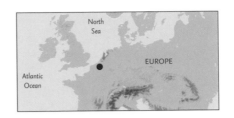

Some might say that the Ghent Six has lost a little bit of its magic in recent years, but in truth all they're referring to is the lack of thick cigarette smoke that used to fill the Kuipke velodrome before Belgium's smoking ban came into effect. The noise, beer-drinking and proximity to the riders on the track are still all there, and it's this really quite special atmosphere, along with its accessibility from the UK, that make the Ghent Six a must-visit event.

First held in 1922, a host of legendary names have graced the boards in Ghent, and in the 1960s in particular, the biggest names would regularly ride the Six circuit, of which Ghent has arguably always

been the most illustrious. Rik Van Looy, Eddy Merckx, Tom Simpson, Peter Post and Roger De Vlaeminck have all ridden at Ghent, and before he became a bona fide Tour de France star, Bradley Wiggins was a regular in the 2000s, partnered with Aussie-Belgian Matthew Gilmore, with the pair winning it in 2003.

Pair a trip to a night or two here with the Koksijde cyclo-cross World Cup just down the road, which tends to fall on the weekend of the Ghent Six, and you've got yourself a grand couple of days out: two very different cycling disciplines, yes, but a trip to Belgium's heartland that you'll remember for a long time to come.

Statistics

Location
Ghent
Distance
Laps of a 168 m/0.1 mile course
Terrain
Velodrome
Record wins
Patrick Sercu (Bel) (11 wins)
First event
1922
Website
www.z6sdaagse.be
Contact
Via website

Kuipke velodrome

Alex Rasmussen won in 2009, partnered by fellow Dane Michael Morkov ▶

Koksijde World Cup Cyclo-Cross Belgium

Cyclo-cross

Top-class cyclo-cross racing accompanied by the best beer and chips ever

The Koksijde round of the UCI Cyclo-Cross World Cup is eagerly awaited each year by locals and foreign visitors alike. The tiny Belgian coastal town makes great use of its geography, and the wild sand dunes provide some steep run-ups and dicey descents, keeping the riders on their toes, not to mention constantly hopping on and off their bikes. The stalls selling beer and chips are extremely welcome, and even more so when it's very cold, which it often is, but time your multiple trips to the tents carefully so as not to miss too much of the racing. Luckily, the racing goes on all day, with junior and under-23 races in the morning, with the women's World Cup race starting off the afternoon, followed by the elite men.

Those spectators taking advantage of the beer tents from the start of the day's programme tend to be in fine voice by the time the men's event gets under way. Think British football-match-style chanting and singing rather than the polite crowds cheering the riders at, say, the Tour de France. It really is a different world, but one that every cycling fan has to see. Then head to nearby Ghent in the evening to make a proper day of it by checking out another must-watch Belgian event – the Ghent Six Day track racing.

Statistics

Location
Koksijde
Distance
60 minutes (2012)
Terrain
Sand, single-track
Record wins
Danny De Bie (Bel) (four wins)
Field size
60
First event
1969
Website
www.veloclub koksijde.be
Contact
cyclocross@ koksijde.be

The loudest cheers are reserved for world champion Niels Albert, a Belgian

Lake Taupo Cycle Challenge New Zealand

Road

Head to New Zealand for a quick lap of the lake – all 160 km of it

Lake Taupo, on New Zealand's North Island, is the stunning setting for this popular event – or, rather, these 12 events – attracting as many as 10,000 participants. There's nothing very standard about the 'standard' challenge – the 160 km sportive is just one lap of the huge lake. Other events include a two , three- or four-man relay over one lap – riders are ferried by bus to their 'leg' – while for those who really want a challenge, there are enduro events consisting of two, four or even eight laps, which start a few days before the main event so that everyone finishes at roughly the same time.

For Penny Comins – a cycling writer from New Zealand, and now a veteran of more sportive events than she can remember – Lake Taupo was one of her first events, and at 160 km was by far the furthest she'd ever ridden at the time, too. Despite the number of sportives she's done since, she says Lake Taupo still ranks right up there among the best.

"The ride itself is really hilly, so it's tough," she says. "Right at the front, some people will really race it, but for everyone else you're in this constant flow of riders, and everyone's having fun. It's held just at the start of the summer, too, so there's this real party atmosphere."

That festival atmosphere continues after the ride, too, she explains. "It really is an all-day event, at this beautiful location, and afterwards everyone sits down for a picnic, and there's a prize draw with spot prizes that in the past have included things like cars and holidays – which means people stay around rather than rushing straight off home like at some other events!"

Statistics

Location
Lake Taupo, North Island

Distance
160 km/99.4 miles (main event, 2012)

Highest point
650 m (2012)

Terrain
Tarmac

Field size
10,000 (all events)

First event
1977

Website
www.cyclechallenge.com

Contact
Via website

Lake Taupo

Tweed Run
United Kingdom
Road

Dressing up time in central London – and further
afield – as cycling in tweed enjoys a revival

Just sometimes, it's nice to take things
down a notch or two. Whether giving it
everything in your latest sportive, doing
battle with the traffic on your commute
to work by bike or sitting on the sofa with
your heart racing whilst watching the latest
pro race on TV, sometimes you just need to
stop, dress up in your favourite tweed and
ride slowly through central London...

The first Tweed Run was held in 2009
and, since then, the event has struggled
to cope with the sheer number of people
wishing to dress up, jump on a vintage
bike, perhaps accessorise with a flat cap

or an extremely well-groomed moustache
– mainly the men – and already similar
Tweed Runs have sprung up as far afield as
Florence and New York, with plans to take
one to Tokyo.

It seems everyone loves a bit of retro
styling, and when you get to combine it
with a gentle, sociable ride around the UK's
capital, and other cities around the world,
complete with a stop for afternoon tea,
of course, it may not be too much longer
before the Tour de France sees sense and
stages its event as a slow bicycle race.

Statistics
Location
London
Distance
20.9 km/13 miles
(2012)
Terrain
Tarmac
Field size
300
First event
2009
Website
http://tweedrun.com/
Contact
Via website

An altogether more genteel way to cycle in London

Tour of Rwanda
Rwanda

Pro stage race

A hilly stage race that pits some of Africa's best national teams against top international pro squads

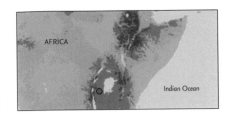

AFRICA

Indian Ocean

The Tour of Rwanda has been held since 1989 and, along with two Rwandan home teams, welcomes national teams from surrounding African countries such as Gabon, Tanzania, Ethiopia and Kenya, and attracts UCI Professional Continental team Team Type 1-Sanofi from the USA and South African UCI Continental squad MTN-Qhubeka.

The seven-day, eight-stage race covers a tough, hilly, but spectacular route, starting and finishing in Rwanda's capital, Kigali. In 2011, US rider Kiel Reijnen, of Team Type 1, triumphed overall, two seconds ahead of compatriot and team-mate Joseph Rosskopf, winning four stages along the way, three of which were back-to-back. The Karisimbi team, containing five-time Tour of Rwanda winner Abraham Ruhumuriza – who had to settle for fifth overall – took the team prize.

Statistics

Location
Kigali
Distance
788.8 km/490.1 miles
over 8 stages (2011)
Terrain
Tarmac
Record wins
Abraham Ruhumuriza
(Rwa) (five wins)
Field size
60
First event
1989
Website
www.en.tourof
rwanda.com
Contact
Via website

Rwanda's capital city Kigali hosts the start and finish

The Rwandan riders are super-motivated for their home race ▶

Country Index

Category Index

Night

Pro one-day race

Road

Road (continued)

Track

Index

T